Personal Finance on the

A practical guide to savings, bankin
insurance, pensions and tax

Internet Handbooks

Books & Publishing on the Internet
Chat on the Internet
Email for Beginners
Find It on the Internet
Finding a Job on the Internet
Free Stuff on the Net
Gardens & Gardening on the Internet
History on the Internet
Homes & Property on the Internet
Internet for Schools
Internet for Students
Internet for Writers
Maths on the Internet
Shops & Shopping on the Internet
Travel & Holidays on the Internet
Wildlife & Conservation on the Internet

Other titles in preparation

internet handbooks

Personal Finance on the Internet

A practical guide to savings, banking, investment, loans, insurance, pensions and tax on the internet

Graham Jones
BSc(Hons)

Internet Handbooks

Other books by the same author

Doing Business on the Internet
How to Use the Internet
Travel & Holidays on the Internet

First published in 1999 by Internet Handbooks, a Division of International Briefings Ltd, Plymbridge House, Estover Road, Plymouth PL6 7PY, United Kingdom.

Customer services tel:	(01752) 202301
Orders fax:	(01752) 202333
Customer services email:	cservs@plymbridge.com
Distributors web site:	http://www.plymbridge.com
Series web site:	http://www.internet-handbooks.co.uk

Produced for Internet Handbooks by Deer Park Productions.

Typeset by PDQ Typesetting, Newcastle-under-Lyme.

Printed and bound by The Cromwell Press Ltd, Trowbridge, Wiltshire.

Contents

Contents

Contents

List of illustrations

Illustrations

Preface

This book is designed to help you use the various financial sites on the internet to run your personal finances. Unlike other books about using the internet, this one assumes that you know the basics and that you already have internet access. If you do not have access to the internet or are unsure about using the internet, you will find an appendix at the back of the book that provides you with all the basics. This appendix also guides you to other sources of information about use of the internet in general.

The bulk of this book, however, assumes a basic level of technical knowledge and that you already have the necessary equipment to log on to the fascinating world of the internet and the world wide web. This book also takes the standpoint that you have some financial awareness and that you understand the basics of finance. Again, there are plenty of books about personal finance if you need help in this area. Instead, what this book will do is help anyone who understands finances, and who has access to the internet, to run any aspect of their financial world using the world wide web.

You will find some debate on the various ways of running finances over the internet. There are discussions on security and electronic cash, for instance. You will also find mini reviews of many sites, together with a list of benefits and disadvantages of the larger, more in-depth sites. There are also some worked examples of how to conduct financial transactions over the internet. However, as with all modern guidebooks on a rapidly growing technology, the information is as up-to-date as possible at the time of going to print. If any of the sites listed have changed since I wrote about them, why not let me know and I can use the information in future updates. Meanwhile, I hope this book will help you gain greater control of your finances using the power of the internet.

What I have written here is based upon direct personal experience. I run my own bank account online, I buy and sell shares over the internet and I do a great deal of shopping on the world wide web. I also use the internet to send faxes and make phone calls. In short, I have been able to save money and make money, thanks to this amazing new technology. I cannot think of a better tool to help you improve your finances today.

Note
Whilst every care has been taken to ensure the information contained within this book is accurate, no responsibility can be accepted for the consequences of any action taken based on the material contained within these pages. Readers should seek professional advice which is suited to their own personal circumstances before proceeding with

any financial matters. Readers may also wish to contact computer consultants regarding security issues. I, Graham Jones, am not authorised to give financial advice and none of the information contained within these pages should be construed as financial advice under the terms of the Financial Services Act 1986.

Please also note that comments made about the web sites and other internet pages mentioned in this book are based on how those sites and pages appeared at the time the book was written. Comments should not be taken as a reflection of how a site may appear at the time you access it, unless the site has remained unchanged since this book was written. All of the web sites shown in this book remain the copyright of their respective owners. The screen shots of web sites were correct at the time of going to press and may appear different now. All trademarks and registered trademarks mentioned in this book are the property of their respective owners.

Locating web site addresses
There are many web site addresses (URLs) in this book. To go to one of the addresses simply type the address, exactly as printed in this book, in the 'address' or 'location' box towards the top of the window of your web browser program. Once you have typed it in, hit the 'enter' key on your keyboard. You will then be transported to the web site you want.

New web site information
If your company has changed its web site or if you want to submit details of a web site you think should be included in a future edition of this book please email the details to the email address shown below. Happy surfing!

Graham Jones

Email:
mail@grahamjones.co.uk

Web sites:
http://www.grahamjones.co.uk
http://www.internet-handbooks.co.uk

1 The financial world and the internet

In this chapter we will explore:

- *major changes ahead*
- *gaining control*
- *doubters exist*
- *using the internet for your finances*

Imagine a High Street that doesn't have at least one bank on it. Or think of a city where insurance brokers don't exist. Consider too what a small town might be like without the local office of a building society. Strange as it may seem, these traditional elements of our national life are set to disappear. Within your lifetime, you will see towns without banks – their old listed buildings boarded up. Already we have seen thousands of bank branches shut across the UK as a result of mergers, improved efficiency and competition. What has happened so far is only the beginning. More, much more, is set to come; and the pace of change is speeding up.

At the heart of this change is technology and the power it provides to individuals. I remember back in the 1970s when I received my first device for getting cash out of a 'hole in the wall' machine. This device was an envelope that contained a pack of five sheets of paper. All you had to do was go to the machine outside the bank, open a large drawer and place your piece of paper carefully over the guide holes. You then shut the drawer and waited for a signal so that you could re-open the drawer – and there you would find a maximum of ten pounds. When

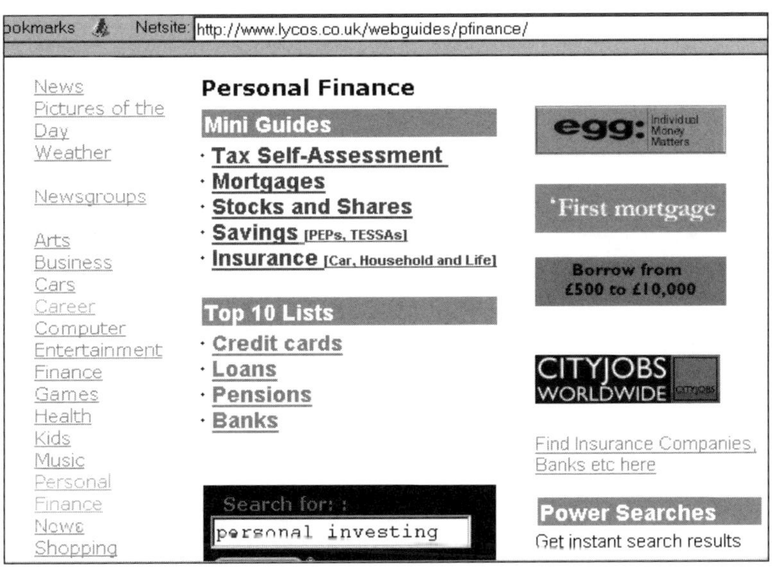

Fig. 1. A vast amount of financial resources can be obtained by using one of the well-known internet search engines, such as Lycos. This is Lycos's page for exploring UK personal finance.

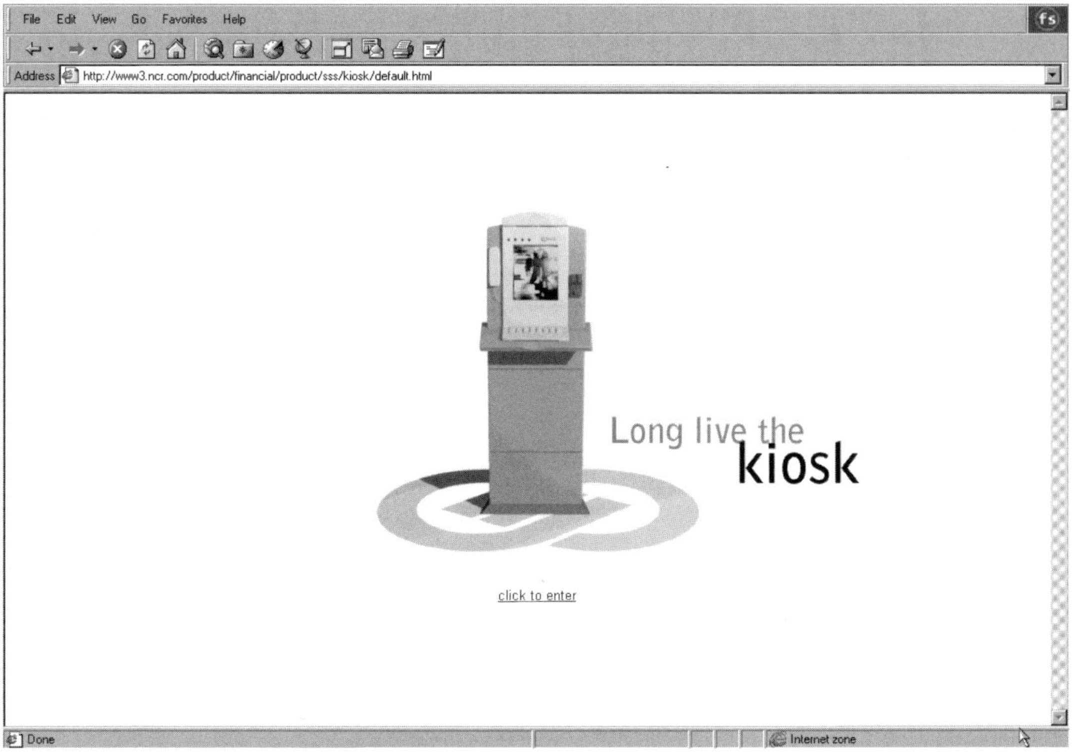

Fig. 2. An example of a 'kiosk', the state-of-the-art public information-processing machine which has evolved from the automated teller machine (ATM).

this system was first introduced, in June 1967 at Enfield, this device was seen as a revolution, but before too long we saw other banks introducing similar machines. Nowadays, we take for granted the new style Automated Teller Machines (ATMs) that sit outside and inside every bank branch. Not only can they dispense cash, you can use them to pay money in and order statements, as well as many other facilities that would have been undreamed of by the pioneers who introduced the paper-based systems of the mid-1970s. Nowadays, across the world ATMs process around 40,000 transactions every second of every day.[1] Clearly their use is so commonplace that we do not take much notice of them.

Yet what happened to all those voices of complaint? All those people saying they didn't want to communicate with a machine, they wanted to talk to a real person? What happened to all those business objections from board members of our major financial institutions who couldn't be bothered with the new-fangled way of doing things and wanted to preserve tradition? What happened is quite clear – customers voted with their feet. Those companies that offered simple, quick, easy-to-use solutions to everyday finances won out. Now, in the UK, all the major banks have joined together so that at long last, as from the beginning of 1999, you could use your cash card in any bank's ATM, rather than having to walk from one end of the High Street to the other. Customer pressure has forced change.

Now, things are changing again in the financial world. ATMs have developed into what the industry calls 'kiosks', which not only provide you with cash, but can also arrange loans, sell you insurance or provide you with tickets for the local theatre. Such kiosks are already popular within the international air transport industry; for instance, at London's Heathrow you can use these kiosks to buy a ticket and check in for your flight. It's simple and quick with no fuss, such as getting annoyed while the person in front of you asks awkward questions. Regular fliers love these kiosks; they can make their flight arrangements, check their frequent traveller reward points and look up flight schedules all at the same time. Traditionally you would have to queue in two or three different places spread across the terminal building. Clearly, kiosk technology helps us as consumers.

In the financial world, such kiosks are only just being introduced. They will help us get automated loan facilities, without having to face an interview with the manager – in spite of what many banks might say in public at the moment. After all, at the beginning of the 1990s, many people in the financial institutions were telling us that telephone banking would never catch on because people liked going into a branch. Now all major financial organisations from banks to insurance companies have telephone-based operations.

So, when you hear people saying that internet banking or share dealing over the world wide web will never catch on, don't believe them. Large businesses, such as financial companies, do not like change. It is awkward and difficult and involves costs that could harm shareholder investments. But changed they have, as we have seen. In fact, more changes have happened in the financial world in the last 15 years than in the previous 150. But hold on to your hats, because we're about to take off!

Major changes ahead

The internet is going to give the financial world the biggest shake up it has ever had. Already, people in financial circles are in awe at the impact the world wide web is having. For example, you can now buy shares directly over the internet (you can find out how in Chapter 7). This did not really begin until the end of 1996 but, between December 1996 and January 1997, the number of shares traded on just one, unadvertised, internet site trebled. In that January there was a further 50 per cent increase in the number of people using the site.[2] Such a huge demand for self-purchase of stocks and shares using the most up-to-date technology could hardly have been predicted. What is known, however, is that back in October 1996 only 1 per cent of financial companies on the world wide web offered any kind of transaction service. Now, 1,500 companies say that they will offer such facilities during 1999.[3] Already in the UK, major financial institutions such as Barclays Bank and the Nationwide will let you run your accounts with them using the internet. We are not talking about pipe dreams here; this is reality.

Indeed, the financial services sector is one of the most established on the internet. By the middle of 1998 it accounted for 16 per cent of all advertising spent on the internet, representing a 120 per cent growth on the previous year.[4] What appears to be taking most financial 'experts' by surprise, however, is the speed of acceptance. Even now, some bank customers do not like using ATMs. Others still insist on using their cheque book even though they have an easier-to-use debit card. Such resistance to new technology appears to the financial institutions to be commonplace, and could explain why they seem to have thought, until relatively recently, that people would not be keen to use the internet for their finances. Yet, as we have seen, the use of internet finance sites is rocketing. Indeed, according to one recent survey more than half the people questioned would like to receive household bills through their internet service.[5] Contrast this with another survey that warned that financial institutions would take time to develop the services that match consumer demand.[6] In other words, financial customers are ready for on-line trading, but the institutions are being too slow.

Unlike the slow introduction of ATMs and the only recently introduced universal card acceptance, the internet poses the financial institutions with something of a headache. In the past, if your bank did not have a cash machine, you simply queued in the banking hall and patiently waited to cash your cheque. There was no other option. Banks were therefore able to control their introduction of new technology, phasing it in to take into account costs, profits and their staff situation. The internet, though, is not like that. If your bank doesn't provide what you want, it only takes a few clicks of your mouse to try somewhere else, sign up and get what you want. Large companies are losing their control and the power now resides in the hands of the customer much more than it ever did. For this reason, banks, insurance companies, stockbrokers and the like, who treat the internet as just another technological change, will not survive for long.

The internet is a complete revolution, not just an extension of existing technology. Those financial institutions that understand this will survive. Those that ignore the technological changes, hoping to phase them in when they want, will disappear. Competition on the internet is keen and easy to find; with the internet you have the power to run your finances the way you want, rather than the way your financial experts want you to. That is proving something of a surprise in the financial world. The speed of take-up can no longer be controlled – as it could with ATMs – and the ease with which customers can depart and move elsewhere is much greater with the internet. Our financial institutions now face the most competition they have ever seen and a new breed of customers who can get their demands met.

Indeed, this is one of the key benefits of the internet – getting what you want when you want it. You are in control; no longer can you be fobbed off by 'procedures' or 'systems'. If a company cannot give you what you want, there is someone else just a few seconds and half-a-dozen mouse clicks away.

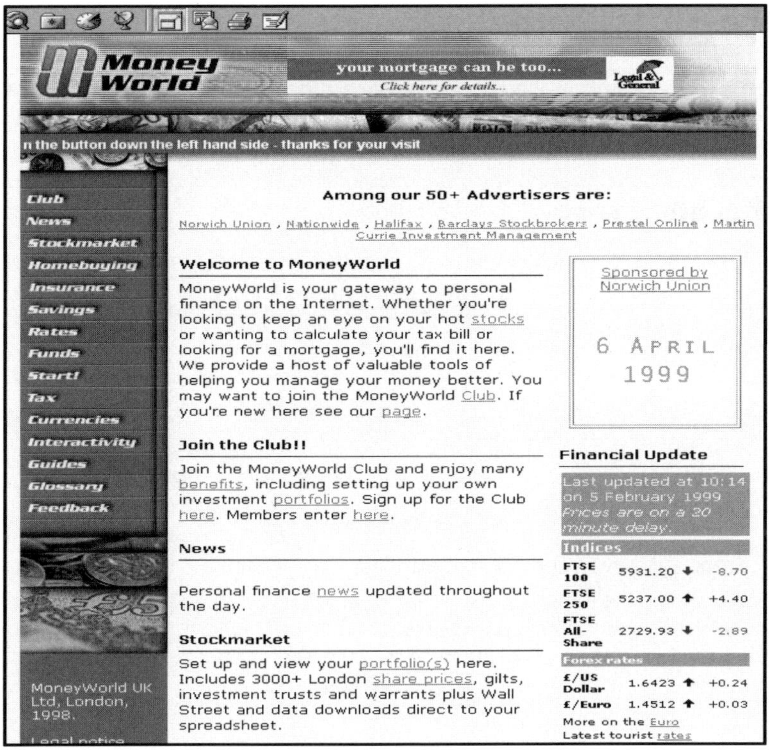

Fig. 3. The MoneyWorld web site. This is an excellent example of the many thousands of UK web sites now offering in-depth information and resources relating to every aspect of personal finance.

Gaining control

The fact that increasing numbers of people should want such control should not come as much of a surprise, as it seems to do to large businesses. Psychologists have known for many years that we like to control the world around us; lack of perceived control contributes to stress, hence we like to obtain as much control as we can of our personal worlds to avoid stressful situations arising. The more out of control we feel, the more stressed or concerned we feel.[7]

For many years, our control over our finances has been comparatively limited. Interest rates are what we are provided with, for instance, and changing to a better rate has been difficult. Trading shares and making informed choices about which companies to invest in has been the domain of our brokers – whose advice we accept, often because we have known no better. Such lack of control makes us feel uneasy about our finances and we worry. Will I have enough for retirement? Is that school fees plan really the best? Is my cash in the best savings account? Such concerns cause stress. Now, thanks to the internet, the control we can regain can reduce that concern.

We are simply being human by rapidly adopting the latest technology – it seems to help us regain control over an important aspect of our life and hence reduces our anxieties. It is this human factor that is likely to be responsible for much of the increase in the interest in internet finances. True, some of the 'early adopters' are techno-freaks who just love using the new ways of doing things – they get a buzz from the excitement of something new. However, the dramatic and rapid rise in interest in financial sites on the world wide web cannot be explained by this phenomenon alone. Suddenly, internet finance has become mainstream; it has already gained acceptance and will soon become the principal way in which we conduct our financial affairs.

Doubters exist

Of course, there are people who say that the internet is fine for young people who understand computers, but what about the rest of us? Well, research from the East Carolina University in the United States puts such a view into perspective. According to the research, people between the ages of 55 and 75 use personal computers for more hours per week than children under the age of 13.[8] Also, elderly people represent the fastest growing group of internet users. Everyone in society is therefore capable of seizing control of their finances as a result of using the internet.

That is why we no longer need High Street banks. You can run your bank account already from a telephone; the internet gives you the same luxury and even more control. You can be your own insurance broker by finding the best deals, often more quickly than a town centre company, you can buy your shares, get a mortgage and arrange a loan – all from the comfort of your study at home. We no longer need big, costly, buildings in our towns and cities for our financial affairs. We can get much, much more from the internet – and you don't have to go out in the cold or get wet. Added to that, think of the environmental benefits – fewer car journeys by customers, and vast numbers of staff no longer making journeys to offices. Even those who need to be retained to run the services can do so from the comfort of their own homes. As you can see, running your finances on the internet is going to have a tremendous impact on society as a whole. That's why this technology is so revolutionary.

Using the internet for your finances

So just what can you do using the internet today for your finances? You can:

- find up-to-date financial information
- check the accuracy of the advice you are being given
- run your bank account
- get loans and credit cards
- obtain 'cybercash' – electronic money for spending online in internet shops
- get a mortgage
- save your money in the best accounts
- buy stocks and shares
- run your pension fund
- buy and sell investments such as antiques or art treasures
- pay your taxes

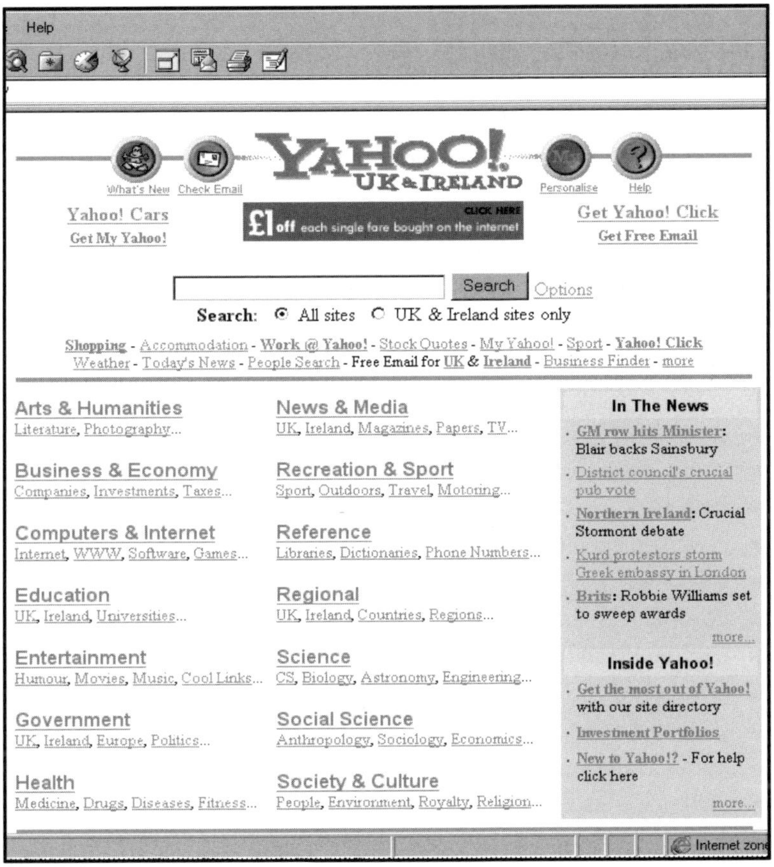

Fig. 4. You can search for financial information of all kinds with an amazingly powerful search 'engine' like the ever-popular Yahoo!. Its ever-expanding directory of web sites runs to millions of pages.

Everything that we can do in the High Street we can now do on the internet. Combine that with the control and convenience we gain with the internet and there can be no reason for ever again popping into town on a financial matter.

References

1 Information based on figures given at NCR web site: http://www.ncr.com
2 *Banking and Finance on the Internet*, Ed: Mary J Cronin, 1998, John Wiley & Sons, p. 247
3 *Banking and Finance on the Internet*, Ed: Mary J Cronin, 1998, John Wiley & Sons, pp. 75-76
4 *Business 2.0* magazine, January 1999, p. 115
See also: http://www.iab.net/news/billion_source.html
5 *Jupiter Communications Survey*, February 1999
See: http://www.nua.net/surveys
6 *Forrester Research Report*, December 1998
See http://www.nua.net/surveys
7 *Hilgard's Introduction to Psychology*, Rita L. Atkinson et al, 1996, Harcourt Brace and Company, pp. 478-479
8 Joyce Philbeck, *Seniors and the Internet*, November 1997
See: http://www.sspp.net/papers/philbeck.htm

2 Finding financial information

In this chapter we will explore:

- *do you need financial information?*
- *performing a simple search*
- *making other refinements to searches*
- *performing a more sophisticated search*
- *searching in a separate window*
- *looking at the finance sections*
- *checking the validity of information on the internet*
- *using independent financial advisers*
- *using links pages*
- *checking on information sites*
- *creating a web page shortcut on your desktop*
- *dealing with small print in web pages*
- *using webcasts*
- *using web chat and forums*
- *gaining financial information outside the web*
- *getting information in your 'inbox'*
- *using usenet newsgroups*
- *finding financial information on the internet in other ways*
- *getting financial information in print*
- *discovering more about the euro*
- *essential tips for finding information on the internet*

One of the most exciting aspects of the internet is its encyclopaedic nature. You can find out anything and everything you want to know. No matter what you want to find out, someone somewhere has the information. All you have to do is find it.

The term 'internet' simply refers to a disparate bunch of millions of computers spread throughout the world and linked together through modems. There is no particular order to it and no one is in charge. Hence information can be repeated and can be widespread. In the early days of the internet (about 1994) searching for the material you wanted to find was like looking for a lost contact lens. You knew it was there somewhere, but could you find it? Such a limitation meant that the internet was of little use to non-computer experts. However, a whole host of new companies quickly sprouted that provided efficient searching methods; in other words, all the hard work was taken away from us, making the internet truly easy to use. Such cataloguing and searching facilities now mean that you can gain access to any financial information you want – and much of it will be free.

Do you need financial information?

Like most of us, you need as much information as you can get. According to a study commissioned by NatWest in 1995, only one in three people knew the difference between 'gross' and 'net' interest. Most schoolteachers accept that teaching children about such financial matters is important, but only one in ten feel confident to do just that.[1] Perhaps the fact that few of us learned anything about personal finances at school lies behind our need for information and support in our adult life.

Nowadays, you can learn more about personal finance in a range of ways, from books to correspondence courses and adult education. But finding out through the internet can be much more exciting. There is an enormous amount of financial information available; there are almost 10,000 web sites that have the word 'bank' in their title, for instance as well as a further 2,000 that include the word 'savings' in their name, to say nothing of the tens of thousands of web sites that include these words somewhere on their pages, not in their title! In addition, a new internet site is added every two seconds of every day – about 175,000 every working week (figures calculated from web statistics[2]). It is therefore hardly surprising that, somewhere, there exists the information you need!

Performing a simple search

Looking for any item on the internet is easy if you use a **search engine**. Essentially, this is a service provided by a commercial company that catalogues sites on the world wide web. These companies make their money from advertising and from selling ancillary internet services. The search engines you may well have heard of come from companies like AltaVista, AOL Netfind, CompuServe, Excite, Infoseek, Lycos, MSN

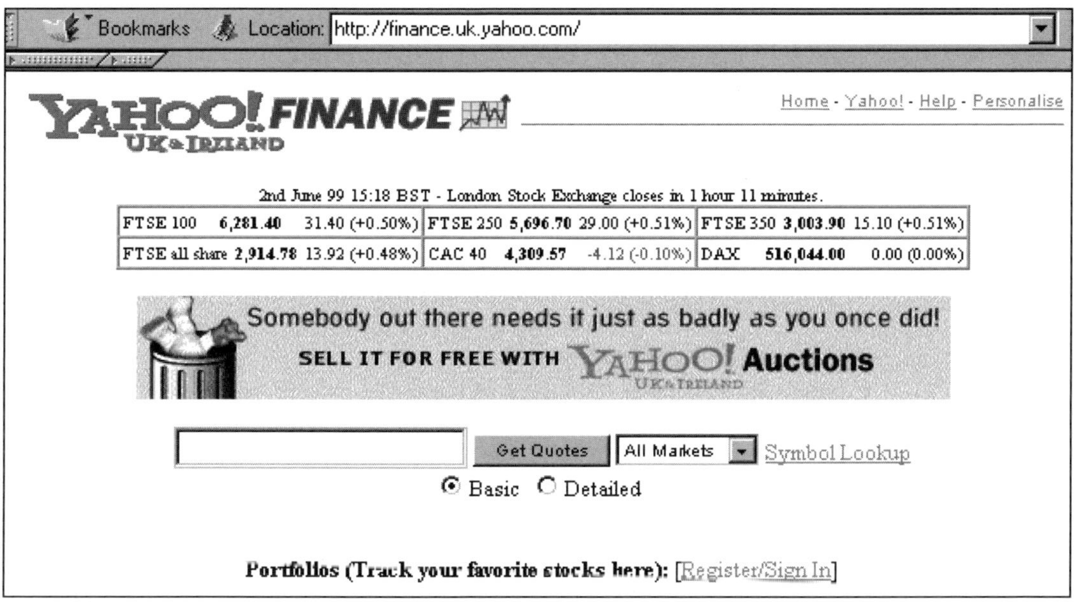

Fig. 5. Search engines like Yahoo! also include specialised financial sections. The services they are offering consumers today are becoming amazingly sophisticated – portfolio management, world wide stockmarket prices, currency and interest rates and more. You can even run a shop on Yahoo!.

Search, Netscape Netcenter, UK Plus, Web Crawler, or the ever popular Yahoo!. Your internet service provider may also have set up search facilities on their home page, though usually this will be just a link to one of the most common services listed here.

To find what you want, all you need to do is type a key word or two in the box – for example 'uk pensions' or 'mortgage interest rates' – and press the search button. Within a few seconds (depending on the speed of your computer and the flow of internet traffic) your screen will display a list of web sites that match your criteria. However, be warned: this is a relatively crude and basic way of searching the internet – you will probably find what you want, but you will also have to wade through a lot of rubbish!

For instance, if you were to enter the words 'interest rates' in the search box, you'd be sent back a list of all the web sites that include the words 'interest' and 'rates'. Using Excite, for example, you would end up with a list of more than 1.5 million pages that mentioned these words. That's because many of these pages have just the word 'interest' or just the word 'rates'. Hence if you were looking for up-to-date interest rates, what use would the site from Cybermarket Strategies be to you? That site appears in the 'interest rates' listing because its site includes the words 'long distance *rates* apply' alongside its advert for live one-to-one phone sex. Hardly what you expected!

To avoid wasting your time, use the search engine dialogue boxes more wisely. One of the best ways is to enclose your search key words in inverted commas: if we had searched for "interest rates", our sexy phone service no longer appears in our list, because the inverted commas tell the search engine that we want *both* words to appear. In this instance, Excite now finds only 42,000 matches, compared with the original vast list. Even so, it's still a long list that would take many hours to wade through.

To refine your searches even further, use the word AND (in capitals). In our example we could search for 'interest rates' AND 'uk'. That reduces the list of sites down to 4,000. This is still not manageable, but much shorter than before. Further refine the search to 'interest rates' AND 'uk' AND 'latest' and we are down to 800 web sites, but still a large amount of information to sift through.

So, to use basic search engines in a refined way:

(a) Put all the keywords together in quotation marks.
(b) Use the word AND (in capitals) to make sure all the words appear in the search results.

Making other refinements to searches

You can also use the following words to help refine your searches:

▷ AND NOT

- ▷ OR
- ▷ For AND or AND NOT you can also use '+' and '–'
- ▷ url: (this means the word you are searching for must be contained in the address of the web page)
- ▷ text: (this means the word you are searching for must not be contained in the address of the web page)
- ▷ You an also use the '*' character to search for 'wild cards'. For instance 'bank*' would find bank, banks, banking, banker, bankers, banknote, bankroll, bankrupt, and so on.

For more information on specific search techniques within your favourite search engine, be sure to click on the 'help' button. Also, many search engines have an 'advanced search' button. Click on this and you will be able to refine your search in even more detail, pin-pointing your precise requirements. Essentially, if you use the basic search facilities of the search engines, you will be faced with an avalanche of material that will bewilder and confuse you. It is much better to learn how to use refined or sophisticated search techniques.

Performing a more sophisticated search

Suppose you want to find out about the latest information on a company that you were thinking of investing in. You could go to their web site (if they have one) and find out, but the information would naturally be biased. How could you find out something independent about a company you want to invest in? You could use a search engine for 'investment advice', but you would end up with a massive list – almost 16,000 sites according to AltaVista.

The answer to this conundrum is to give your search some thought before you start typing in keywords. It is terribly easy to get enthusiastic and simply type in the first few words that come into your head, but they will inevitably lead to rather poor results. With some careful thought and planning, your search terms can be quite sophisticated and lead you almost directly to what you want.

However, there is an easier way. All the major search engines have put the sites they list into categories. You can 'drill down' through these categories until you get to the information you want. For instance, in Yahoo! you would need to click on the 'Investments' button, select 'commercial investment services' and you would then be faced with an array of choices already sorted for you. In other words, you will just need to make a few mouse clicks, rather than spend ages trawling through long lists because your search terms are too vague.

It's a good idea to try a couple of different search engines, too. If, for instance, you have found something on Excite that may be of interest, also go to Lycos to see if anything else is listed. Not all web sites are listed by all search engines, so it's worthwhile zipping across to another search page to see what's available.

Checking the validity of online information

Searching in separate windows

You can easily search in different search engines at the same time by opening up a separate window in your browser.

Microsoft Internet Explorer
To do this in Microsoft Internet Explorer:

1. Position the cursor over the item you want to select.
2. Click and hold the right mouse button.
3. Select 'Open in New Window'.

You will then see the page you wanted open up in a second window, leaving your original window untouched. Using this technique you can browse through a couple of different search areas at the same time.

Netscape Navigator
You can do the same with Netscape Navigator. To do this you should:

1. Select the File menu.
2. Choose 'New Navigator Window'.

Looking at the finance sections

All the major search engines and content providers such as CompuServe and AOL have financial sections. These are often a good starting point for finding financial information on the web. The material on these pages is categorised so you can easily find your interests. However, be warned: even though the companies running the search engines take great care to ensure the pages they refer you to are valid, they do not guarantee their content or in any way endorse the information provided on them. You should take care yourself to make sure that the information you get from the web is valid.

Checking the validity of information on the internet

One of the benefits of the internet is also one of its downfalls. Anyone can set up a web site, put virtually anything they like on it and easily pass themselves off as experts in a field. Just how can you work out whether the sites you find in your searches are valid and reliable? One way is to look at the bottom of the home pages you enter. See if the small print mentions such organisations as

- ▷ The Personal Investment Authority (PIA)
- ▷ The Securities and Investment Board (SIB)
- ▷ The Investment Management Regulatory Organisation (IMRO)
- ▷ The Securities and Futures Authority (SFA)

During 2000, the UK regulatory authorities will be combined into a single regulator, The Financial Services Authority (FSA). These are the

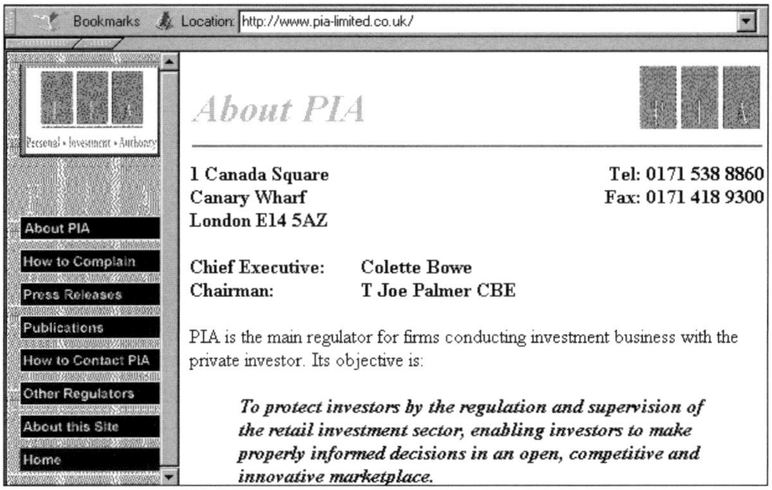

Fig. 6. Make sure that the advice you get is authorised by one of the regulatory authorities, such as the Personal Investment Authority (PIA).

regulatory bodies covering companies that operate from the UK. In the United States, the Federal Reserve Regulations only apply to US citizens. In Europe, a new EU directive was drafted at the end of 1998 to cover web-based financial services.[3] However, web sites that quote the regulatory authorities which cover their activities are likely to be acceptable to you.

If you are still unsure, check with the regulatory authorities themselves. The relevant web sites are:

PIA	http://www.pia-limited.co.uk/
IMRO	http://www.imro.co.uk/
SIB	http://www.sib.co.uk
SFA	http://www.sfa.org.uk/home.htm

Using independent financial advisers

One way of making sure the information you receive via the internet is valid is to get it checked by an Independent Financial Adviser (IFA).

Fig. 7. This is the web site of IMRO, the UK Investment Management Regulatory Organisation.

Fig. 8. Another UK financial regulatory body you can explore online is the Financial Services Authority (FSA).

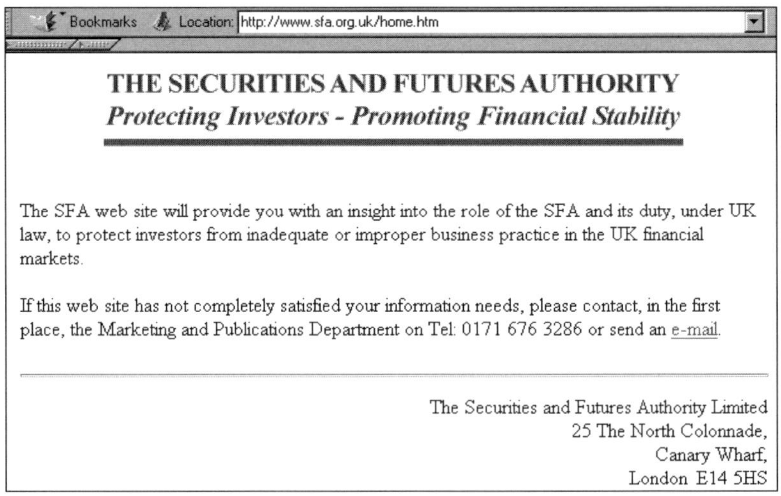

Fig. 9. The Securities and Futures Authority (SFA) also fills a regulatory role.

These people are regulated by the Financial Services Act 1986 and must give advice that is suited to your particular circumstances. In order to gain IFA status, individuals need to pass certain tests and gain specific qualifications. Their supervisors also have to pass more stringent examinations. Hence, if you are unsure about any financial information you gain from the internet, you may wish to check it out using an IFA. An IFA near to you can be found on the MoneyWeb site, listed below.

Using links pages

Another method of determining the validity of the data you get over the internet is to go to well-respected and known sources of financial information first and then use their pages of links to take you to the kind of sites you want. Although most companies say they haven't checked out the various sites they list and can't be held responsible for their contents, there is a good chance that a major financial institution is not going to list dubious sites on its own pages. Well-known and respected financial information sites include:

AAA Investment Guide
http://www.wisebuy.co.uk/sg-tx0.htm

The Financial Times
http://www.ft.com

FIND – Financial Information Net Directory
http://www.find.co.uk/

Money Central
http://www.moneycentral.com/home.asp

MoneyExtra
http://moneyextra.com/

MoneyWeb
http://www.moneyweb.co.uk/

Moneywise magazine
http://www.readersdigest.co.uk/finance.htm

MoneyWorld UK
http://www.moneyworld.co.uk/

The MoneyZone
http://www.lineone.net/moneyzone/content.fhtml

The Motley Fool
http://www.fool.co.uk/

Times-Money
http://www.times-money.co.uk

This Is Money
http://www.thisismoney.com/

UK Portfolio
http://www.ukportfolio.freeserve.co.uk/research2.htm

You could also try looking at the links on sites set up by personal finance software specialists such as Quicken and Microsoft Money:

Quicken
http://www.quicken.co.uk

Microsoft Money
http://moneyxtra.com/default.asp

Checking on information sites

Each of the sites mentioned above has its good and bad points. The main bad point that applies to all of them is the fact that they do not provide everything for everyone. However, they are comprehensive information sources and by using a couple of them you will be able to find information on all of your financial concerns. It's a good idea to find a couple of sites that you like and which provide the information you need and then 'bookmark' them. You can also create a 'shortcut' on the desktop to your favourite sites.

Creating a web page shortcut on your desktop

In either Microsoft Internet Explorer or Netscape Navigator:

1. Make sure you are viewing the page you want as your shortcut.
2. Click and hold the right mouse button.
3. Choose Create Shortcut from the pop-up menu that appears.

A shortcut to your favourite page will then appear on your desktop. To view it at any time, all you need do is double click the shortcut icon for this page. If you are not already connected to the internet, and providing your connection software is correctly set up (see Appendix 2), you will be automatically connected to the up-to-date version of the page.

AAA Investment Guide
This is really a guide to financial terms and products. For instance, if you never knew what 'ground rent' was, this site will explain it to you. As such, many of the pages you can access are educational. However, you can subscribe to the service at a cost of £39.99 for the entire contents of the site. This site is useful if you want some background, but it doesn't provide you with comprehensive financial data. It is easy to understand and well written.

▷ *Key benefits of the AAA Investment Guide Site*
Crammed with essential facts
Well written and easy to understand

Fig. 10. This is the AAA Investment Guide web site from the UK-based information service Wisebuy.

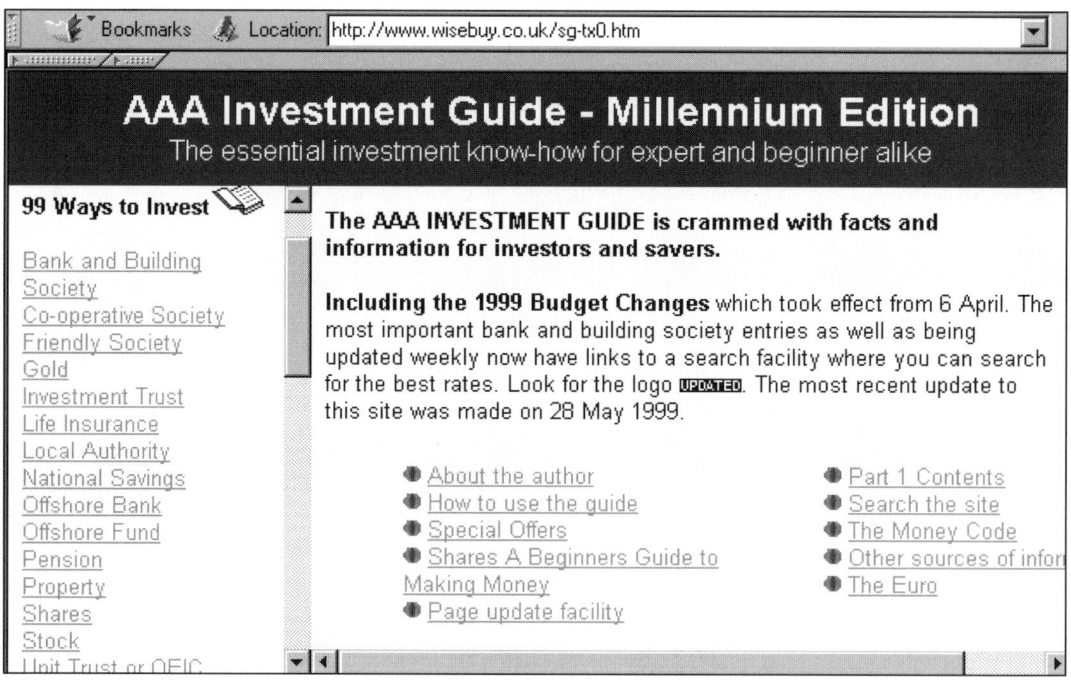

▷ *Disadvantages of the AAA Investment Guide*

Looks rather untidy in places

No extensive financial data

The Financial Times

You need to register to use the site. This is free, but you will not get access unless you give some basic details about yourself. Once registered, you get full access to the FT site. This site has a leaning towards business users and is heavily geared to the stock market, international finance and the like. It is very well organised, easy-to-use and has vast amounts of in-depth research available. There are occasional banner advertisements, but they do not slow down the site, which operates very quickly. Naturally, the site contains news from the *Financial Times* itself, but there are also special reports on a host of economic and financial matters. Stock prices are updated every 15 minutes and you can order annual reports of companies you may wish to invest in.

Fig. 11. The web site of The *Financial Times*. Among the resources available on this very impressive site is an online library of more than 4 million articles gathered from 3,000 different publications.

▷ *Key benefits of the Financial Times site*

Comprehensive and authoritative economic and financial information

Full information on companies, including annual reports

▷ *Disadvantages of the Financial Times site*

Aimed more at business than personal finance

You need to understand financial and economic terms

FIND

This site provides a comprehensive listing of financial information. Essentially, it is a series of pages of links to other financial web sites. For instance, if you did not know where to look for 'pet insurance', for instance, this site can point you in the right direction. The site is supported by a number of banner adverts (which can sometimes be annoying) but, unlike many sites that contain banner adverts, FIND is

Fig. 12. The FIND site is an excellent starting point for finding information on the world wide web. There is much more on its home page than there is space to show here.

very fast. That, combined with its daily updating and comprehensive nature, is probably why it has received accolades from the press. The *Financial Times* said that FIND was 'the best UK directory for financial services'[4] and the *Wall Street Journal* said that FIND should figure at the top of a 'must visit' list[5].

▷ *Key benefits of the FIND site*

Clear and easy-to-find directory of information on all areas of finance

Fast and accurate listings

▷ *Disadvantages of the FIND site*

No information of its own – it is just a directory

Adverts can sometimes be annoying

MoneyCentral

This is the site you are taken to when you use Microsoft Money. It is crammed with information and advice. Also, there are some excellent 'how to' articles that lead you through, for instance, budgeting. However, this site is heavily biased towards American users and even

Fig. 13. The MoneyCentral site is run as part of MicroSoft Network (MSN), Bill Gates' global internet service provider.

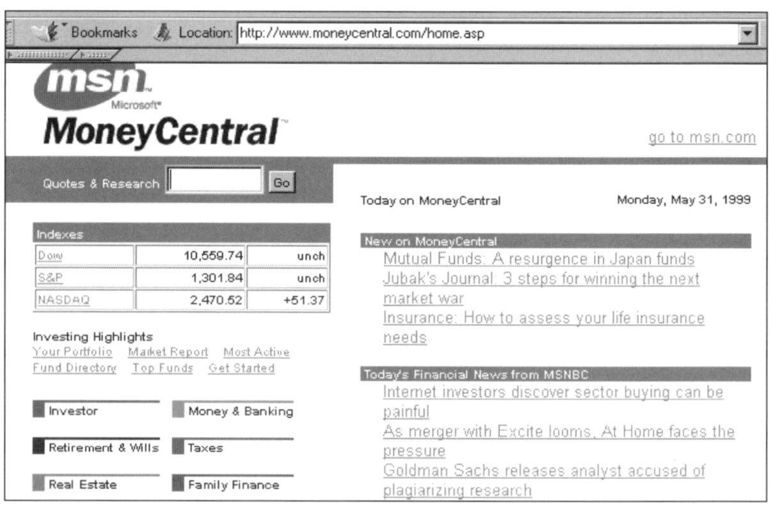

though much of the basic information is helpful, unless you own shares in American companies or have other financial interests in the USA, much of the detailed information may not be very useful.

▷ *Key benefits of MoneyCentral*

Can link to Microsoft Money, if you use that for your accounts
Has excellent 'how-to' style guides to almost every financial matter

▷ *Disadvantages of MoneyCentral*

Large American bias
Lots of text to read

MoneyExtra

This site is also produced in association with Microsoft Money and, thankfully, is UK-biased. It provides a range of information, but does not have the 'how-to' style articles of MoneyCentral. There are, however, plenty of links and the latest financial news. The site also lists tables of interest rates and so on. To get the full benefits of the site, such as portfolio listings, you need to register. This service is, though, free.

▷ *Key benefits of the MoneyExtra site*

Up-to-date British information
Plenty of background material to help boost your knowledge

▷ *Disadvantages of the MoneyExtra site*

Text is sometimes confusing
At first sight, MoneyExtra doesn't appear to contain much

Moneynet

Moneynet (http://www.moneynet.co.uk) is a site that offers a great deal of practical information on a whole host of financial matters. Unlike many of the other general personal finance sites, Moneynet is not

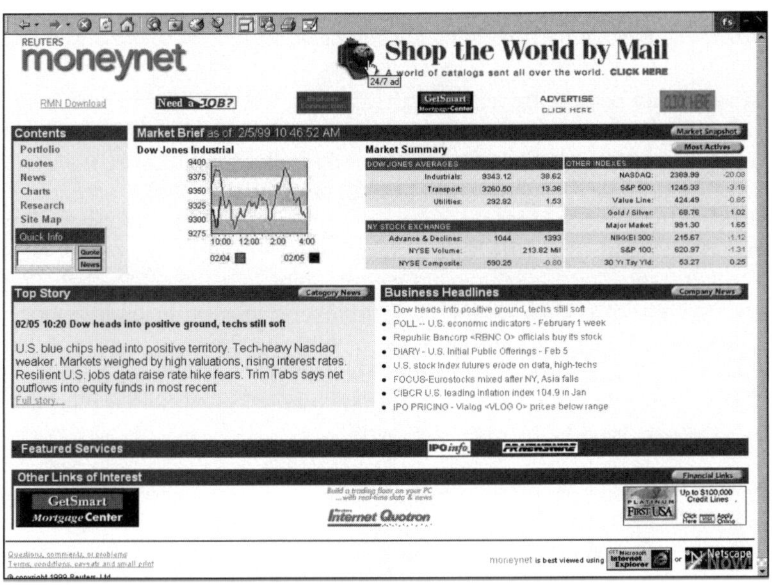

Fig. 14. The Moneynet web site is a typically impressive US financial resource.

about general advice. This site is geared towards products. It is an excellent way of scouring the internet for the specific products you need. The site is updated every day so you can be sure that the product information you receive at this site is the most recent. You can therefore compare a range of financial products to ensure you are getting the best deal. There is also a complete A-Z of financial terminology.

▷ *Key benefits of the Moneynet site*

Quick search of financial products in all categories (mortgage, savings etc)
Daily updates so it is the latest information

▷ *Disadvantages of the Moneynet site*

The amount of information you get can be confusing
It's a huge site with a great deal to see

MoneyWeb

This site is heavily geared towards pensions, mortgages and insurance. Also contained within the various pages is a range of 'calculators'. For instance, you can enter in your age and how much pension you want when you retire and it tells you how much more you need to invest. There is also an extensive range of links to Independent Financial Advisers (IFAs), listed helpfully by post code. However, the site does not have the same degree of professional look and feel about it as the other directories.

▷ *Key benefits of the MoneyWeb site*

Essential background on pensions, mortgages and insurance
Good guide to IFAs

▷ *Disadvantages of the MoneyWeb site*

Poor look and feel
Does not provide a comprehensive guide to all financial matters

Moneywise magazine

This site appears to be the *Moneywise* magazine on the web. There is a range of articles providing financial advice and information as well as a comprehensive listing of interest rates, performance tables and so on. However, the site annoyingly does not provide helpful links. For instance, there is a very useful page of information on credit card interest rates. This lists the various companies offering credit cards and the interest rates they charge, but the listing only provides telephone number contacts, rather than web or email addresses, even though many of the companies listed have an established internet presence. This severely limits the Moneywise site, even though there is plenty of useful background financial information.

▷ *Key benefits of the Moneywise site*

Up-to-date financial advice
Performance tables to help make comparisons

▷ *Disadvantages of the Moneywise site*

Few links to gain further information
Lots of text

MoneyWorld UK

MoneyWorld UK is a comprehensive site full of information and useful links. In a sense it combines the best of the directory-style sites with the best of the information sites. In this way you can find out basic financial information or go straight to more detailed advice, such as a specific quote for insurance. It has links to other sites so that you can get quotes and information, plus it has a great deal of background information of its own. The site also has its own 'Club'. You can join this free of charge, though you do enter your details onto a mailing list. In return you get valuations of your own portfolio, regular emailed financial news, and a range of other offers such as money-off vouchers.

▷ *Key benefits of the MoneyWorld site*

Helpful information in an easy-to-read 'questions and answers' style
Good range of 'calculators' and quotations services

▷ *Disadvantages of the MoneyWorld site*

Much of the information is sponsored
Some pages are text heavy

MoneyZone

This site is run by LineOne, a content provider. Although anyone can access this page, you do not get the extra benefits until you sign up for

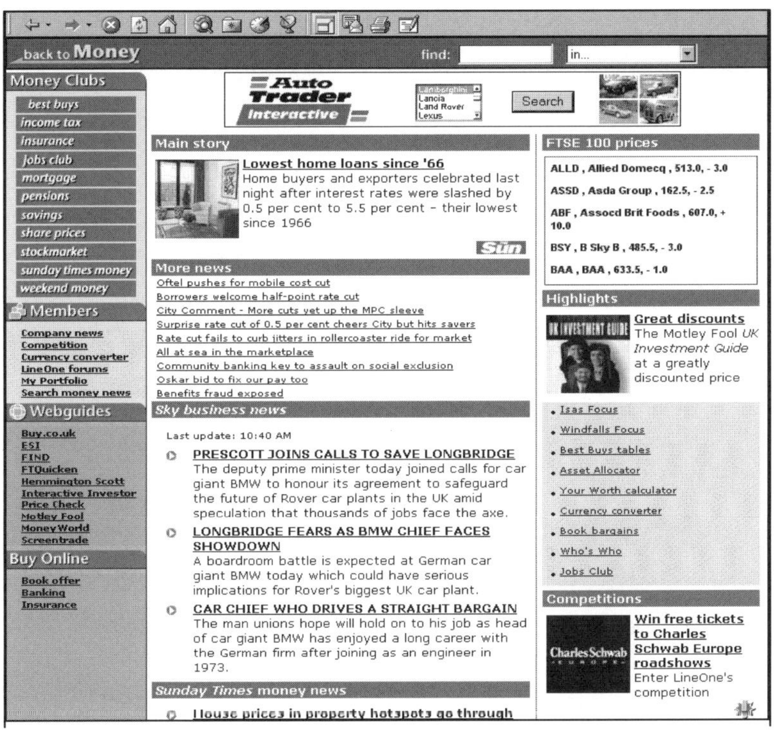

Fig. 15. The LineOne Money Club web site is a must for financial information.

the LineOne service. This costs £9.99 per month. The extra benefits include internet access, email, and a specialist range of exclusive pages of UK-focused material. This extends beyond financial information, but there are extra pages to the MoneyZone that you can only access if you are a LineOne member. These pages include specialist advice, for instance. Even so, the information you get without paying the LineOne charge is extensive. There is a host of links to financial news and star ratings of other financial web sites.

▷ *Key benefits of the MoneyZone site*
- Focused clearly on the UK
- Extensive up-to-date financial news and features

▷ *Disadvantages of the MoneyZone site*
- You have to pay for the full service (though you do get additional benefits)
- Returning to the main page can be awkward and involves lots of clicking

The Motley Fool

The Motley Fool web site is renowned. It is fun, quirky, but very approachable and appears embedded in the real world. The advice and information available is direct and to the point and gives you clear, step-by-step guidance on particular financial objectives. The site is UK-focused, though there is an American version as well if you have financial interests in the USA (http://www.fool.com). In either case, the

Fig. 16. The quirkily named Motley Fool has established itself as an impressive information point for personal finance.

Motley Fool is about investments. Borrowing money, banking and the like is not the domain of this site. Hence it is not comprehensive, but for investment information there are few that can beat it. There is also a message board system so that you can share ideas and thoughts with other users.

▷ *Key benefits of the Motley Fool site*

Down-to-earth practical advice and information
Solid international reputation

▷ *Disadvantages of the Motley Fool site*

Heavily focused on investment side of finance
Lots of text on some pages (more than 1,000 words)

Quicken

Quicken is one of the most popular computer-based personal and small business accounts programs. It has an internet site packed with information on financial matters. This site is a good starting point, but its links are not very extensive and point largely to sources of financial news, rather than hard information on specific financial products and services. Even so, such news-based information is very important. You can get a picture of what is happening in a particular industry sector, for

Fig. 17. General financial sites like Quicken can provide an excellent starting point for locating the right information.

instance, or find out about new products and services as they are launched. However, many of the news sites are American-biased.

▷ *Key benefits of the Quicken site*

Can link to Quicken accounts if you use this software
Up-to-date trading prices

▷ *Disadvantages of the Quicken site*

Heavy American bias, particularly in the news section
Not all its features are useful if you don't use Quicken software

Times-Money

The *Times* newspaper has its own personal finance web site which is a highly useful source of general information. There are also statistical data, such as the latest share prices. The site includes a useful mortgage calculator so that you can work out how much you can afford to borrow. In addition, there is a comparison on loan interest rates, helping you find the best deal. Other useful information includes foreign exchange rates and a guide on completing self-assessment tax returns. The Times-Money site also has a handy glossary of financial terms, in case you need anything explaining. It's a quick site, easy to use and comes with the authority of the *Times* newspaper's financial section, which has a solid reputation.

▷ *Key benefits of the Times-Money web site*

Comprehensive coverage of British finance
Handy reference tables and data

▷ *Disadvantages of the Times-Money web site*

Lots of relatively small text
Annoying 'marquee' (a moving line of text at the bottom of the screen)

This Is Money

This Is Money is produced by the publishers of the *Daily Mail* and the *Evening Standard*. Both of these newspapers have a solid reputation in financial reporting. The web site is nice and clear and has a number of useful tools available. For instance there is a mortgage calculator and an exchange rate converter. In addition, you'll find tables of interest rates on offer for savings and borrowings, as well as all the latest financial news and a useful 'ask the expert' section, where you can submit a question and it will be answered on the web page itself. You can also review the questions asked by other web surfers. Overall, this is an interesting site that is full of useful information and is more approachable for the lay person than some of the other sites.

▷ *Key benefits of the This Is Money site*

Comprehensive, easy to understand coverage
Useful calculators and financial tools

Fig. 18. The web site of 'This is Money', an online service developed by the *Daily Mail, Mail on Sunday* and *Evening Standard.*

▷ *Disadvantages of the This is Money site*

Some of the great mass of information seems to be repetitive

The pages contain a lot of data and can be slow to load (the home page is some 20 times larger than the home page of a typical search engine, for instance)

UK Portfolio

This site is simply a list of financial links. As such it can be a useful starting point on your search for financial information. The site can direct you to a wide array of information, but it is not clearly listed. The site presents you with questions, the answers to which are specific web sites. However, these are not listed in a logical order.

▷ *Key benefits of the UK Portfolio site*

Quick listing of potentially interesting web sites on finance

Heavily biased towards the UK

▷ *Disadvantages of the UK Portfolio site*

Not apparently logical presentation

Not as comprehensive as some other sites

AOL, Compuserve, Freeserve

Each of these popular internet content providers has specialist financial information pages that are available only to members. If you access the internet using AOL, Compuserve or Freeserve, your starting point for financial information may well be their finance channels.

Dealing with small print in web pages

If a web page has small type you can change it so you can see it more clearly in your browser window:

In Microsoft Explorer
Choose the 'View' menu.
Select 'Fonts'.
Choose 'larger' or 'largest'.

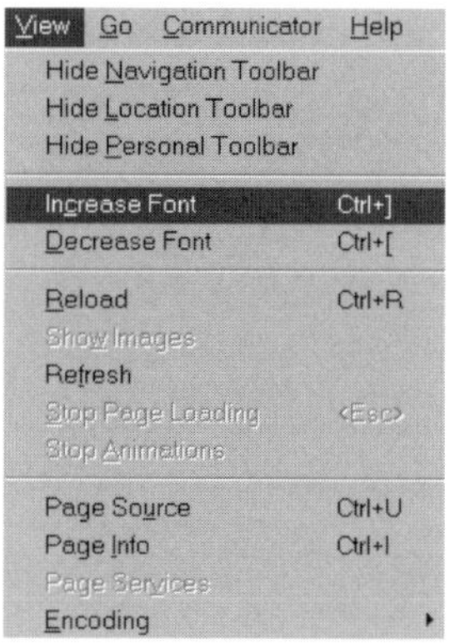

In Netscape Communicator
Choose the 'View' menu.
Select 'Increase Font'.

Using webcasts

The world wide web is increasingly being used for broadcasting. Video and audio technology has improved dramatically in the past couple of years and watching live TV or listening to audio broadcasts is now feasible. There are regular daily financial programs, including, for instance, live coverage of equity trading. To find out what's on, go to sites that list schedules, such as:

http://channelseek.com
http://www.onnow.com/
http://www.real.com/realguide/index.html

If you don't have the software to let you see web TV or listen to web audio you can download it from:

http://www.real.com

Using web chat and forums

Other useful places for financial information are the 'chat rooms' and the forums that are springing up. These allow you to talk or type direct, often live, to people in the know, or to others like you looking for information and advice. The result is that you can share ideas, web addresses, and other material with like-minded people. Most of these forums are 'unmoderated' – no one is in charge and there is no 'editor' making sure the information you get is accurate. However, they are useful places to go if you are really stuck and can't find what you want elsewhere on the internet. Also, these forums allow you to share tips and ideas with people in a similar situation.

Example
Investorville (http://www.investorville.com) is a popular forum for discussing investments. You can share ideas with others on this site and swap stories about how your investments are doing. Such sites are electronic versions of clubs or chatting with mates down the pub! Although many such sites exist, most are US-biased and geared towards online discussion between traders and brokers. However, they do provide interesting snippets of information and news. You should be able to find a list of the many forums available categorised on your favourite search engine.

Gaining financial information outside the web

The internet has more to it than the world wide web, though this is where the vast majority of people spend their entire time.[6] Two other areas that are important are:

▷ email

▷ usenet (newsgroups)

Getting information in your 'inbox'

You can subscribe to various services, often free of charge, so that you can obtain up-to-date financial information in your email inbox. Some of the web sites listed earlier in this chapter have subscription services that provide you with email newsletters of the latest information. Often, these will just highlight the new information on the web page, but such newsletters are worthwhile since you don't need to keep revisiting the page to check for updates. There are also mailing lists you can join for up-to-date financial information. There are several hundred of these, so it would be impossible to list them here, but if you want to check out which mailing lists are available go to:

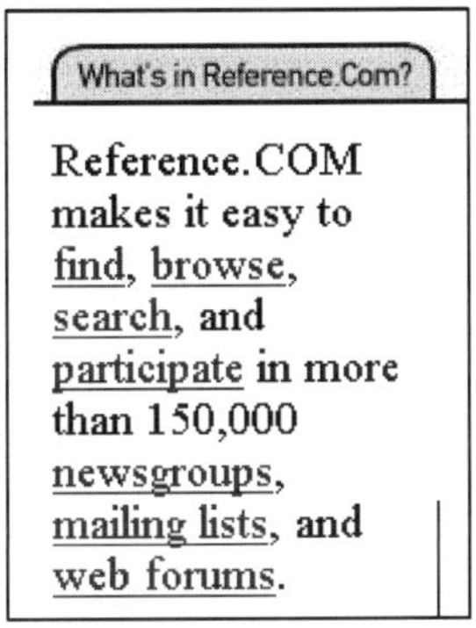

Reference.com
http://www.reference.com/

Some of the popular email newsletters include those listed below. To subscribe send an email to the address shown, with the word 'Subscribe' in the subject box.

Personal Finance Digest
persfin-digest@shore.net

Prodigy
business-finance@listserv.prod

Soros
sfn-finance@soros.org

Using usenet newsgroups and financial information

Newsgroups are found on 'usenet' – the part of the internet that is written, run and set up by 'users', hence its name. This is the area of the internet that is least frequently used, but which nevertheless is interesting, though somewhat dangerous at times! That's because it is even less moderated than the web forums. At least with a web forum, if something is said or a message is posted that is not in the best interests of other users, the people running the page can remove it. With newsgroups, for the most part, no such filtering or editing takes place, and information can be unreliable.

However, the usenet area of the internet is also the area where the

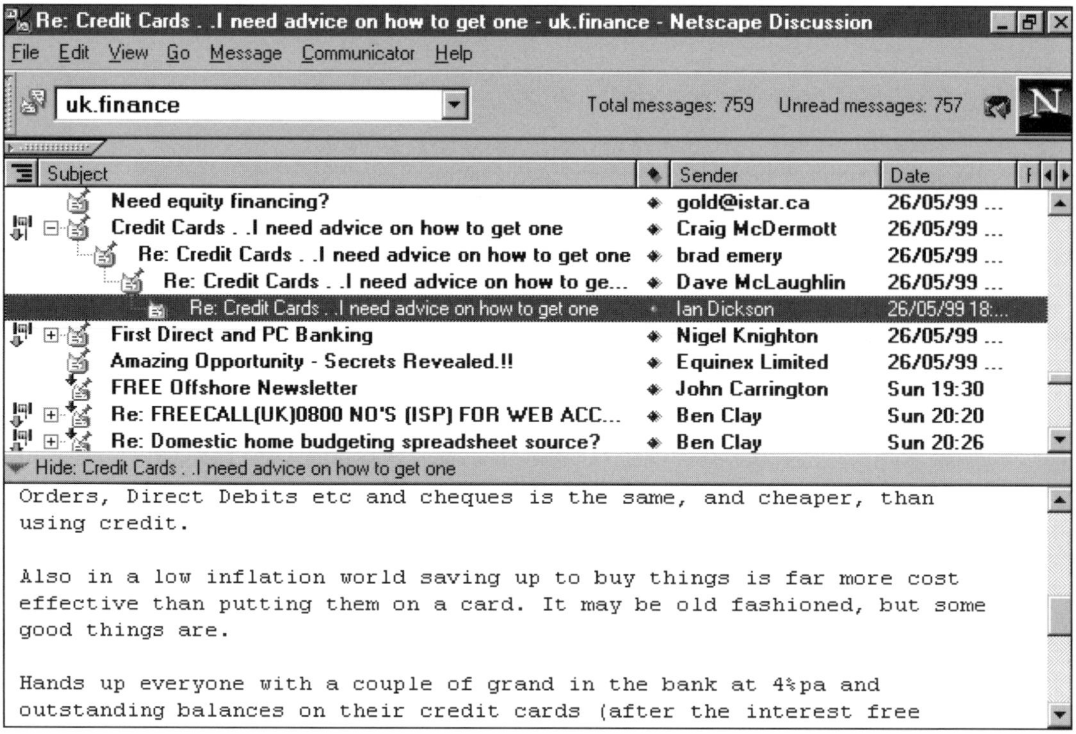

Fig. 19. A typical public usenet session in progress. This particular newsgroup is called uk.finance. There were 759 messages when accessed. You just highlight any message header to read a particular message.

'hottest' news and tips will be found. News of great national or international importance can flash round the newsgroups in seconds. This is very important for people with large investments at stake, for instance. Also, many people in the financial world keep an eye on the usenet newsgroups for the latest rumours and gossip about what is really going on within companies.

There are literally tens of thousands of newsgroups available. Your web browser (Microsoft Internet Explorer or Netscape Navigator) will let you access these newsgroups on usenet as well as the world wide web. Just select 'news' and you will be connected. The first time you do this you will be prompted to download to your machine a list all of the newsgroups that are available. This may take some time, typically between 10 and 30 minutes but, once you have the list on your computer, you only need to update it from time to time. You will need to search through the list until you find one that suits your needs. Once you have found a title that sounds interesting, you 'subscribe' to it. This doesn't mean you have to pay for it. It is your computer's way of knowing that you want to see the messages posted in that newsgroup. It just involves a couple of mouse clicks, and you can just as easily 'unsubscribe'.

Finding financial information on the internet in other ways

To save you searching through newsgroups or the web itself, you can get various software tools that will do it for you. These are a couple of the well-known commercial programs:

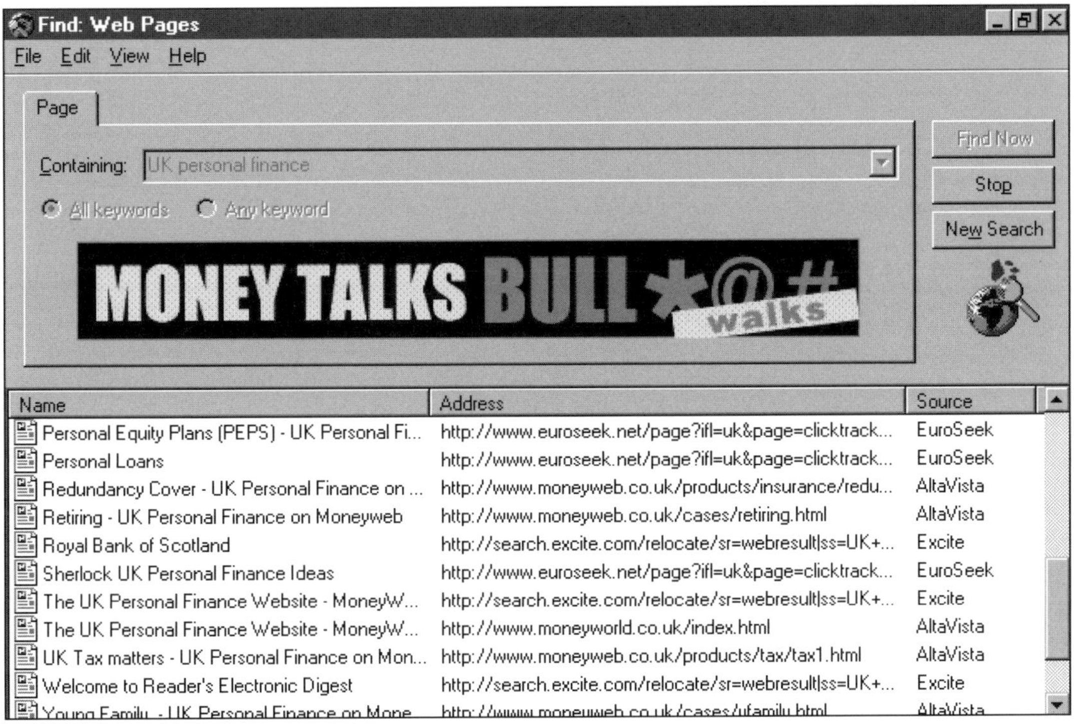

Fig. 20. A search using an 'agent', in this case the popular Web Ferret, available free from Ferretsoft.com. Web Ferret makes things easy for you by searching several of the top search engines at the same time and at high speed.

▷ Autonomy Agentware

▷ Webcompass

There are also free tools that will search the internet for you. These handy tools are called 'ferrets' and you can download them in a few minutes from:

FerretSoft
http://www.ferretsoft.com
The free ferret programs will search in a range of different places, saving you the time and trouble of ferreting about yourself. You can upgrade the free versions to professional ferret programs, which have more capacity and capabilities. There are web ferrets, news ferrets and email ferrets.

Getting financial information in print

Of course, the internet can provide you with millions of pages of information, but you might like something more permanent. You can keep up to date with all the latest financial books in print by going to one of the leading online bookshops:

Amazon Books
http://www.amazon.co.uk

The Internet Bookshop (WH Smith)
http://www.bookshop.co.uk/hme/hmepge.asp

These bookshops allow you to purchase books over the internet, but they have an added extra. Just sign up to their email service, at the bottom of the home pages, and you can receive emails when books on your favourite subjects are published. You could also try:

Blackwells Bookshop
http://bookshop.blackwells.co.uk/

You can also obtain regular information on financial matters on the internet in the weekly column inside the old-established magazine *Investor's Chronicle*. The other financial magazines also contain articles on the internet from time to time. Newspapers also contain information on finances on the internet. For instance there is a column 'Internet Investor' every Saturday in *The Independent*. A similar column ('Techno Investor') also appears on Saturdays in *The Daily Telegraph*. The *Sunday Times* has a column called 'Internet Shopper'.

Discovering more about the euro

Now that the single European currency is in existence you can find out a great deal more about it, and what it means for your finances, at a number of sites. A good place to start is the official government site on the euro at:
http://www.euro.gov.uk/

You can find up-to-date news about the euro at:
http://www.euro-emu.co.uk/

The official EU site on the euro is at:
http://europa.eu.int/euro/html/entry.html

If you want to convert any currency from or to euros, you can go straight to a conversion program at:
http://195583.com/

Business-based information on the euro can be found at:
http://www.eubusiness.com/emu/euroamue.htm

For critical views of the euro, visit:
http://www.eurocritic.demon.co.uk/

Essential tips for finding financial information on the internet

- ▷ Use the search engines fully.
- ▷ Get yourself some 'ferret' software to search extensively and very easily.
- ▷ Find some comprehensive sites that suit you and put their shortcuts onto your desktop.
- ▷ Subscribe to some quality email newsletters to keep you up to date.
- ▷ Check out what you are told with a professional adviser.

Fig. 21. You can search for American financial information at a vast range of internet sites, such as this one run by MS-NBC.

References

1 An early start on the financial facts of life, *The Independent*, 3 February 1999, Wednesday Review, p. 12

2 http://www.statmarket.com/

3 'Legal Briefing: Buying financial services online', *Internet Magazine*, February 1999, p. 101. See also: http://www.ffwlaw.com

4 *Financial Times*, 3 January 1998

5 *Wall Street Journal*, 19 June 1998

6 See: http://www.commerce.net/research/stats/wwwpop.html#COMBINED

3 Running your bank account on the internet

In this chapter we will explore:

- *making the move to online banking*
- *getting benefits from online banking*
- *checking on security issues*
- *comparing security risks*
- *considering the benefits of online banking*
- *looking at the changes*
- *comparing internet versus online banking*
- *what do you need for internet banking?*
- *obtaining an internet bank account*
- *gaining from internet banking*
- *what you should use your internet bank account for*
- *case study*
- *the internet banks*
- *banking abroad*
- *running your internet bank account*
- *reducing your workload*
- *essential tips for internet banking*
- *banking checklist*

Imagine that you have just arrived on Earth from the planet Zog. You are an intelligent being and want to settle in to your new world, so you talk to your new-found friends about financial matters. You discover that cash is fine for small transactions, but for larger purchases you need a bank account.

'So what happens to my cash?' you ask.

'The bank looks after it for you,' explains your new friend. 'They store it, invest it and give you a share of the proceeds in the form of interest – extra cash added to your account.'

'So how do they get hold of *my* money?' you ask.

'You take it to the bank and give it to them. They then give you a receipt showing they have your money and the amount appears on your statement.'

'Ah, I see. They keep an up-to-date record of money going in and out of my account,' you say as you begin to realise the strange ways of these Earthlings.

'Not quite,' is the reply.

If you were from the planet Zog you would then begin to ask a whole host of questions as to why the bank does not give you a true picture of your finances. You would no doubt be stunned to hear that even if you pay a cheque into your account, for most banks it doesn't appear as 'your money', until two or three days later. In the meantime it is

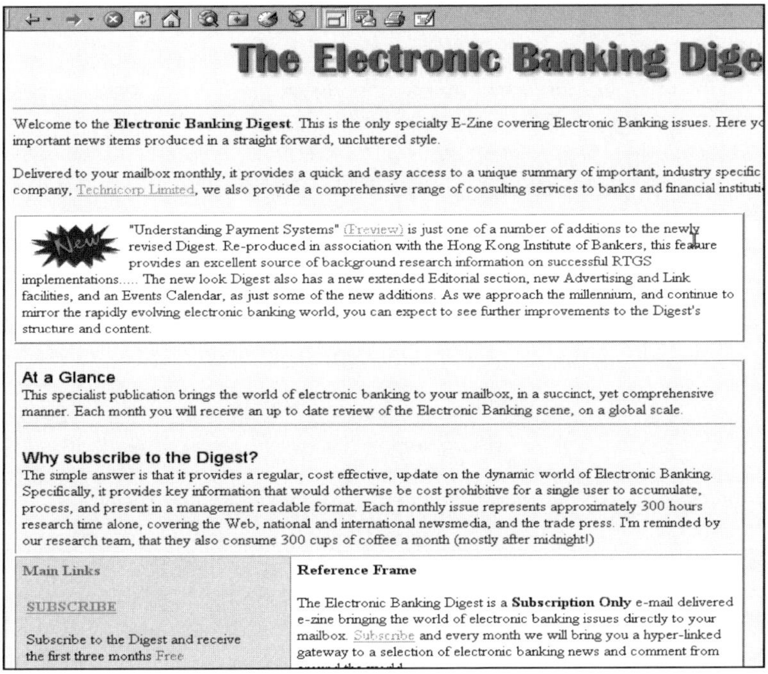

Fig. 22. The Electronic Banking Digest is an online in-depth global banking magazine which you can receive monthly by email.

effectively the bank's money to invest and make interest on. Meanwhile, your cheque is put in a bag, collected by a van driver, taken to a regional 'processing centre', where bank clerks enter the details into a computer. Another van then collects the cheque, takes it to London, where another clerk enters the details into another computer on the following day. A day later, yet another van collects your cheque and drives it to the bank where the account is based. Your cheque may travel a thousand miles or more and take three days to appear back in a bank branch.

Now, what would you say coming from the planet Zog? 'Are you all crazy? Doesn't this swirling mass of paper actually cost tons of money to transport around? Isn't the country's economy missing much of the financial activity that could be taking place if you had the money straight away? And what about the cost to the environment of hundreds of vans driving bits of paper around the nation? On Zog we don't do any of this.'

Well, welcome to the planet Zog because, thanks to the internet, such a ridiculous way of paying money into and out of your bank account can be swept aside. Using internet banking you can pay bills, have money credited to your account and deal with a range of other financial matters without contributing to the nonsense that is called 'clearing'. At the moment, though, many banks still take two or three days to 'process' your transactions – even though it could be instant. There are various reasons given for this delay, but banks make considerable profits from delaying money transfer and investing the funds overnight, making extra money on the international money markets and other investment systems. As internet banking takes hold, this situation is bound to change. Already, in the United States, the system has moved from banks making money using customers' funds overnight towards making more profit from fee-based operations. These fees are also under increasing pressure from credit unions and online banking systems.[1] In short, you can benefit from reduced fees and an improved banking system if you join the growing band of people running their account online.

Making your move to online banking

There is also political pressure to encourage more online banking. In the past decade about 3,500 bank branches have been closed in the UK. This has resulted in many people complaining that their community is without banking facilities. Some villages and small towns, for instance, only have one bank or, in some instances, no branch at all. Politicians have discussed providing powers to financial regulatory authorities to make banks provide people with banking facilities so that they are not 'financially excluded'.[2] The reason why banks have closed so many branches is because keeping them open is expensive. The only way to meet the political pressure to maintain banking facilities to all, and to keep costs down, is for internet banking to become the norm. Even if this means banks buying computers for its customers, it would still be cheaper than re-opening old branches or keeping existing branches open.

Getting benefits from online banking

There are several key reasons why you should consider running your bank account online. These include:

1. greater control
2. reduced charges

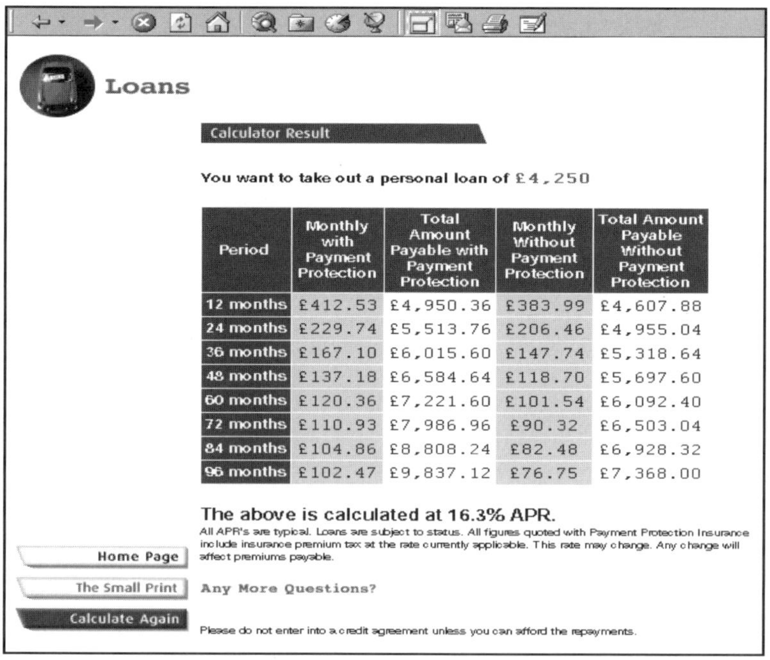
Loans

Calculator Result

You want to take out a personal loan of £4,250

Period	Monthly with Payment Protection	Total Amount Payable with Payment Protection	Monthly Without Payment Protection	Total Amount Payable Without Payment Protection
12 months	£412.53	£4,950.36	£383.99	£4,607.88
24 months	£229.74	£5,513.76	£206.46	£4,955.04
36 months	£167.10	£6,015.60	£147.74	£5,318.64
48 months	£137.18	£6,584.64	£118.70	£5,697.60
60 months	£120.36	£7,221.60	£101.54	£6,092.40
72 months	£110.93	£7,986.96	£90.32	£6,503.04
84 months	£104.86	£8,808.24	£82.48	£6,928.32
96 months	£102.47	£9,837.12	£76.75	£7,368.00

The above is calculated at 16.3% APR.

All APR's are typical. Loans are subject to status. All figures quoted with Payment Protection Insurance include insurance premium tax at the rate currently applicable. This rate may change. Any change will affect premiums payable.

Home Page

The Small Print

Any More Questions?

Calculate Again

Please do not enter into a credit agreement unless you can afford the repayments.

Fig. 23. An example of a loan calculator at an internet bank. Just input the amount and period of the loan you want, and the interest rate, and your estimated monthly payments will appear on the screen in seconds.

3. a clearer picture of your financial position
4. the ability to link direct to your accounts program or spreadsheet
5. the ability to access your financial data from anywhere in the world (if you access your account via the internet).

In addition, banking through your computer can also allow you to:

1. pay bills
2. transfer funds from one account to another
3. communicate directly with bank staff
4. have other internet bank users pay you directly.

You may have noticed the words 'banking through your computer', rather than 'banking through the internet'. This is because some leading financial institutions offering bank accounts have decided that the internet is too insecure to allow you to run your bank account through it. Instead, these banks use web browser technology to allow you to bank 'online', but through a dedicated telephone number that accesses only their computers. In Britain, NatWest, First Direct (HSBC) and the Bank of Scotland have all opted for online banking rather than internet banking. According to these banks, this followed a review of security issues and it was decided that being separate from the internet provided greater security to customers.

Checking on security issues

If you bank online, there is a risk, albeit small, that someone can access your financial details, even remove money from your account. The banks that have opted to offer online banking, rather than internet banking, believe that such risks are minimised if you access their computers direct, rather than via the internet. Clearly, those banks that offer internet banking don't agree. So what are the real risks of internet banking?

The risks of the internet have almost certainly been heavily overplayed and hyped up. People just do not trust the internet. According to one survey, only 5% of PC users trust the internet to transmit financial information; that's compared with 62% who are prepared to take part in telephone banking.[3] Some people would argue that much of this hype has come from people who have an interest in making us nervous – such as those offering security software solutions. Whether or not this cynical view is true is not the real issue. What is important is to balance the risks with the benefits.

For instance, let's say you want to buy a product you have seen advertised in a newspaper or magazine. You call up the advertiser, give your credit card number and the item is delivered the following day. This is a normal, routine, everyday activity – mail order shopping or telephone-based shopping is a fact of life and we regularly quote credit card or debit card numbers over the phone. Yet do we worry? Rarely. But think about it for a moment. Do you really know what the person you are talking to will do with the information? Will it be kept securely? Will it be scribbled down on a piece of paper for anyone to pick up? Is the person a trustworthy employee of the company, or a criminally minded temp?

Have you also considered the implications of faxing your credit card details? Gosh, a permanent record of your signature, your credit card number can be sent to anyone, if you press the wrong digit on the fax machine! Yet this is an everyday occurrence which does not get anywhere near the same level of attention as does the potential risk of giving the same information on the internet. According to one of the leading internet software companies – Netscape – they don't know of any individual person who has lost money over the internet.[4] Equally, Visa doesn't have any evidence of internet fraud involving their credit cards.[5]

So, let us now consider what happens to your credit card information on the internet. Assuming your bank or other financial institution has set itself up on a 'secure server', the information is 'scrambled' by your web browser making it impossible for a casual glancer to identify your credit card details. The company you are making a purchase from unscrambles the information. So what are the risks here?

- ▷ *Interception* – Financial data sent via the internet can be intercepted, but is not understandable unless the person making the interception has computer skills to unscramble the coded material. Compare this with data sent by phone or fax. This is 'raw' and can be intercepted more easily and does not need unscrambling. Consequently, the ways in which we send credit card numbers, or other financial information, outside the internet are actually more risky than sending via the internet.
- ▷ *Routing of information* – True, using the internet does pose other risks. Your message containing your financial information may go on a convoluted route around the world, passing through several computers of which you are unaware.
- ▷ *Tracking down* – Also, tracking down any interception of your financial information is difficult. At least if your credit card number is stolen after you make a telephone purchase, you can be fairly sure where the problem occurred – at the other end of the line! So let's compare the risks and benefits.

Comparing security risks

'Traditional' transmission of financial data	*Internet transmission*
Easy to intercept	Difficult to intercept
Easy to understand	Needs special skills to understand
Easy to trace interception	Difficult to trace interception

Few opportunities for interception	Large number of opportunities for interception

As you can see from this list, the security issue is largely about the difficulty of tracing those people who could intercept your financial data. In addition, those people need special skills and software. Indeed, according to an influential group of banking experts from Basle, Switzerland, the threat to online banking is not really that different from traditional banking security problems.[6] In fact, the Basle Committee of Banking Supervision said that one of the real issues was the need to educate bank staff about technological issues. Taking these comments into account, together with the fact that most credit card fraud results from physical theft of the cards, it seems that the perceived risks of internet problems are exaggerated. Transmitting your financial information over the internet is probably no more risky than doing the same by phone, fax or mail.

Considering the benefits of online banking

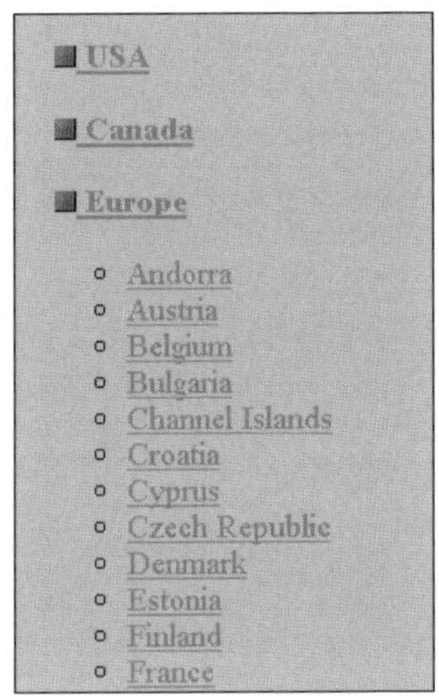

Even if you think the risks are high, why not consider the tremendous benefits of internet or online banking? Your bank charges will definitely fall. It costs 107 times more for a bank to process a transaction if you go into a branch, than if you use the internet.[7] Already, using online banking, charges are reduced compared with ordinary cheque accounts. Added to that, consider the additional services on offer already from banks through the internet. Citibank has a service where you can apply for a car loan, via the internet, and the motor dealer can access the web to be sure your loan is properly set up.[8] In fact, the list of potential benefits of internet banking is growing each day, as banks and their customers and suppliers dream up new ideas. Most of all, though, internet banking means you can run your account any time, anywhere. All you need is a computer and a phone.

Looking at the changes

The changes being made to internet banking are proceeding with rapid pace. The first bank account transaction on the internet was made on 18 October 1995.[9] This was a donation to the American Red Cross by the Security First Network Bank, the Atlanta-based financial institution that was set up from the outset as an internet bank. Within a year, 28 banks had joined SFNB. Now, in just a few years since this breakthrough, several hundred banks provide internet banking with thousands more saying they will do this imminently. Only a handful have opted to provide online direct-access banking. Clearly, the mass of opinion within the banking world is for internet access for its customers. Indeed, the venture capital group APAX has joined forces with Intel, the chip manufacturer, to launch the first European internet-only bank.[10] These companies are clearly confident that internet banking is the future, since they have invested more than £10m in the venture.

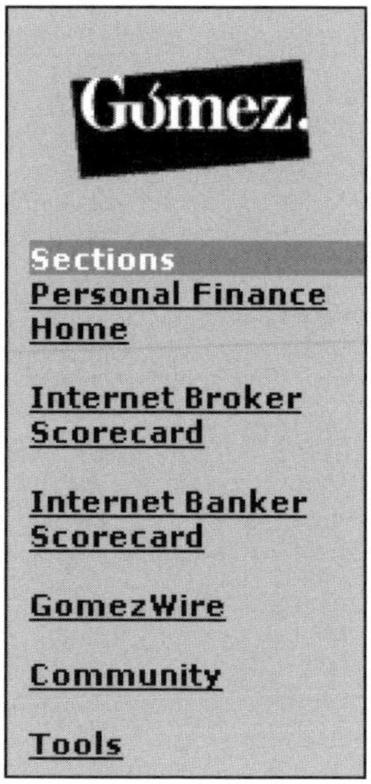

Comparing internet versus online banking

The security issues that have led some banks to provide direct online services, rather than internet banking, will work against customers and almost certainly against these banks. Such a position appears to trade on the nervousness that exists about internet security. However, the comparative advantages of internet banking will probably outweigh these security issues.

Internet banking	*Online banking*
Access from any computer in the world, allowing you freedom to control your finances while away from your desk	Access from one computer only
Ability to compare prices, products services etc with other suppliers	No comparisons possible as you are only online to the bank itself
Flexibility to handle financial matters at the same time as sending email, or downloading files from another part of the internet	Can only access the bank's computer – no other online facilities available at the same time
Ability to transfer funds from your bank account to an internet shop using 'cybercash' (see Chapter 4).	No way of transferring funds for same-time online purchases

As you can see, internet banking offers you a whole lot more – specifically, greater control and flexibility, something that direct-access online banking only half-heartedly provides.

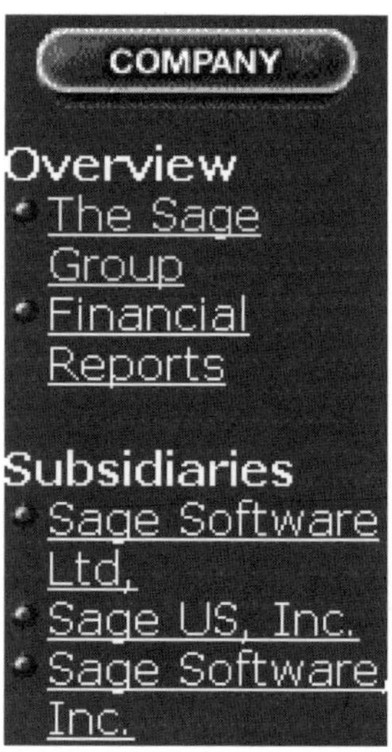

What do you need to use internet banking?

One of the best ways of internet banking is to use an accounts program on your computer, or a spreadsheet that you have developed yourself. Accounts programs you might consider include:

- ▷ Microsoft Money
- ▷ Quicken
- ▷ Sage

There are other accounts programs, but by using these well-known programs you will be able to keep a close eye on your personal finances and, in many instances, compare your bank's details with your own records so that you can reconcile your statement, making sure you know your exact position. These accounts programs can do this automatically, using the data that comes from your internet banking service. You could also set up a spreadsheet in something like Microsoft Excel or Lotus 1-2-3 to do much the same thing. In any event, using the internet banking service together with your accounts program or spreadsheet will provide you with a level of control that you cannot achieve in any other way.

Obtaining an internet bank account

You can get an internet bank account from most of the main High Street banks. Others are being added each month, but the main players include:

Barclays
Citibank
Co-operative Bank
Lloyds TSB
Nationwide
Norwich and Peterborough Building Society

Online banking can be obtained from:

Bank of Scotland
Barclays
First Direct
NatWest

As you can see, all the major banks now offer banking from your PC. You will need to make the choice depending on your own personal circumstances and views on security. An advantage of internet banking is that you can open an account with another bank, use its services online and 'test' it out. If you like it, you can then transfer all your

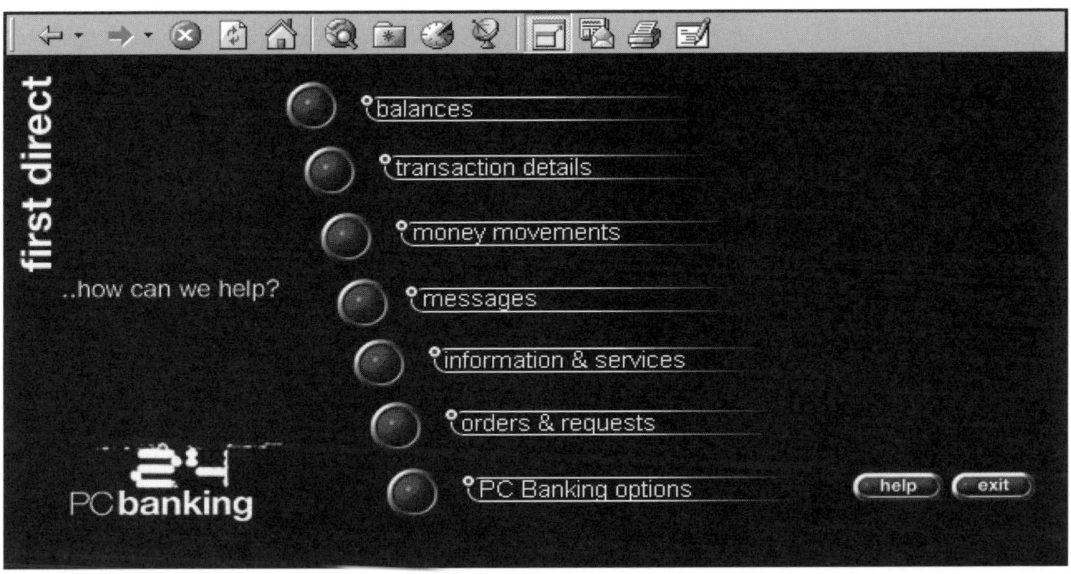

Fig. 24. As a customer you can use the First Direct service to check out your balances, transaction details, money movements, messages and more.

Fig. 25. Example of a First Direct bank statement. Why wait weeks for a statement to arrive in the post when you can access the information you need 24 hours a day?

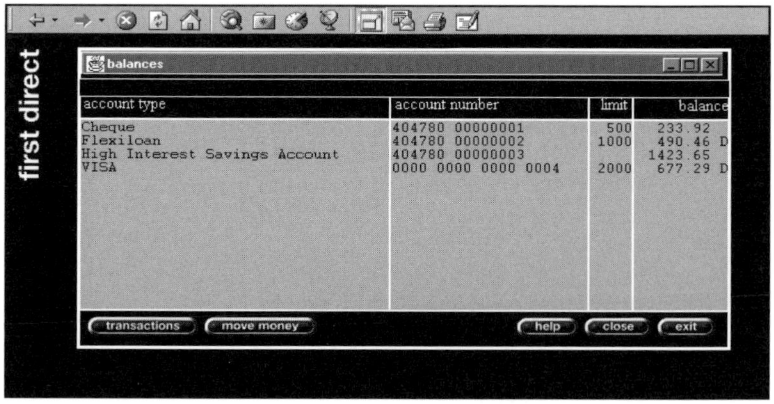

banking to that service. This is something you cannot do easily with traditional banking or with direct-access online banking.

Gaining interest from internet banking

Apart from the reduction in bank charges that is inevitable with internet banking, working online with your bank account also helps ensure you gain money. That's because you can monitor your money and transfer funds to savings accounts to gain interest. You can keep your current account as low as necessary, ensuring you make the maximum amount of interest possible. All you have to do is transfer funds from one account to another.

Theoretically, this is all you have to do with an ordinary bank account. Just write to your bank, or pop in to the branch to arrange the transfers, or complete the transaction over the telephone. Yet this rarely happens. Many of us have great intentions to transfer money in and out of our accounts, maximising our returns, but the inconvenience of performing the task prevents us from doing it. The only winner in this situation is the bank – which makes interest on your funds, but doesn't pass any of the return on to you. With internet banking, the situation is wholly different. For the cost of a one-minute local telephone call, you can monitor your funds each day and transfer money from one account to another. This ensures you gain the maximum interest. Internet banking

Fig. 26. NatWest's web site offers business and economic news as well as personal and corporate banking services.

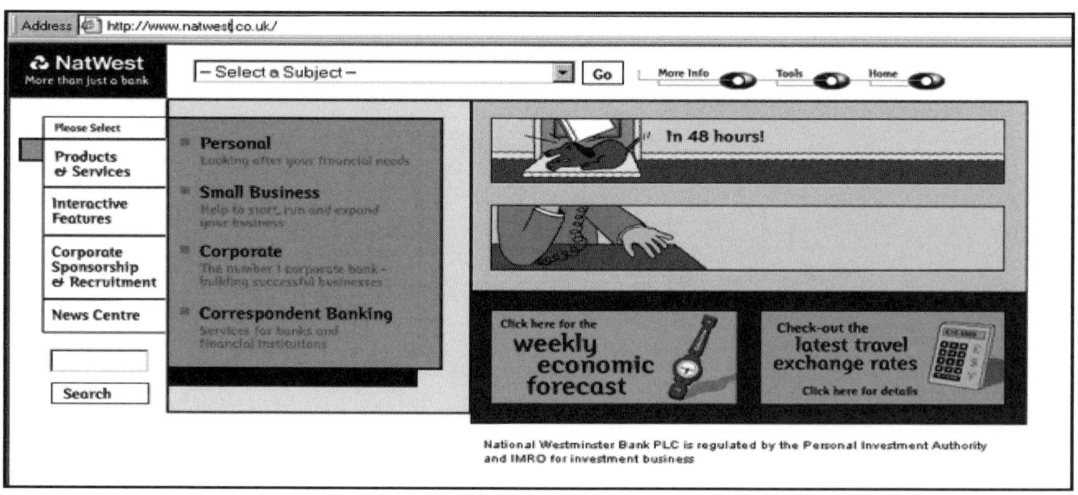

therefore not only saves you money, it can help you make it as well.

Step by step
To ensure you gain the maximum return on your internet bank account, it is a good idea to:

1. set a specific time each day, or week, to log on to your bank's service
2. check your statements, if necessary comparing these with your accounts program
3. transfer excess funds to your savings accounts.

These three simple steps should help boost your financial position, though you will need to check on charges made by your bank for the transfers. Sometimes these will be higher than the money you gain in interest, so be careful!

What you should use your internet bank account for

Your internet bank account will have different facilities, according to the bank you use. However, you should be able to:

- ▷ check balances
- ▷ transfer funds
- ▷ pay bills
- ▷ check on other services and products
- ▷ apply for new products or accounts
- ▷ send email to the bank

If you do nothing else with your internet banking service other than arrange transfers and pay bills, you should benefit. This is because of the lower charges and the control you get – for instance you can pay a bill as soon as you receive it but ask the bank to delay it until the last moment. That way, you can be sure your bill is being paid and that you will gain the maximum interest possible on the funds. Many people with traditional accounts pay bills early, for fear of forgetting them, and hence lose interest on the money. Alternatively, they forget the bill and face late payment charges from suppliers. With internet banking linked to your accounts program you will be able to reconcile your financial position once the bill has been paid. In this way, you will have a precise picture of your finances.

Case study – the freelance graphic artist

John is a freelance graphic artist, but is in a wheelchair following a motorcycle accident. He works from home producing designs for various commercial clients. He rarely has to leave home, which is quite convenient since he lives out in the country. His nearest town is 18 miles away. He sends all of his designs to clients via email and attracts extra business using his own web site. However, his biggest problem has always been getting to the bank to pay in the cheques he receives and to pay bills. Now, though, he has signed up for his bank's fully interactive internet service. His customers have been given his bank account details so they can pay directly into his account. He has also set up his internet bank account so that he can pay all his bills online. In fact, there is no need for John to visit his branch at all. Because he is wheelchair-bound he finds this service particularly useful.

The internet banks

The banks that offer internet banking all differ in what you can do online and in the way in which their sites work. No matter who you bank with, you can get a feel for the way the online system operates as each of the main internet banks has demonstration pages, showing you how a fictional account works. It is worth looking at these pages.

Barclays
http://www.personal.barclays.co.uk
Barclays Bank offers internet banking as well as direct-access online banking. The internet service is less well featured than the online service; for instance you cannot pay all your bills using the internet service. Also, the direct access 'PC Banking' service allows you to download information into Microsoft Money, something that you cannot do with the internet service. However, Barclays was one of the first of the high street banks to offer internet banking and has a wealth of experience in this area. Also, Barclays has an 'Emerging

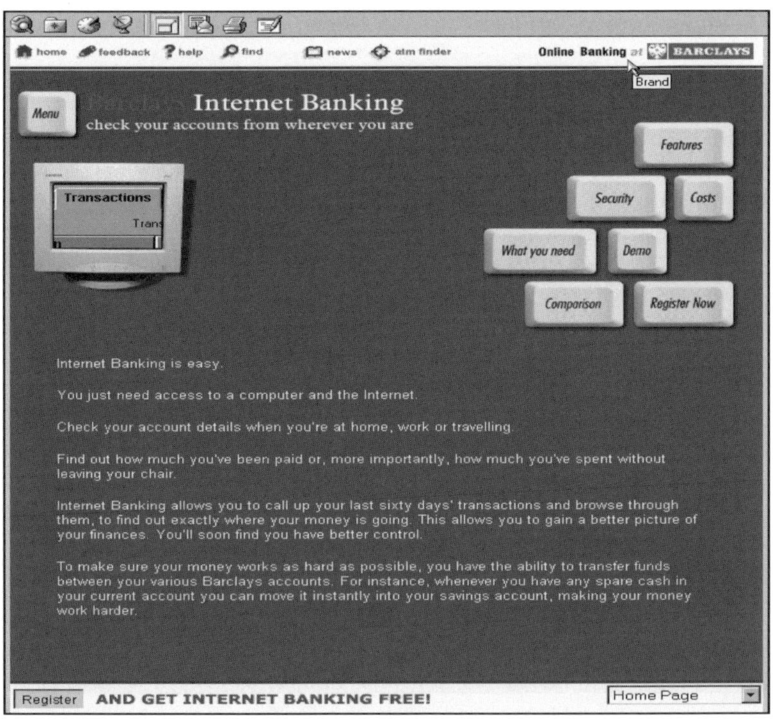

Fig. 27. Internet banking with Barclays. 'You just need access to a computer and the internet'.

Markets Group', based at its Barclaycard offices in Northampton. This group is internationally regarded as one of the most knowledgeable organisations in new banking technology. Though the Barclays internet banking service may appear limited at the moment, you can be fairly sure that redevelopment work is going on behind the scenes, updating the offering as new ideas and technology take hold. To open a Barclays internet account go to:

http://www.personal.barclays.co.uk/online/

and then select 'register'. You can complete an online application form. You will then be sent an application form in the post to complete, if you do not already have a Barclays account. As with all banking services, there are charges to pay. Barclays Internet Banking has a low annual service fee, which is waived for the first year. In other words, internet banking with Barclays is free, for a year – though transaction charges and other normal bank account fees would apply.

Citibank
http://www.citibank.com/
Citibank has been heavily promoting its service with national press advertising. Internet banking is an important future strategy for Citibank, hence its continued promotional work. Citibank is also making it worth your while considering their service, since there are no monthly fees and no sign-up fees – apart from normal transaction charges, this is a completely free service. In addition, the account can be linked to Quicken or Microsoft Money, to enhance your financial control. Citibank Internet Banking also allows you to pay bills and transfer funds; some banks will only allow you to do this with direct-access, online, non-

Fig. 28. Internet banking with Citibank. As one of the biggest financial institutions in the world, Citibank is well established as a global internet bank. This is the home page of its UK arm.

Internet banking. To open a Citibank internet account go to:

http://www.citibank.com/uk/intbank/index.htm

However, you will discover that Citibank requires you to deposit a minimum of £2,000 in the account in order for it to be opened or have your salary paid into the account each month. This may be limiting if you are simply trying to open an account for 'testing' purposes. As with most banks, you will need to sign the application forms. These must be original signatures, not scans or electronic signatures; you will need to print out the application form and send it by post. This is not really Citibank's fault; it is largely due to legislation that is way behind the electronic signature capabilities of your web browser!

Co-operative Bank
http://www.co-operativebank.co.uk/
The Co-operative Bank's internet service has a demonstration available that shows you what can be done. You can access this demonstration at:

http://www.co-operativebank.co.uk/ib_registration.html

You will need a Co-operative Bank account to register for internet banking. Unfortunately, unlike some banking web sites you cannot do all this in the same registration area. You need to leave internet banking and go back to the accounts pages of the bank's main site and open an account from there. There is a comprehensive online application form, but you will be sent a printed version of this after you have submitted it, so that you can sign it. The Co-operative Bank does appear to let you open a current account with no minimum amount and without your paying in your salary each month; this is an ideal account to try out for internet banking. In addition, Co-operative internet banking accounts are free of all charges while you remain in credit, making them highly

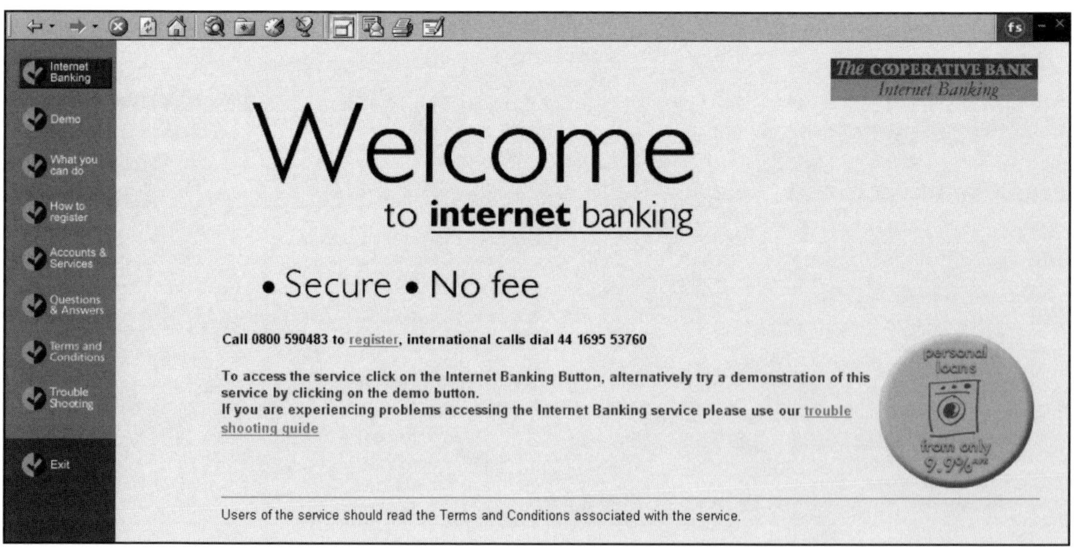

Fig. 29. Internet banking is now available with the Co-operative Bank.

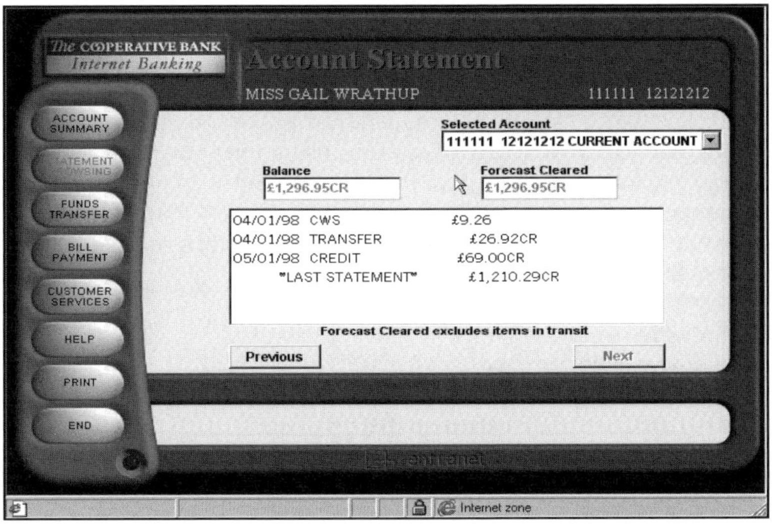

Fig. 30. This how your statement might look if you are banking online with the Co-op.

attractive. In addition, if you have Sky satellite television, you can access your account through the Teletext service.

Lloyds TSB
http://www.lloydsbank.co.uk
Lloyds TSB offers internet banking only through its Lloyds Bank network – the TSB arm offers direct-access PC banking instead, via CompuServe. You can access the Lloyds internet service at:

http://www.lloydsbank.co.uk/ibank/index.htm

You can register online, but only if you already have a Lloyds account. Sadly, you can only find out information about such accounts online. To apply for an account you will need to visit a branch, something most of

Fig. 31. Lloyds On-line. Their web site includes a helpful online banking demo.

the other internet banking services don't force you to do since they can at least send you account information. This is a serious limitation of the Lloyds service, which otherwise is excellent with very clear screens and an intuitive way of working. To help you locate your nearest branch, this web site has a very useful 'find your bank' facility that allows you to type in the name of your town or your post code and receive a list of nearby branches.

Nationwide
http://www.nationwide.co.uk
Nationwide, like Citibank, has been heavily promoting its internet banking service. You can access this service at:

https://olb.nationet.com/onlinebanking/olbHomePageSetup.htm

You have to already be a Nationwide account holder in order to register. Registration, though simple, is not ideally set up. To open an account you have to complete an application request here:

http://www.nationwide.co.uk/fserv/fserv.htm

and then wait for the post to deliver an application form to you. Then, once you have an account, you can go back to the site and register. This is a cumbersome approach, considering that other banks offer online account application. Even so, unlike some of the other internet banking operations, the offer from Nationwide does allow you to integrate the information with Microsoft Money, providing you with extra control. The Nationwide 'Flex account' (a current account) has no transaction charges for normal day-to-day banking.

Fig. 32. The Nationwide was one of the first UK institutions to go onto the internet, and it has also become an internet service provider.

Fig. 33. The Midland Bank web site. Midland are part of the mighty HSBC (Hong Kong & Shanghai Banking Corporation).

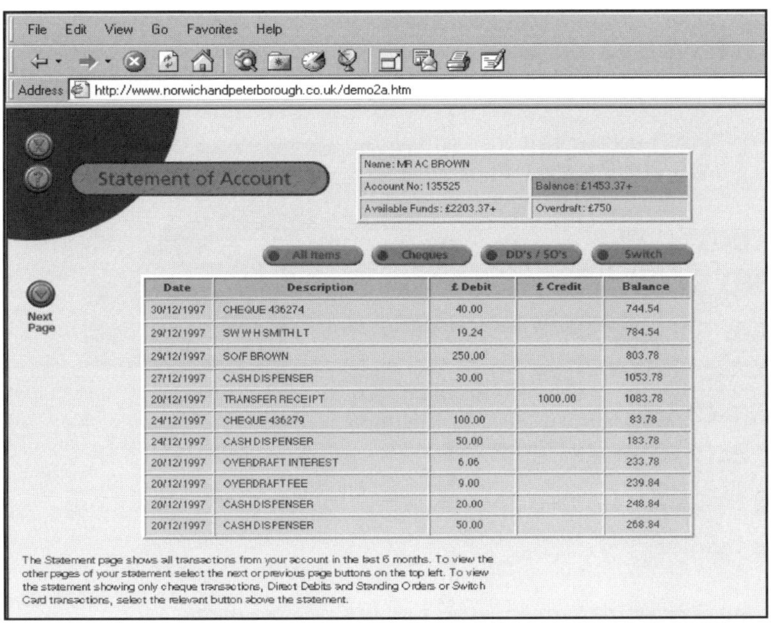

Fig. 34. A typical online customer's statement of account at the Norwich & Peterborough Building Society.

Norwich and Peterborough Building Society
http://www.norwichandpeterborough.co.uk
It's not just the big High Street names that are developing internet banking. Outside East Anglia, the Norwich and Peterborough is not widely known, but it has its own internet banking service that allows you to manage all your accounts with the Society. You can find out more from:

http://www.norwichandpeterborough.co.uk/intro.htm

There is a demonstration at this site and you can also click on 'register' to request an information pack. Sadly you cannot apply online for an account and for the internet banking service the Norwich and Peterborough calls 'NetMaster'.

Reviewing internet banking

The British banks that offer internet services are conservative in their approach. Security is a clear watchword within this industry, and rightly so, but the lack of flexibility and the lack of full use of the internet's capabilities indicate that the high street giants are ripe for attack. You can be certain that, before too long, British internet-only banks will start springing up, with full capabilities, able to utilise the full facilities of the world wide web. At the moment, most British banks appear to be using the web as an afterthought, rather than in a strategic way. This means the young upstarts of the financial world will overtake them. Banks that think this cannot happen should be reminded of the building societies that converted to banks in the past ten years, or the insurance companies, such as Legal & General, which set up a bank recently. You can find more information about banking and recent developments in this industry by visiting these web sites:

The British Bankers Association (BBA)
http://www.bankfacts.org.uk/

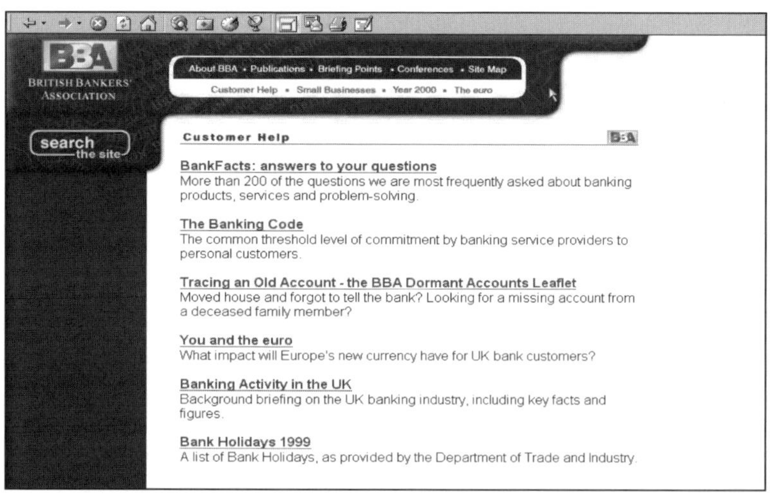

Fig. 35. The British Bankers Association web site. You can find out a great deal about the banking system in the UK. Among many resources available here, the site answers 200 common questions about UK banking.

The BBA is the representative body of British banks and its web site includes a copy of the Banking Code as well as answers to many of the questions you may have about banking in general. This web site works very quickly and has a whole host of fascinating facts and figures about the financial world.

Online Banking Report (OBR)
http://www.onlinebankingreport.com
This free information site is reporting on the progress of banks all over the world towards internet banking. Check out its latest report on the UK banks, and compare what is happening in the UK with other countries around the world.

Banking abroad

Fig. 36. The Online Banking Report is one of the best places to follow what banks around the world are doing in response to the internet. Needless to say, there are direct hyperlinks to the web sites of literally thousands of banks all over the planet. Fancy banking in Switzerland or the Bahamas?

Thanks to the internet, it is now much easier to find out about foreign bank accounts and even place your money in tax havens offshore. Indeed, it is now possible to open a Swiss bank account on the internet. Go to:

http://www.bekbnet.ch/eng/

Most of the banks on the internet are based in the USA. You can open an account in America and use it online. However, for most banks you will need a US mailing address, a Social Security number, or some other form of US identification. Security First National Bank (the first internet bank) is looking at alternative ways of offering banking to non-US citizens, as are other banks on the internet. Remember that if you are looking for an American bank account, current accounts are called 'checking accounts' and deposit accounts are called 'savings accounts'. Also, don't forget that the accounts will be in US dollars, so you will need to take into account any losses or gains due to currency fluctuations. Remember too, that if you are a UK resident, company or partnership you will be responsible for declaring any gains made to the

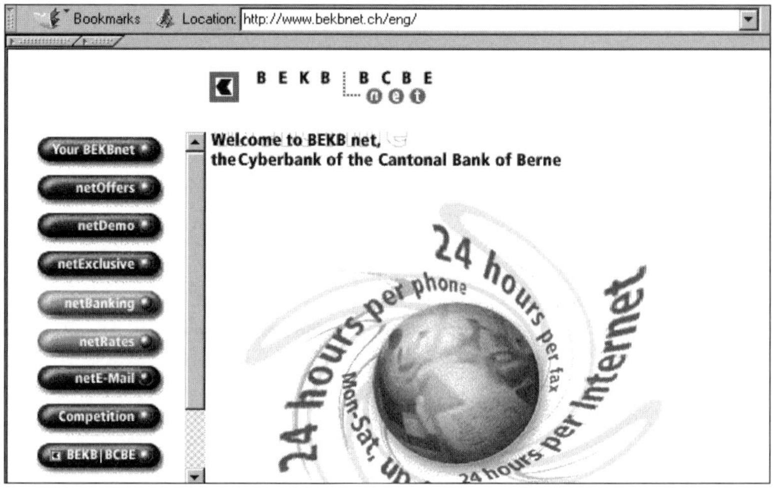

Fig. 37. BEKB is an example of a Swiss bank in cyberspace. Just send them an email to find out more.

Inland Revenue, even though the money was not earned in the UK.

Running your internet bank account

Whether you have an account in the USA or the UK, or any other country, there are some key things you need to do to ensure your account runs smoothly. Firstly, ensure that your password is memorable only to you. Don't use your name as your password or your birth date, house number or some other easily identifiable word. If you simply cannot remember your password, write it down in some code, such as in the middle of a sentence that makes sense. For instance:

Password	fellow
Sentence	Success comes to every fellow who waits

The sentence makes sense and has no link to your bank account. You can then keep the sentence on the wall in front of you – it makes no sense to anyone and looks like a motivational statement. However, if you can avoid such prompts, so much the better. Web browsers allow you to save passwords in the Microsoft Windows password list. While this helps you log onto sites quickly, it is also problematic for two reasons:

1. Anyone can log on to your bank account if they start up your web browser.
2. You will not remember your password and won't be able to log on using another computer, such as when you are in an internet café while away on holiday.

Don't save your passwords, even though your browser will give you the opportunity to do so.

The next thing you must do is create a regular back-up schedule for your bank account information. This is particularly important if you use your internet bank account together with accounts software such as Quicken or Microsoft Money. If you don't back up your files, you will waste time in the future downloading all the data again. To create an efficient back-up system do the following:

(a) Once a week copy all relevant files to a removable disk, such as a floppy, Zip, Jaz, SyQuest or CD-ROM. Call this disk your back-up master.
(b) Every time you use the software, copy the files to another removable disk. Call this disk your daily back-up.

In this way, your files on your master back-up will only be, at the most, a week out of date. You can then update these with the relevant data on the daily back-up set. Having two back-ups protects you in case one back-up fails. Ideally, store a third back-up disk in a safe place, such as a fire safe. Paying attention to password issues and back-ups will help ensure that you have a trouble-free time with your internet bank account.

Reducing your workload

Another good idea when working with your internet bank account is to establish a regular routine. Perhaps, dial up once a week, or daily if necessary, but always do it at a specified time. Save up all your banking tasks until this time and do them in a batch. This will save you online connection charges, if you pay them to your internet service provider. It will also help cut down your phone bill, as you will only need to spend time connecting once. In addition, you will find that your use of the web site is faster as your computer will only need to cache (temporarily store) the graphics and other items once. This speeds up your use of the site. So in short:

1. Dial up your internet bank at a regular time (create a habit).
2. Save up all your banking tasks and do them at this time.
3. Don't be tempted to dial up again until your next scheduled contact.

Essential tips for internet banking

▷ If possible use your existing bank's service.

▷ Use as many of the services as possible (such as bill paying, transfers etc.).

▷ Make your use of internet banking a habit.

▷ Batch your banking activities to save time.

▷ Email your bank's internet service with comments to help them improve their use of the new technology.

▷ Be aware of security issues and keep your password secret.

▷ If possible, integrate your internet banking facilities with an accounts program such as Microsoft Money, Quicken or Sage.

▷ Back up your accounts files regularly.

Fig. 38. DigiCash is pioneering the use of e-cash (electronic cash). This is how it could work.

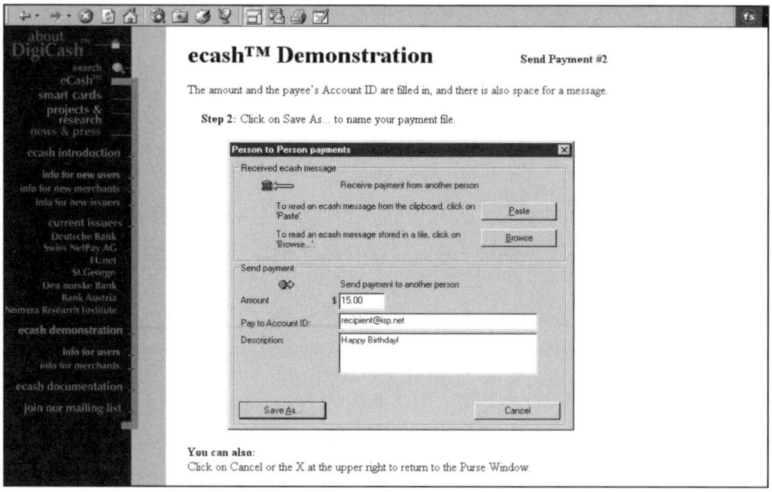

Banking checklist

▷ Personal current accounts usually pay little, if any, interest. So only keep the minimum amount you need in such accounts.

▷ Transfer as much money to 'notice' accounts as possible – this will give you higher interest rates. Remember though, you need to give advance 'notice' if you wish to withdraw cash so that you don't lose interest.

▷ If you are a UK higher rate taxpayer, you should declare your savings on your tax form and pay additional tax. You can avoid this extra tax if all your savings are in an account owned by a lower rate taxpayer. For instance, if your partner is a lower rate taxpayer, transferring your excess cash to their account could save money.

▷ You can have accounts at more than one bank. Sometimes you might want to do this to separate household expenditure from, say, a holiday savings account.

Fig. 39. BankNet web site. BankNet is supported by Secure Trust Bank plc.

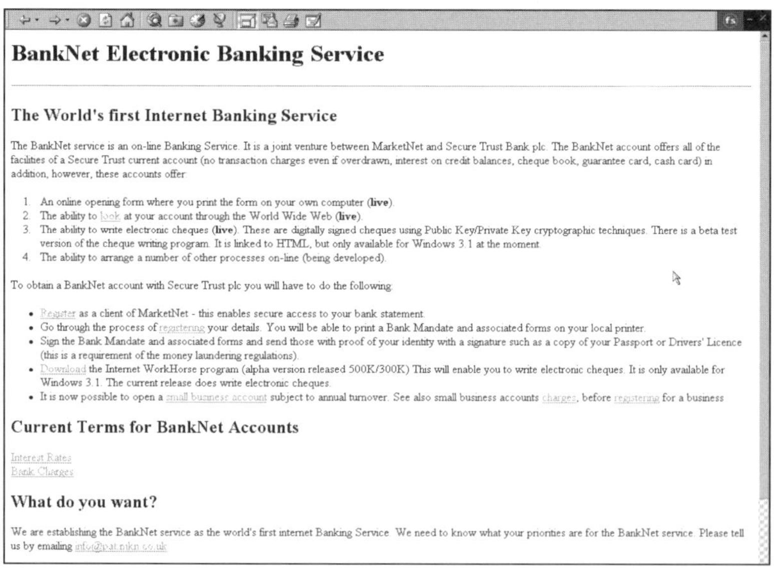

References

1 See: http://www.reporternews.com/opinion/molly0319.html
2 *The Independent*, 22 February 1999, p. 19.
3 *Banking and Finance on the Internet*, Ed: Mary J Cronin, 1998, John Wiley & Sons, p.184.
4 *Going Digital*, The Economist, Profile Books, 1998, p. 149.
5 *Going Digital*, The Economist, Profile Books, 1998, p. 149.
6 See: http://www.commsec.com/news/980320.htm.
7 *Net Future*, Chuck Martin, 1999, McGraw-Hill, p. 30. See also: *Sunday Telegraph*, 28 February 1999, p. 2b.
8 *Net Future*, Chuck Martin, 1999, McGraw-Hill, p. 31.
9 *Banking and Finance on the Internet*, Ed: Mary J Cronin, 1998, John Wiley & Sons, p. 55 and p. 73. See also: http://www.sfnb.com/infodesk/bankinfo_menu.html.
10 *Sunday Telegraph*, 28 February 1999, p. 2b.

4 Getting credit via the internet

In this chapter we will explore:

- *what to remember when borrowing*
- *checking your credit status*
- *understanding credit scoring*
- *getting credit scores repaired*
- *example of repairing poor credit*
- *checking credit suppliers*
- *finding information on credit*
- *finding out about loans*
- *applying for a credit card*
- *applying for loans*
- *getting 'cash' you can use online*
- *getting electronic cash*
- *example of using electronic cash*
- *essential tips for getting money on the internet*
- *loans and credit card checklist*

We would all like to borrow money at some stage. Whether we want a new car, a special present for someone, or that luxury for ourselves, we often need to borrow some funds to finance the purchase. Even if the borrowing is only short term, until we can pay off the loan in full when we get our pay cheque, we all borrow. Most of us borrow on a regular basis using charge cards, or credit cards. Others borrow using a regular overdraft facility. We can also get loans or, increasingly these days, use 'credit unions'. All of these facilities – and more – for borrowing money can be found on the internet.

What to remember when borrowing

Wherever you raise credit, remember you will have to pay the money back, usually with some interest. Credit facilities available via the internet are no different. Before taking up internet credit and loan facilities you will need to:

- provide detailed personal financial information
- be prepared to wait for credit checks to take place
- agree to pay the money back by a specified date
- agree to pay a specified amount of interest.

The internet is no different from traditional methods of raising money, except for two key factors:

1. Faster access to a variety of lenders
2. More rapid processing of applications

In other words, the internet gives you the ability to make more informed choices about potential credit facilities. It also enables you to set up credit facilities much faster than normal postal applications; getting the best credit for you in a hurry is just what the internet can help with.

Checking your credit status

Before you start looking for credit card companies or loan arrangers, you might like to check out the sites that provide information and news on your chances of gaining credit facilities. The first place you might like to visit is the 'UK Credit Files'. This site has an application form that you fill in, and seven days later in the post you receive a complete list of all the credit information stored on you at credit reference agencies. This service is an ideal way of ensuring that information on you is accurate, so that when you do apply for credit facilities you will be sure the companies are using the right data to assess you. To gain your own information go to:

http://www.ukcreditfiles.co.uk/

Another source of useful personal credit information is:

http://www.instant-search.com/

Although this site does not have online capabilities for personal credit

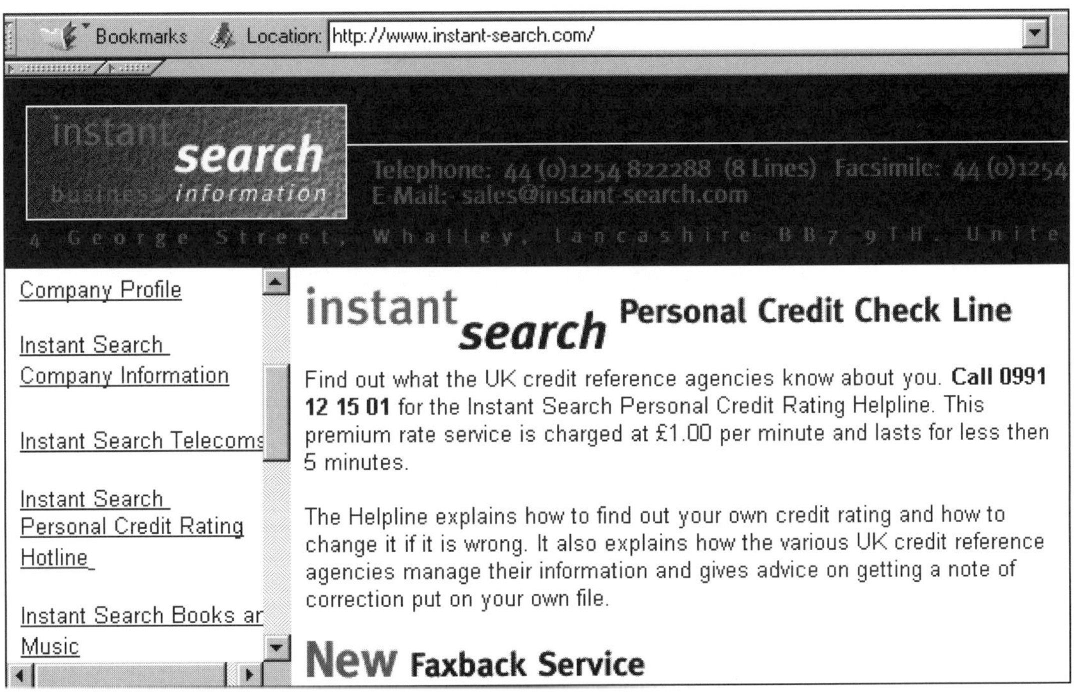

Fig. 40. The Instant Search web site is one of several you can explore if you want to find out about your personal credit rating.

searches, it provides phone numbers and a fax back information service so that you can check your credit status quickly. Under the terms of the Consumer Credit Act 1974, if anyone has inaccurate information on you, corrections must be made. You have to contact the agency that stores the information on you and arrange for them to alter their records. It is worthwhile checking your records to ensure that any credit applications you make online will use up-to-date and accurate information.

Understanding credit scoring

The reason you need to check your credit status with various agencies is that companies which provide loan facilities do not have the information they need to assess your creditworthiness. Instead, such information is collected by a handful of credit-scoring agencies who supply the details on a one-off basis to loan companies each time you apply for credit. The information stored on you relates to your address, any other credit facilities you already have and your bill-paying habits.

Your creditworthiness is reduced if you move home frequently, if you owe a lot of money to other companies or if you are a poor payer, missing payment dates regularly. You are also less likely to have an application accepted if others with your surname who live at your address also have poor credit status. All the information collected by the agency is 'scored' for each bank or loan company that is processing your application. It is this score, almost always alone, that decides whether or not you will be granted credit. If the agency has inaccurate information, such as the amount of credit you already have, your application is less likely to succeed. Other items will also reduce the likelihood of your gaining credit:

(a) frequent applications for credit

(b) previous refusal of credit

(c) frequent changes in employment

(d) county court judgements against you.

You should check your credit status so that any information is accurate and your chances of gaining future credit increased. However, remember that frequent applications for credit may reduce your chances of success. It is better to choose one credit card company and stick with it, rather than change regularly. Losing a percentage point here or there in interest may be more trouble than it is worth in the long run. That's sad, but true.

Getting credit scores repaired

If you find that your credit status is inaccurate, there are companies on the internet who can help. Companies you might like to try include:

Jonathan Comerie
http://www.knowledge.co.uk/xxx/credit/

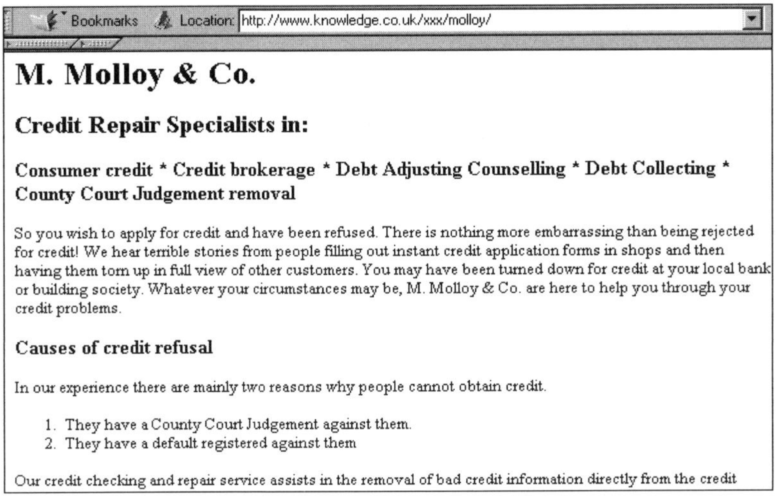

Fig. 41. You can use the internet to get a bad or inaccurate credit record repaired. Molloy and Co is one of several online companies than can help you.

M Molloy
http://www.knowledge.co.uk/xxx/molloy/

The Judgment Removal Company
http://www.judgmentremoval.demon.co.uk/

Lawrights
http://www.lawrights.co.uk/
Another useful area for legal information is Lawrights. This is a very helpful site that provides background information on legal issues that you may find of use.

You could also seek advice from your local Citizens' Advice Bureau. Many individual Citizens' Advice Bureaux offices have web sites, but

Fig. 42. The Judgment Removal Company is another web site that can help you repair your credit record.

Fig. 43. Lawrights can help you find out where you stand in any legal matter. The internet offers a vast amount of UK and international legal information and advice, much of it free.

most do not. You should therefore look up your local office in the telephone book.

Another method of correcting your credit references is to employ the services of a lawyer. As in choosing other professional advisers, personal recommendations from others that have used a lawyer's services are the best way of selecting someone suitable. However, there are many lawyers who advertise their services on the web. You can find a local lawyer by visiting:

Fig. 44. Want to track down some good legal advice near where you live or work? Use an internet site like LawGuide to find the contacts you need.

LawGuide
http://www.lawguide.co.uk/
All you have to do is enter your postcode and you will then be provided with a list of local lawyers, together with their contact details.

The Law Society
http://www.lawsoc.org.uk/
Another useful site is the Law Society's own selection of pages. Here you can also check out the credentials of solicitors you may want to use.

Chartered Accountants
http://www.chartered-accountants.co.uk/
Another useful source of advice and support would be an accountant. You can locate an accountant from this web site. Once again, you might like to seek personal recommendation for an accountant. If you do not know anyone who uses an accountant or who can recommend one, try your local Chamber of Commerce:

British Chambers of Commerce
http://www.britishchambers.org.uk/public/index.htm
You should be able find your local Chamber here.

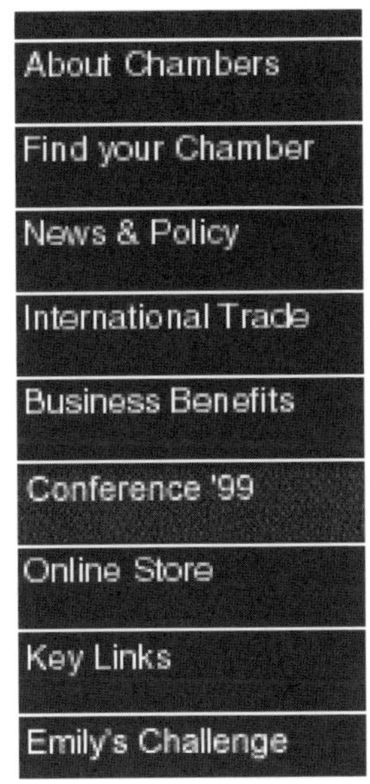

Case study – repairing poor credit

Sally has a busy life, working four days a week in a local shop, as well as being a leading light in the local amateur dramatics society and bringing up three children. She tries to take up as many offers as she can, in a bid to keep her costs down. Recently, she discovered that a local store was offering its own credit card and holders would receive an automatic 15% discount. So, Sally applied. Sadly her application was rejected, which she found unusual because she has never had a credit request refused before. Being an internet fan, Sally sought some advice. She found some credit repair companies and emailed them for information. She also discovered her local Citizens Advice Bureau had a web site, so she searched that for support. She sent an email to an online lawyer and waited for all the replies. Within 24 hours she had been given a host of advice and was able to get her re-application successfully accepted. It turned out that the credit scoring agency had made a mistake. Using the resources on the internet, Sally was able to get the decision revoked much more quickly than would have been possible using traditional methods.

Checking credit suppliers

Once you have checked your data and corrected the information held on you if necessary, you might wish to check the people who lend you money. Big names, such as American Express, Diners Club, MasterCard or Visa are so well known that their brand name exemplifies trustworthiness. But what about other loan companies? You may wish to obtain information on these before asking for credit. Some shops on the internet, for instance, offer their own credit facilities. Just how can you rate such facilities? Happily, information services on the world wide web can come to the rescue. A number of companies can perform checks on your supplier of credit to help set your mind at rest. The companies you might like to use include:

Business Credit Management
http://www.creditman.co.uk/

Credit Status
http://www.creditstatus.com/

Instant Search
http://www.instant-search.com/

Status International
http://www.status-int.co.uk/

UK Data On Line
http://www.ukdata.com/

Each of these companies provides reports that will show you whether the company lending you the money can afford to do so.

Finding information on credit

There is a range of sites that can provide detailed information on credit facilities. These include magazine or newspaper sites that give up-to-date details on credit companies, and specialist sites. A useful place to start is the Moneywise site, mentioned in Chapter 2. Although not as interactive as others, it does include a reference table of credit companies and their interest rates. You can check this out at:

Readers Digest
http://www.readersdigest.co.uk/mstat_09.htm

MoneyWorld
http://www.moneyworld.co.uk/faqs/ccfaq.htm
Other useful general sources of information are the credit card pages of MoneyWorld. These provide useful information on all aspects of credit and can be found at the URL above.

Times-Money
http://www.times-money.co.uk
You should also try Times-Money, which has a useful comparison of credit cards and loans on its web site.

Indeed, many of the general financial information sites mentioned in Chapter 1 also have information on obtaining credit. You may find it useful to check out what's on offer on your favourite financial information site.

MasterCard
http://www.mastercard.com/press/
Another useful source of information, obviously biased, is the press office of MasterCard. This has its own web site as shown above. Although many of the press releases clearly promote MasterCard services, there is useful background information.

VISA
http://www.Visa.com
Useful information, particularly on credit card safety, can also be found at the Visa web site at:

http://www.Visa.com /cgi-bin/vee/ct/main.html?2+0

MasterCard
http://www.mastercard.com/mcu/credit.html
Another useful site is this one. This is part of the 'MasterCard University', a fancy name for a set of pages that contains essential financial information, with a particular emphasis on credit.

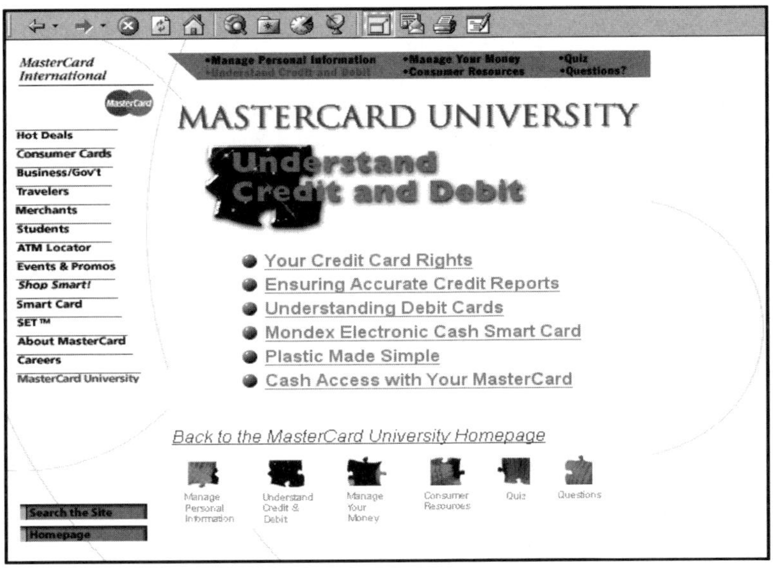

Fig. 45. MasterCard University. Well, there are no exams! Just lots of helpful and practical advice for cardholders of all kinds.

Finding out about loans

There are various places where you can find out about loans on the internet. For instance, if you want to buy a car, then instead of looking in the financial pages you have already found, go to some car-buying pages, which may offer special deals. Equally, if you are looking for a new computer, some of the computer stores on the internet can offer their own finance deals. Don't restrict yourself to looking for 'finance' or 'loans' in your searches; instead, browse through the specialist shops that offer the goods you want to buy, and you may well find that these companies can also offer finance, provided that you make a purchase from them.

▷ *A word of warning* – Most online stores offering financial services to buy their goods are American. While you can buy the goods and import them into the UK, arranging finance may be more difficult. The finance company backing the loan may require an American Social Security number from you. If you don't have such a number, or a proper US mailing address, you might not be able to arrange the loan. So check with each shop before you apply or try to buy something. You can make this check by sending an email to the site that is offering the loan – most have a 'contact us' button or something similar. Almost all sites have an email button for the 'webmaster', the person who runs the site. If in doubt, send an email to the webmaster and ask them to forward it to the appropriate people.

Although loans are widely available on the internet, you may find it better to use a credit card, rather than a specific loan, since you can make international purchases much more easily.

Applying for a credit card

Obtaining a credit card online is nowhere near as easy as using one! Most of the companies that provide credit cards do not allow you to apply online. Instead, you have to give the company your details and they post you an application form. This really is quite ridiculous, considering the security measures available at even a basic level on the internet. Far too many of the credit card companies are treating the internet as just another advertising medium, rather than as an alternative way of doing business, or as a revolutionary tool for gaining new customers. Such a dinosaur attitude will certainly see them disappear or forced to make major changes because of intense competition.

Barclaycard
http://www.barclaycard.co.uk
Barclaycard is a breath of fresh air amongst the credit card companies operating on the internet. You can apply for Barclaycard's range of credit cards with an online application form. You can also use the Barclaycard site to administer your credit card. For instance, you can check your balance and pay what you owe, using your Barclay's bank account. If you use another bank's online account service, you can check your balance on the web site and then switch to your bank account to pay

Fig. 46. The home page of Barclaycard.

what you owe direct to Barclaycard. The Barclaycard web site itself is easy to use and is bright and clear – just what you want when you are worried about your mounting debts!

▷ *Key benefits of the Barclaycard site*

Able to apply for a card online
Able to manage your credit card online

▷ *Disadvantages of the Barclaycard site*

Lots of text
Sometimes easy to get lost!

MasterCard
http://www.mastercard.com
The MasterCard organisation does not issue cards itself; instead, cards are provided by individual banks. Barclays, for instance, has its own MasterCard, as do Lloyds, HSBC/Midland, Bank of Scotland, Abbey National and MBNA. To find out about credit cards from your bank, visit your own bank's web site. MasterCard, though, has a comprehensive web site covering all its products and services. This is a very busy site, packed with information. It even includes a useful links page to banks that offer MasterCard credit cards, many with online application forms. Sadly, however, none is in the UK. Indeed, applying online for a MasterCard appears to be possible only using the Barclaycard site.

▷ *Key benefits of the MasterCard site*

Comprehensive and easy to use
Useful supporting information

Fig. 47. MasterCard has become one of the most widely used pieces of plastic on the planet. You can apply for a card online and check out their latest special offers.

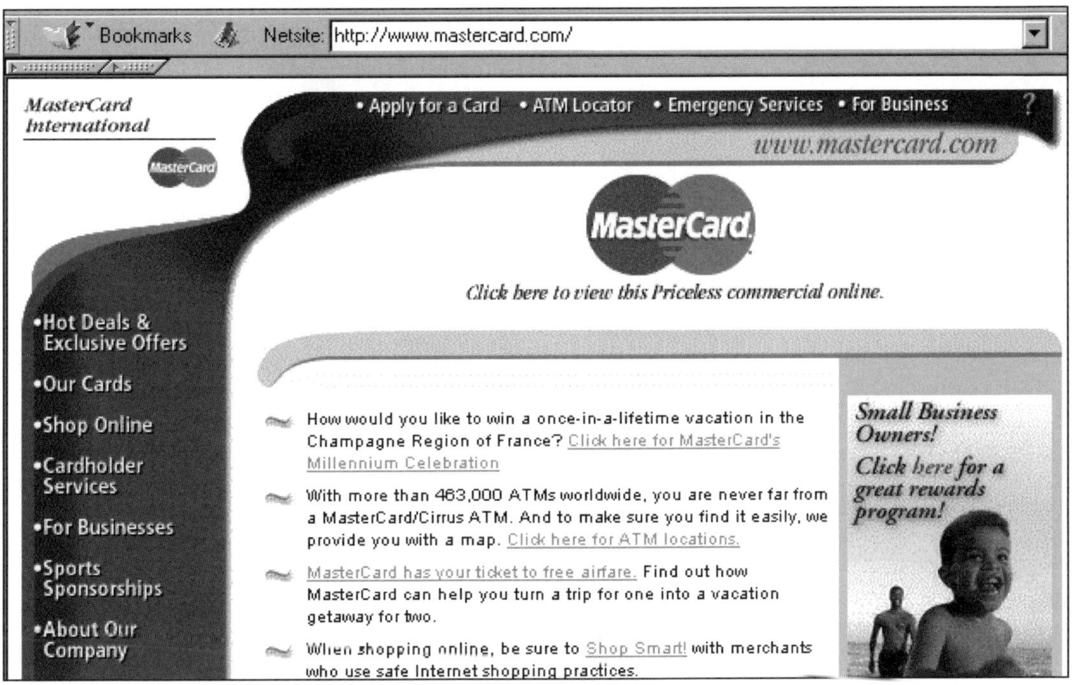

▷ *Disadvantages of the MasterCard site*

Not enough focus on the UK, since the site is international
No online application form

Visa

http://www.Visa.com

The Visa organisation is similar to MasterCard. It is a group of financial companies that issue credit cards – Visa will not provide you with a card itself, but one of the issuing banks will. As with MasterCard, you need to visit bank-specific web sites to apply for a Visa card. Happily, the Visa organisation does provide a list of links direct to UK issuing banks. To reach this page go to:

http://www.Visa.com/cgi-bin/vee/pd/cards/eu/uk.html?2+0

You can then select a bank's site to apply for a Visa card. The Visa site also allows you to report a stolen card, should you be so unfortunate; you can halt all payments made with that card. This is a highly useful security feature and one that should be standard on all credit card sites.

▷ *Key benefits of the Visa site*

Alert system for stolen cards
Links to issuing banks

▷ *Disadvantages of the Visa site*

Some of the links to issuing banks are not to useful sites
This is a large site and you might find it too detailed

Fig. 48. The web site of Visa. Don't miss it if you are thinking of changing your plastic.

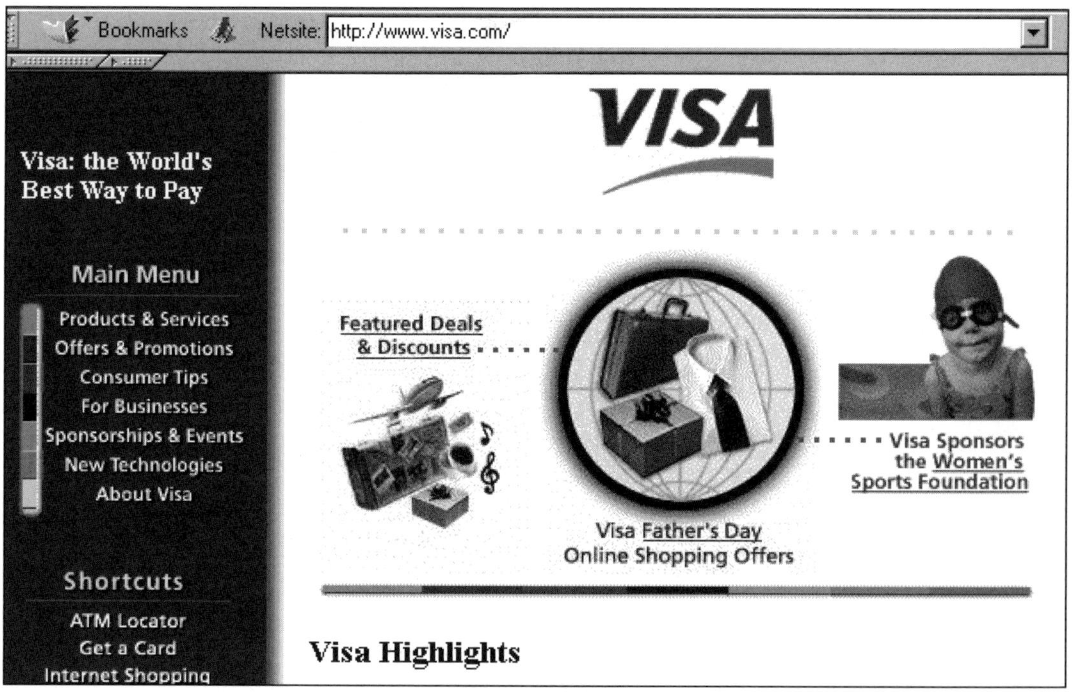

Bank of Scotland
http://www.bankofscotland.co.uk
Information on credit cards is hidden under 'Personal Banking Package' which is at:

http://www.bankofscotland.co.uk/NEWPERSONAL/personal.html

All you get is a couple of lines of information. You then have to give them your name and address so they can send you even more information in the post.

Bradford & Bingley
http://www.bradford-bingley.co.uk
The Visa site lists the Bradford & Bingley Building Society as a Visa card issuer, but the bright and clear Bradford & Bingley web site has no information at all about Visa cards on it.

Egg
http://www3.egg.com
Egg is the unusual name given to the personal finance company owned by The Prudential. The company offers a range of loans from its site at:

http://www3.egg.com/loans/default.asp

However, you need to register in order to access the useful areas of the site, such as an application form for a loan. To register, you enter your name and Egg allocates you a password. This is a random series of eight characters, which is hardly memorable. Other sites that ask you to register at least give you the option of choosing your own password.

Fig. 49. Egg is a totally internet-based personal finance project of the London-based Prudential.

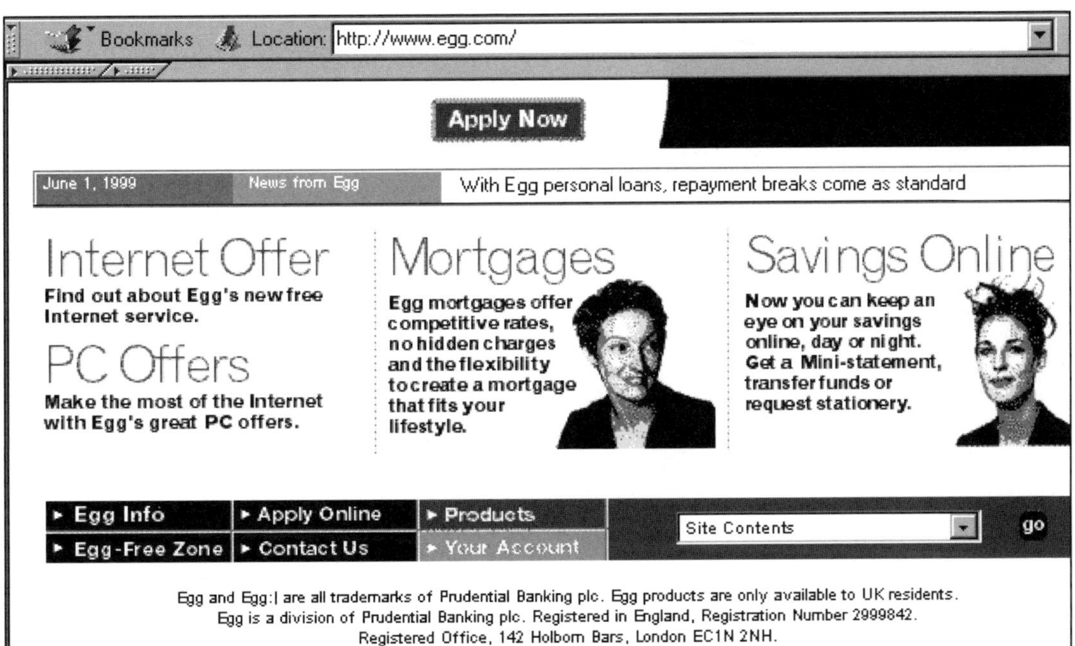

Credit card web sites

Once you can remember your Egg password, you can gain access to a useful loan calculator and apply for the money you want.

Halifax
http://www.halifax.co.uk
This is a well-designed and rapid site which appears to have been produced by a team that has realised the advantages the internet can bring. That's because you can apply online for a credit card – you don't have to submit a postal application. The online application form is clear and easy to understand. Go to:

http://www.halifax.co.uk/card/card.html

Halifax also has a series of credit cards that can be used to donate money to charity. The bank donates a specified amount based on the level of your credit card expenditure. More details are on the web site.

Hamilton Direct Bank
http://www.hdb.co.uk/
Hamilton Direct Bank is part of HFC Bank and issues Visa cards. You can go to the online application form here. It's a simple web site, but is ideal if all you want to do is apply for one of the bank's Visa cards.

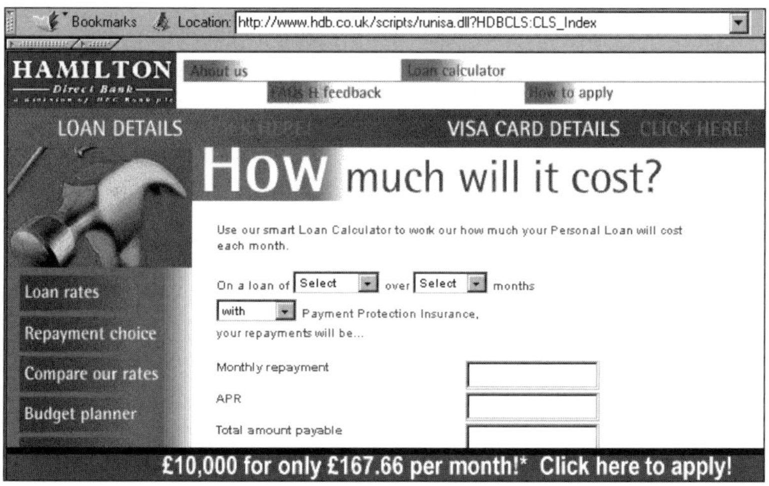

Fig. 50. The Hamilton Direct Bank web site. It includes an instant loan calculator.

Lloyds Bank
http://www.lloydsbank.co.uk/
Lloyds Bank issues Visa cards in the UK, but does not include any information at its web site about such cards, even though the Visa site refers you there. Also, the Lloyds site has no method of online application for its products. In fact you can't even submit an application form to ask for information, you have to go to a branch. This makes the Lloyds web site of little use if you want to apply for a credit card *now.*

MBNA
http://www.mbnainternational.com
MBNA is an American Bank, but has a UK operation and issues cards

here. At first sight, MBNA appears to be much more go-ahead than many of the British financial institutions. For instance, you can apply online for an MBNA credit card (which can be a Visa or MasterCard). Just go to:

http://www.mbnainternational.com/cards/index.htm

However, don't go there unless you have a US Social Security number. The MBNA web site is American and aimed at US citizens. Even though they have a British operation, you can't apply for your UK credit card here. Indeed, the MBNA web site doesn't appear to acknowledge the company's existence outside the USA. If you want an MBNA credit card you will have to contact the UK company direct, using old-fashioned technology.

Midland Bank
http://www.midlandbank.com
Midland is part of HSBC, the Hong Kong & Shanghai Banking Corporation. It issues Visa cards and MasterCards. You can find out more about these products at:

http://www.midlandbank.com/cards/

Don't get too excited – there is not much information at all at this site. Also, you cannot apply online. You have to request a booklet that will be sent to you in the post.

Nationwide
http://www.nationwide.co.uk
The Nationwide Building Society offers Visa credit cards since you can jump there from the link provided at the Visa web site. To get to the information via this link you need to select 'online banking', which is a rather strange route. You can save lots of clicks and go direct to:

http://www.nationwide.co.uk/fserv/banking/credit/creditcard.htm

Like almost every other credit card issuer in the UK, though, Nationwide has opted to use the postal route to let you apply. You can fill in an online form, but then you will have to wait for an application leaflet to pop through your letterbox.

Royal Bank of Scotland
http://www.royalbankscot.co.uk
Like most other banks, the Royal Bank of Scotland issues Visa and MasterCard credit cards. You can find out more at:

http://www.royalbankscot.co.uk/personal/credit/

This page provides information about the credit cards in general. But click on one of the pictures of the cards available and you will be sent to an interesting page: a calculator allows you to see in a few seconds the savings you might make if you transferred your existing credit arrangements to a Royal Bank of Scotland credit card. This is an excellent use of internet technology, but the Royal Bank of Scotland lets itself down by insisting that you telephone for an application form, rather than allowing an online application. Even so, this web site is worth a visit, simply to help you recalculate your existing credit card arrangements!

TSB
http://ww.tsb.co.uk
You are referred to the TSB by the VISA web site, since this part of the Lloyds TSB group issues Visa cards. However, in common with the Lloyds site, the TSB pages do not provide any information on credit cards. Indeed, if you want detailed information about TSB products and services you will have to call them or visit a branch.

Woolwich
http://www.woolwich.co.uk
The Woolwich bank offers credit card information at its web page:

http://www.woolwich.co.uk/creditcard/

All you can do, though, is submit a form asking for details to be sent to you in the post, together with an application form.

Affinity credit cards
There are a number of organisations that issue 'affinity cards'. These are credit cards that are operated by a bank, but look as though they are run by your favourite sports club or charity, for example. A range of affinity cards appears on the internet.

Football Card
http://www.footballcard.co.uk/
One group of affinity cards on the internet is the 'Football MasterCard'. You can access this site and find out if your team has its own credit card. If so, you can send in a request for further information, though you cannot actually apply online for the cards.

Union Card
http://www.unioncard.co.uk/
Another affinity card is the Union MasterCard, which can be emblazoned with the name of your trade union, if you wish. You cannot apply for the card online, but you can request more information.

Graduate Card
http://www.graduatecard.co.uk/
A number of universities also offer 'affinity cards'. To find out if your *alma mater* has its own credit card, go to Graduate Card. You will find a list of universities that have credit cards issued by the Bank of Scotland. You can only apply for more information, though; you cannot get a credit card online.

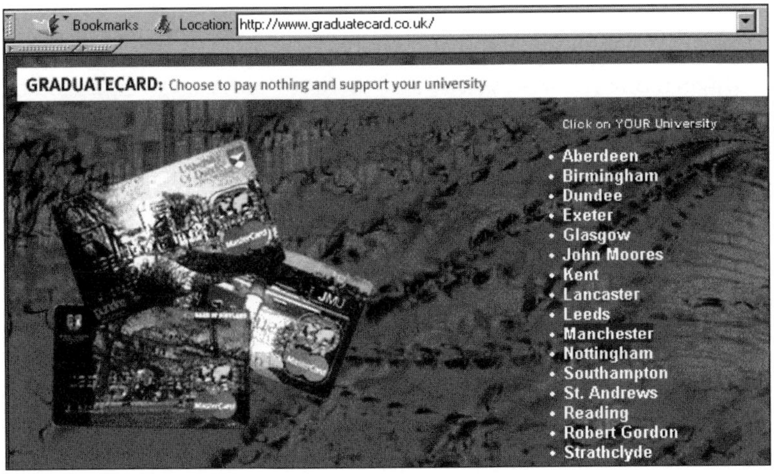

Fig. 51. Why not apply for a Graduate Card, and manage your personal finances while supporting your own university?

Supermarket credit cards

Supermarkets such as J. Sainsbury and Tesco have their own 'banks' and their own credit cards. However, even though these companies have pioneered internet shopping and are using internet technology very effectively, they do not have information about their financial services on their web sites. This is a strange omission, considering the supermarket sites themselves offer internet shopping you can pay for with your credit card! It seems, for the moment at least, if you want to apply for your favourite supermarket's own credit card, you will have to visit the store and pick up an application form.

Applying for loans online

Getting a loan appears to be a whole lot easier on the internet than applying for a credit card. This is strange, because if you want to shop on the internet, you need a credit card, not a loan! Loans are usually only provided for a specific purpose, such as buying a car or a boat, or for some other major expenditure. Also, check carefully with loan suppliers since it may sometimes be cheaper to finance a major purchase using an agreed overdraft with your bank, rather than a separate loan. In fact, for many years, agreed overdrafts have been the cheapest way to borrow money. As with many other aspects of financial services, you may wish to start your search for a loan at the web site of your own bank. Some mention their loan facilities, some don't.

Find
http://www.find.co.uk/
To find a list of companies that offer loans go to Find. Scroll down the page and you will find a link to companies offering loan facilities. Some of these links are to banks and building societies, but other financial institutions are also mentioned.

Abbey National
http://www.abbeynational.co.uk
The Abbey National web site has a useful calculator and budget planner on its loan pages:

http://www.abbeynational.co.uk/chile.cgi?id=35844133-6476&hr=loan/index.hot

You can use these to work out how much you can afford, or the size of loan you can get. To apply for a loan you have to click 'Any more questions', which is not the most obvious place for applications. Even so, once you click on this, all you are 'applying' for is more information to be sent to you.

Barclays
http://www.personal.barclays.co.uk/
Barclays has an efficient and friendly loans web site which has a useful 'calculator' to let you work out what you can afford. Also, you can apply for a loan online. There is a six-page application form that you can submit for a decision, which is guaranteed within 24 hours.

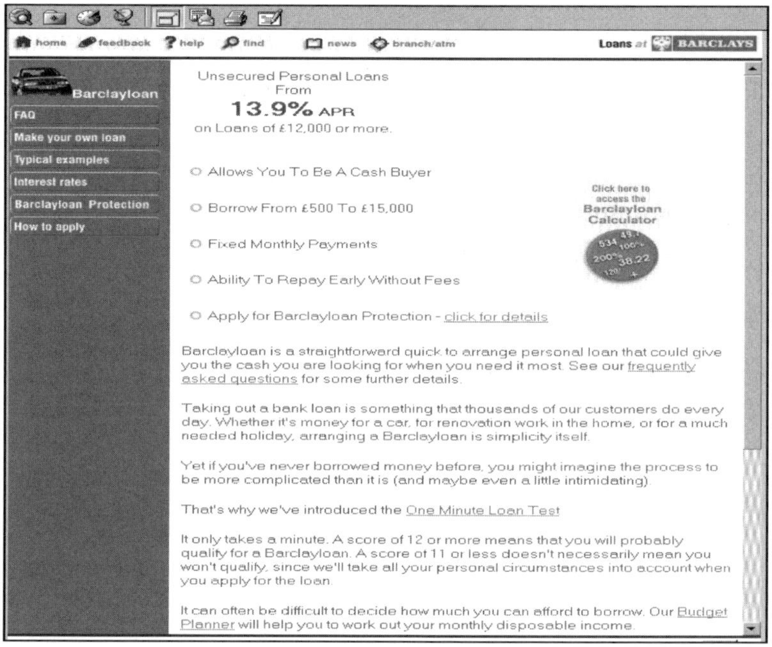

Fig. 52. 'Make your own loan' online with Barclayloan. This web site helps to take the mystery out of the cost of borrowing.

Bank of Scotland
http://www.bankofscotland.co.uk
This is an extremely annoying site that forces you to click past lots of images, or wait for them to lead you to the eventual page that you want. Don't go to the Bank of Scotland's main site for a loan, instead, go here:

http://www.bankofscotland.co.uk/nws/lifestyle.html

You can then make an online application for a loan and get an answer within 24 hours. Although there is no calculator on this site, there is a clear table showing you how much your loan will actually cost.

Capital Investors
http://www.capital-investors.co.uk
This is a loan company with a rapid and clear web site. You can find out

Fig. 53. The internet is greatly intensifying competition for customers. If you need a car loan, why not try a web site like Freeway, which specialises in online auto finance?

how much a loan will cost but you cannot apply online. You need to request an application form that will be sent in the post.

http://www.capital-investors.co.uk/main.htm

Freeway
http://www.freeway.ltd.uk
Freeway offer loans over the internet for car purchases only. The site has a very comprehensive list of cars and purchase methods. You select the car you want, say how you want to pay and you are given an online quotation within minutes. If that is acceptable to you, you fill in an online form and a company representative then calls you to finalise the details.

Halifax
http://www.halifax.co.uk
The Halifax has a very comprehensive and easy to use web site that is an example for other financial institutions to follow. You can apply for a loan at:

http://www.halifax.co.uk/loan/loan.html

There is an online application form, but no 'calculator' or easy method of finding out exactly how much your loan will cost. The charges are all well explained, there is just no instant calculation or budget tool to use.

Hamilton Direct Bank
http://www.hdb.co.uk/
Hamilton Direct is part of HFC Bank. You can apply for a loan online here. It's a simple site, with not much detail. However, it does have the advantage of having a 'commitments calculator'. Using this you can work out your current financial commitments and then see whether a Hamilton loan would work out any cheaper.

Interactive Finance Services
http://www.loancorp.co.uk/index.htm
Interactive Finance Services is a loan company offering funds to home owners. This site has a table showing what you will pay for a specific loan. There is also an online application form.

Lombard
http://www.lombard.co.uk/index.htm
Lombard is one of Britain's largest loan companies. However, they have one of the smallest web sites. However, once you access this site and compare it with other loan companies you will realise that it provides comprehensive information, but nothing more. To get a loan, you have to phone the company.

Marks and Spencer
https://www.marks-and-spencer.co.uk
Marks and Spencer Financial Services is at this page:

https://www.marks-and-spencer.co.uk/financial-services/

Using this site you can find out more about loans. You can also apply for a loan online, up to a maximum of £10,000. There is a handy calculator, as well, to help you work out what you can afford. You can use this site to apply for a Marks and Spencer 'Personal Reserve' account, which comes with a cheque book. You can write cheques, almost as though you had an overdraft with Marks and Spencer. Paying back the borrowed amount, though, is flexible, allowing you to operate the account almost like a credit card.

NatWest
http://www.natwest.co.uk
NatWest has a nice, easy-to-use web site, but sadly it doesn't use the technology to its best advantage. Instead, the site is more of an

Fig. 54. Marks and Spencer Financial Services also offer the ability to play with figures and apply for the loan you want. You are invited to send them feedback through their web site.

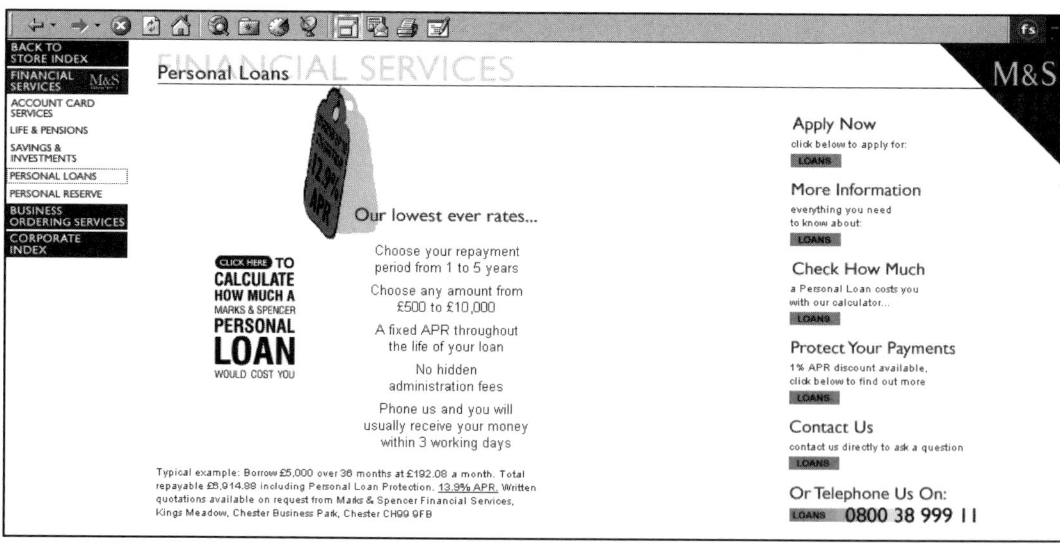

advertisement for its branches, rather than an interactive tool. There are a few interactive features; unfortunately, though, unlike its competitors, NatWest has not introduced many of these for loans. You can calculate your loan repayments, but to apply you have to go to a branch.

Paragon
http://www.paragon-cars.co.uk
Paragon is another company that specialises in the car loan market. When you access this comprehensive site you can select the make and model of the car you are interested in buying, add on any optional extras you want included, and then get the calculator to work out your total price. You then get to select a choice of payment options before applying online for your loan. This is a highly efficient web site and an excellent example of what the technology can achieve.

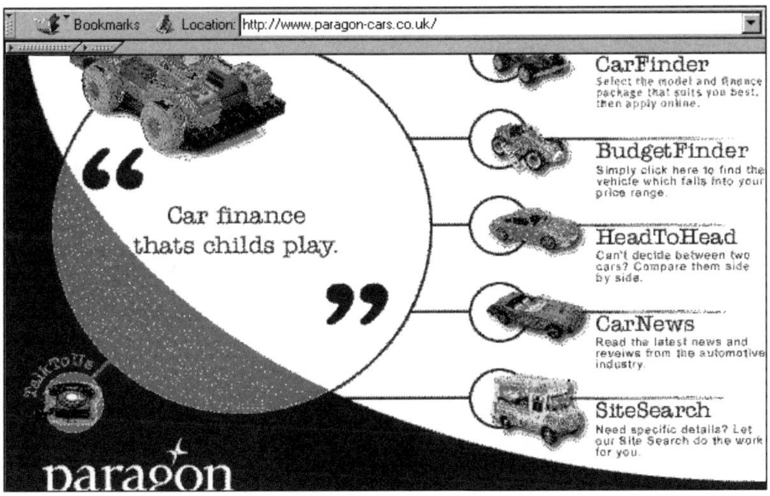

Fig. 55. Paragon is another web site offering finance for motor purchases.

Priority Loans
http://www.btinternet.com/~priorityloans/index.htm
This company offers loans for a variety of purposes. You can use a repayment table to work out the cost of your loan and you can apply online using the form provided.

Purple Loans
http://www.purpleloans.com
Purple Loans is another independent loan company that offers online application facilities for all-purpose finance. You can get to this form by going to its web site here.

Sterling Direct
http://www.sterlingdirect.co.uk/Home.htm
Sterling Direct is an independent finance company providing all-purpose loans. This site, though, is purely informational. To apply for a loan you have to contact the company using more traditional means, or send an email saying you want them to contact you.

Templeton Ross
http://www.templeton-ross.co.uk
Templeton Ross is an independent financial company. You can apply online for a loan, though there is no calculator to help you work out the costs. Full information comes when your application has been processed. You can go to their main index page by pointing your browser to:

http://www.templeton-ross.co.uk/index2.html

Universal Finance
Universal Finance is a licensed credit broker that is based at:

http://ourworld.compuserve.com/homepages/universal_finance/uftop.htm

This is a very simple site, but there are forms with which you can apply for loans.

Wilmslow Financial Services
http://www.ukloans.co.uk
Wilmslow Financial Services provide a range of loans from their web site here. You can get a clear indication of the costs you are likely to incur, and can also apply for a loan online. Your application will be assessed, and details posted to you, on the same day you submit your form.

Wisemoney
https://www.wisemoney.com
This site comes from a financial institution with international interests, e.g. the USA and China. Before you can get any real benefit from the site, you have to register by filling in a lengthy form, including a great deal of financial information. If you are just browsing for quick quotes and information on loans, this is not a very good idea since it is quite off-putting for casual queries. You can go direct to the UK site at:

https://www.wisemoney.com/homepage.asp

Getting 'cash' you can use online

The emergence of 'e-cash' or 'cybercash' is one of the most exciting advances in internet technology in the last year or two. In essence you can arrange for funds that you can spend only with online traders. It is a new form of currency; as such, you can borrow it, just like any other form of money. According to *The Economist,* there are problems with cybercash or 'e-money' as some people call it; this leading commentator on international finance predicts that the current crop of cash cards and payment card systems will naturally evolve online.[1] Other commentators are less pessimistic. For instance, the internet analyst Dr Mary J. Cronin, from Boston College, says that e-cash systems have advantages over credit cards in some instances.[2] These include very small transactions of single-figure sums, as well as occasions when people wish to buy anonymously (something you cannot do if you give your credit card number).

A number of e-cash systems are being pioneered at the moment. You can sign up with a company and buy some cash credits using your credit card. This cash can then be stored in your electronic account and used at web sites to pay for items you wish to buy. The idea is that, before too long, you will be able to add a 'smart card' reader to your PC and load up a payment card with your e-cash credit. You could then use this electronic money on your smart card to pay for small items, such as car park charges. If you insert the card back into your PC you can use the money to buy things from the internet as well. Commentators believe this will be the most popular way of using e-cash.

In essence, the idea behind such smart cards is that we will be able to dispense with cash altogether. This has a number of advantages:

1. Cash is insecure.
2. Cash is heavy and inconvenient.
3. Cash is only useful in a specific country.

Digital money doesn't have these problems:

1. Your smart card or electronic cash file is password protected; even if it is stolen, your cash is secure.
2. The card can have hundreds of pounds in it and won't weigh your pocket down.
3. E-cash can be used internationally.

The pursuit of e-cash is developing very quickly, with backing from major companies such as Barclays, which has already experimented in the North of England with an 'electronic purse'.

To find out more about how you can get electronic cash credit go to:

Finance Hub
http://financehub.com/emoney
This page provides links to a range of information sites on electronic money and payment systems. You might like also to look at the pages of:

The Electronic Banking Association
http://www.e-banking.org/
Another useful way of gaining information on electronic cash systems is to put yourself on a mailing list run by Mondex (see later this section). You can register for this mailing list at:

http://194.112.42.30/mondexuk/cgi-bin/printpage.pl?fname=agent.html&doctype=page

Barclaycoin
http://www.barclaycoin.co.uk/
This is a payment system being pioneered by Barclays Bank. It allows

you to load up an 'electronic purse' with cash credits. You can use this purse to purchase small value items on the internet. You can get your Barclaycoin purse by going to this web site. There you will find you can download your own 'wallet' that you can load up with cash deducted from your credit card. You can then use the wallet to purchase small items on line. For instance you can buy individual recipes, pay donations to charity, electronic books, or information from *Which?*.

Check Free
http://www.checkfree.com/index-ecomcon.html
You can access the Check Free consumer information here. This site has a variety of useful links, plus you can download an application form to get their electronic cash system. However, to get the form you will need a well-known piece of software called Adobe Acrobat Reader. If you don't have this software go to the Adobe page at:

http://www.adobe.com/prodindex/acrobat/readstep.html

CyberCash
http://www.cybercash.com/
CyberCash Inc is an American company offering electronic cash credit. This company has a partnership with Microsoft to offer complete trading solutions to businesses. CyberCash offers a range of services including Cybercoi and Electronic Check. Sadly, the company does not yet offer its services outside the USA. However, you can find out a great deal of useful information at this site.

Fig. 56. CyberCash is a web site to visit if you want to glimpse the future of electronic money in today's expanding financial world without frontiers.

DigiCash
http://www.digicash.com/
DigiCash is an American company offering electronic cash services. It has a European subsidiary based in Amsterdam. You can't sign up for e-cash with DigiCash, though. As with a credit card organisation, such as Visa, DigiCash offers the system and then banks issue the accounts. Banks that issue DigiCash include Bank Austria, Deutsche Bank and EU

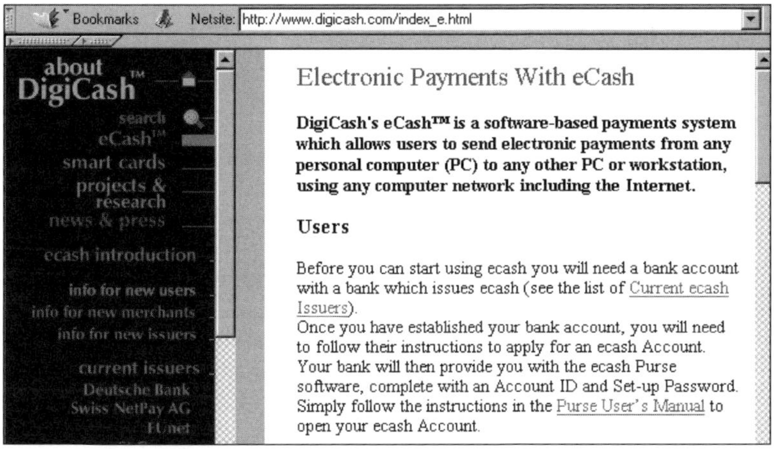

Fig. 57 . DigiCash is another pioneer in the development of electronic money for cyberspace. The impact of cyber money could be as far-reaching as the invention of bank notes in the eighteenth century.

net (Finland). You can find out more about the DigiCash e-cash system at:

http://www.digicash.com/index_e.html

Mondex
http://www.mondex.com
Mondex started life with an experiment in Swindon. People were provided with smart cards that could be loaded up with cash credits. They could use these cards instead of cash in local shops. Now, though, the Mondex company has expanded into a major international electronic payments organisation, part of MasterCard and backed by NatWest and Midland Bank. Be warned, though, the site opens with a simple graphic and no obvious route to anywhere! All you have to do is run your mouse pointer over the various parts of the graphic and up will pop the names of all the locations on the site. (In fact this is a growing technique on the internet known as mapping. An image can be used as a map of the web site, with different 'hot spots' that direct you to other pages on the site.)

Netchex
http://www.netchex.com/
This is another American company offering services aimed at 'merchants', in much the same way that credit card companies operate. There is little of direct interest to consumers, but you can find out more information at its web site.

Even though many of these sites are very interesting and provide a fascinating insight into the future of commerce and financial technology, it has to be said that digital cash systems are still in their early stages. Most of those available are only for US citizens, except Barclaycoin or Mondex. If you want to download a credit account for use on the internet, UK residents appear to be restricted to Barclaycoin, though expect this to change fairly rapidly.

Case study – using electronic cash

Anne's hobby is cooking. She loves inventing new recipes and entertaining her friends and family at dinner parties where she has produced something new. However, like all cooks, she needs a source of ideas. She has a range of cookery books, but many have similar recipes and this is an expensive way of seeing repetitive ideas. Anne has been searching the internet for recipes and has come up with many ideas this way, but now she has found a better way of getting good value recipes. She has loaded up a Barclaycoin account with £10 from her credit card. She can use her Barclaycoin wallet to buy recipes from people selling them on the internet. The average price of each recipe is just 25p and she is able to check first whether the recipe is likely to be of any value before making a purchase – something that is much more difficult when buying a book.

Essential tips for getting money on the internet

- ▷ Use the web to ensure your financial status is recorded properly.
- ▷ Make sure you have all your financial details at your fingertips before you go online, as you will need this information to complete an application form.
- ▷ Use the calculators available on sites so that you can check what you will actually pay.
- ▷ Open up a number of different loan or credit card sites in separate windows so you can make comparisons between different company's interest rates. (See Chapter 2 for more information on how to do this or access the 'help' facility in your web browser.)
- ▷ Go to the Moneywise site so you can compare interest rates: http://www.readersdigest.co.uk/finance.htm
- ▷ Get a Barclaycoin account so that you can experience the potential benefits of future electronic cash trading.

Loans and credit card checklist

- ▷ Loans come in two varieties – secured and unsecured. Secured loans will offer you more money, usually, though you need to offer something as 'security' should you default against the loan (usually your house).
- ▷ Interest rates vary – check you will get the best deal. Compare the 'APR' (the annual percentage rate) since this will show you exactly what you will repay.
- ▷ Credit cards vary according to the moment when interest starts to accumulate. Some provide an interest-free period, others start clocking up the interest from a specified date. Check the small print if you wish to avoid paying excess interest.

References

1 'Going Digital', *The Economist*, 1998, p. 148.
2 *Banking and Finance on the Internet*, Ed: Mary J. Cronin, 1998, John Wiley & Sons.
3 *Personal Computer World*, April 1999, p. 36.

5 Mortgages and the internet

In this chapter we will explore:

- *finding out about mortgages*
- *using magazines*
- *comparing mortgages with specialist software*
- *using accounts software for mortgage information*
- *finding out about properties for sale*
- *finding property on the internet in other ways*
- *types of mortgage*
- *locating a suitable mortgage lender*
- *using a bank for a mortgage*
- *finding out about building society mortgages*
- *using a broker to find you a mortgage*
- *choosing between brokers and mortgage companies*
- *getting a specialist mortgage*
- *considering other factors in home buying*
- *essential tips for getting a mortgage on the internet*
- *mortgage checklist*

Your mortgage is likely to be the biggest financial commitment you will ever make. Most people take 25 years or so to pay back the money they have borrowed. That's because the average mortgage in Britain in 1998-99 was £60,000.[1] At 7% interest on this average loan you would have to pay back a whopping £130,000 – more than double the original amount lent. This is why most of us are forced to spread the cost of buying a home over such a long period. It is also why most of us want to pay off our mortgage sooner rather than later. The earlier you can pay off your mortgage, the better. You will reduce your interest charges significantly – even a modest overpayment each month can substantially reduce the amount in interest you pay. For example, if you overpay a £100,000 mortgage by as much as £100 a month, you'll knock off about eight years and around £50,000 in interest.[2] It is therefore an excellent idea to make sure you have the right mortgage for you – one that you can make inroads into and one that you can afford. Choosing the right mortgage is fundamental to your entire financial position. Making a mistake with your mortgage could have an impact on all your other financial arrangements. Choosing the right mortgage is essential.

Finding out about mortgages

Most people only really start to consider mortgages when they move house. This is a mistake. Mortgage rates and products vary tremendously and new offers are being made all the time. You can always change your mortgage even if you do not move home.

Admittedly there will be some charges to do this, but you need to weigh up the costs and benefits of change according to your own individual circumstances. However, if you do not keep up to date with what is happening in the mortgage world, you could pay more interest than necessary, pay higher charges than you should, and lose out on a potential increase in money in your pocket. It is therefore advisable to keep a constant eye on mortgages so that you can make sure you benefit if necessary.

This means you need to make a regular time slot, say once every three months, to find out the latest on mortgages. So where should you get the information you need? If you go into a high street estate agency that offers mortgages you won't get a great deal of help. They would rather sell you a house since this is where they make most of their profit—the mortgage business for estate agents is only a comparatively small slice of their income. Your high street bank could provide you with information on mortgages, but it will be biased; your bank will want to sell you its products rather than tell you how wonderful the competition is!

Fig. 58. Make sure you get independent financial advice by checking that your advisers have this logo.

To get truly unbiased advice you need to talk to some specialists. There are mortgage brokers in some towns and cities, but usually they work in offices above shops and are not immediately noticeable. You can find these brokers listed under 'Mortgage Brokers' in *Yellow Pages*. If you choose one near to you, make sure you are protected in some way – they should be regulated by one of the authorities mentioned in Chapter 2. Also, they should say they are 'Independent Financial Advisers' and should have the appropriate logo on their stationery. You can find out more about independent financial advisers at:

Independent Financial Advisers
http://www.ifap.org.uk/home/homeword.htm

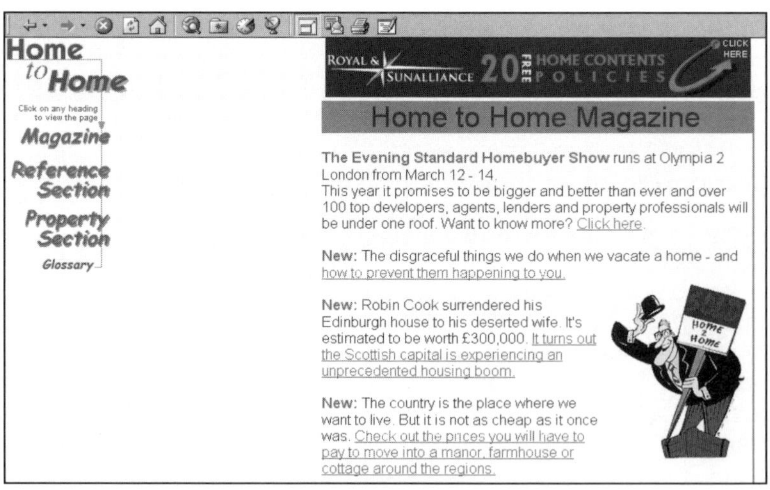

Fig. 59. *Home to Home* is a useful electronic magazine published by Royal & SunAlliance.

Using magazines

There are many magazines that will provide you with unbiased mortgage advice. You can get these magazines in most major high street newsagents. Remember, too, that any newsagent can order any magazine for you. Here are some magazines to try – they contain details of the latest mortgage offers and many have useful comparison tables:

Bloomberg Money | *Money Observer*
Moneywise | *What Mortgage*
Your Mortgage

Fig. 60. *Your New Home* is another internet magazine aimed at the home buyer, with the latest information from McAlpine, Barratt, Beazer, Bryant, Fairview, Laing, Persimmon and other house-builders.

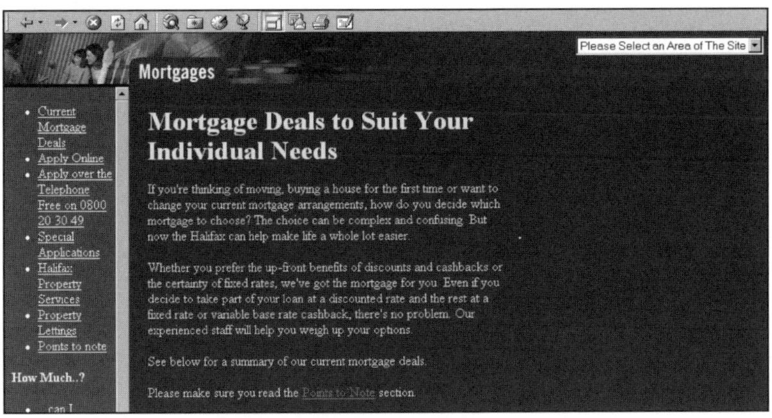

Fig. 61. You can explore the best mortgage deals by visiting a web site like this.

Comparing mortgages using specialist software

Trying to work out all the different offers that are available can be a nightmare. You are faced with a variety of interest rates, payment schemes and so on. It can all become bewildering. To overcome this difficulty, you can get some software that will do all the hard work for you. If you have a spreadsheet program, such as Microsoft Excel or Lotus 1-2-3, you can construct a table that will work out the comparisons for you. If you don't have the skills or the time to produce such a table for yourself you can download many examples

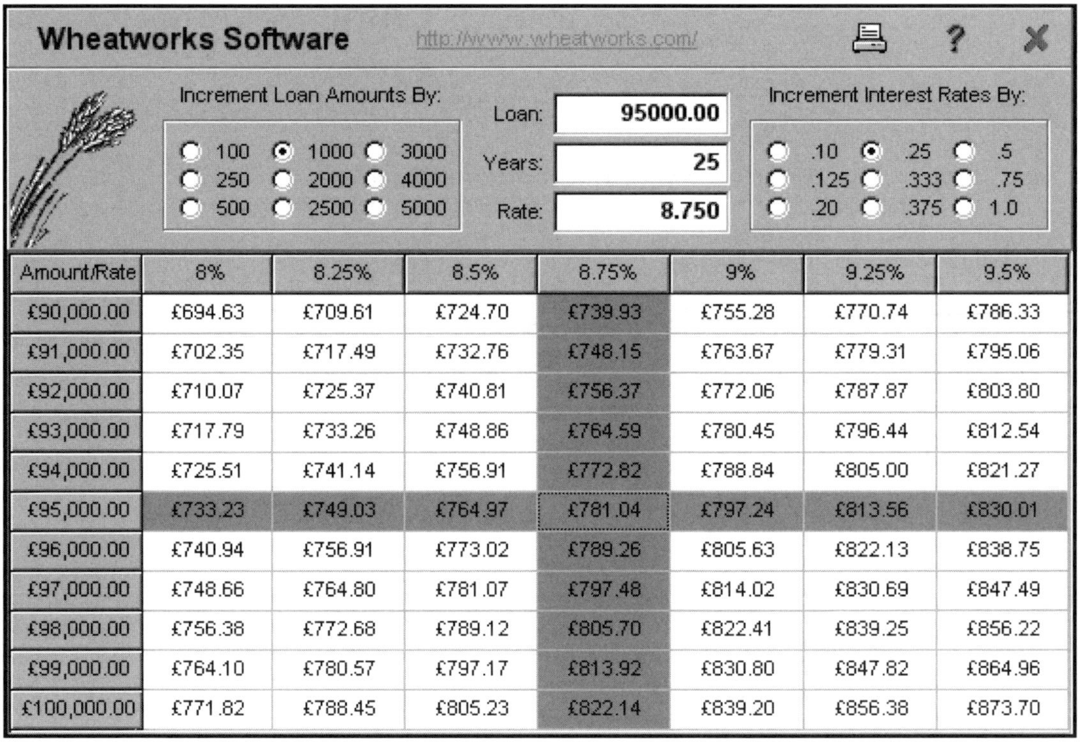

Amount/Rate	8%	8.25%	8.5%	8.75%	9%	9.25%	9.5%
£90,000.00	£694.63	£709.61	£724.70	£739.93	£755.28	£770.74	£786.33
£91,000.00	£702.35	£717.49	£732.76	£748.15	£763.67	£779.31	£795.06
£92,000.00	£710.07	£725.37	£740.81	£756.37	£772.06	£787.87	£803.80
£93,000.00	£717.79	£733.26	£748.86	£764.59	£780.45	£796.44	£812.54
£94,000.00	£725.51	£741.14	£756.91	£772.82	£788.84	£805.00	£821.27
£95,000.00	£733.23	£749.03	£764.97	£781.04	£797.24	£813.56	£830.01
£96,000.00	£740.94	£756.91	£773.02	£789.26	£805.63	£822.13	£838.75
£97,000.00	£748.66	£764.80	£781.07	£797.48	£814.02	£830.69	£847.49
£98,000.00	£756.38	£772.68	£789.12	£805.70	£822.41	£839.25	£856.22
£99,000.00	£764.10	£780.57	£797.17	£813.92	£830.80	£847.82	£864.96
£100,000.00	£771.82	£788.45	£805.23	£822.14	£839.20	£856.38	£873.70

Fig. 62. A mortgage calculator from Wheatworks.com. This one is very easy to use and well laid out.

from the internet to do the job for you. To get a specialist mortgage calculation program go to:

Mortgage Calculation Program
http://www.magma.ca/~yjlandr/
Towards the bottom of this web page you can download a spreadsheet model (in dollars) which shows you how much you would pay on a certain amount at a certain interest rate. The larger stand-alone program mentioned at the top of the screen is much more sophisticated, but is really aimed at mortgage professionals. Whichever version you use, remember that these programs are 'shareware', i.e. you are expected to pay for them. The spreadsheet model costs $19.

Mortgage Calculation Program
http://www.softseek.com
Another useful mortgage calculator is Mortgage Calculation Program, which produces a comparison table of different mortgage products. Indeed, SoftSeek is a useful site of shareware, demonstration programs, and free snippets for your computer. You can access SoftSeek's own search facility at the main web address shown above. You can get the Mortgage Calculation Program from:

http://www.softseek.com/Home_Family_and_Leisure/Home_Finance/Review_15425_index.html

ZDNet
http://www.zdnet.com/swlib
A similar collection of software can be found at this site. Both ZDNet

and SoftSeek include a whole host of mortgage analysis software. You might like to download a few to find the one you like most.

Using accounts software for mortgage information

It is worthwhile remembering that accounts programs such as Microsoft Money and Quicken have sections on mortgages. For instance, within Microsoft Money Financial Suite you will find an extensive array of information on mortgages. You could access these pages for details on mortgages and for some tips on improving your own mortgage position. Quicken, meanwhile, has a remortgage calculator that will help you see whether or not any change in an existing mortgage will save you money.

Finding out about properties for sale

You might not just want a new mortgage – you might want a home to go with it! If that's the case, there are plenty of sites on the internet to help you locate a property to buy. Indeed, there are many online estate agencies. One very useful place to start is:

Up My Street
http://www.upmystreet.com/
This enables you to locate estate agents by post code. This site also contains a whole host of information useful to people who are moving. Items include average house price sales for the area, a guide to the best schools and lots more. You can also compare one area of the country with another, using a range of parameters.

▷ *Key benefits of the Up My Street site*

Able to locate properties and agencies by post code
You can compare your own area to your new location

▷ *Disadvantages of the Up My Street site*

Redrawing of graphs can sometimes be slow
Occasional gaps

You can also find properties for sale at the following sites:

Home Hunter
http://www.homehunter.co.uk/

Home pages
http://www.homepages.co.uk/index.html

Homes UK
http://www.homes-uk.co.uk/hfs_home_uke.html

Homes On Line
http://www.homes-online.co.uk/

House Directory
http://www.house-directory.co.uk/

HouseWeb
http://www.houseweb.co.uk/

Internet Property Finder
http://www.propertyfinder.co.uk/

Internet Property Register
http://www.propreg.com/

National Property Register
http://www.national-property-register.co.uk/

Premier Property Network
http://www.premier-property.net/home.asp

Prestige Properties
http://www.prestigeproperty.co.uk/

Property Bunny
http://www.propertybunny.co.uk/

Property Gold
http://www.ukpg.co.uk/

Property Platform
http://www.property-platform.com/

Fig. 63. The UK Property Gold web site. With access to more than 40,000 properties for sale and to rent, this is a great place to start your house-hunting.

Property Sight
http://www.property-sight.co.uk/

Property Warehouse
http://www.uk-property.com/

The Property Zone
http://www.property-zone.com/uk/

UK Property
http://www.uk-property.co.uk/

UK Property Sales
http://www.ukpropertysales.com/

House-builders' web sites
A number of house-building companies have web sites. You can contact them at:

Beechwood Homes
http://www.beechwood.co.uk/

Berkeley Homes
http://www.berkeleygroup.com/index2.html

Bewley Homes
http://www.bewley.co.uk/

CALA Homes
http://www.pwave.co.uk/pwave/cala/

Fairclough Homes
http://www.fairclough.co.uk/

Persimmon Homes
http://www.persimmon.plc.uk/

Premier Property
http://www.premier-property.net/home.asp
You can also find a list of local developers by region at this web site.

Finding property on the internet in other ways

Many estate agents have their own web sites. There are too many to list here, but you can use your favourite search engine to find them. It's a good idea to restrict your search to the part of the country in which you want to buy a house. For instance your search keywords might be:

"estate agent" AND "Berkshire"

In this way, you would only get a listing of Berkshire estate agencies, rather than a long list of companies, most of which would be of little use to you. Interestingly, more and more people are also advertising their own properties for sale as individual web pages. The plethora of free web space offered by internet access providers has helped create this boom. You can find a list of current properties offered for sale on an individual basis at this Yahoo! page:

http://www.yahoo.co.uk/Regional/Countries/United_Kingdom/Business_and_Economy/Real_Estate/Listings/For_Sale_By_Owner/

As you can see, there are many different ways in which you can use the internet to find somewhere to buy.

Types of mortgage

Type	*How it works*	*Advantage*	*Disadvantage*
Repayment	You pay interest and capital back at the same time.	The least risky mortgage. Provided you pay up each month, you are guaranteed to pay off the debt.	If you move or change mortgage early, you won't have made any inroads into paying off the capital, as the early years are interest payments.
Endowment	You pay only the interest and take out an endowment policy to cover the capital cost on the last day of the mortgage.	Lower cost than repayment mortgage.	Higher risk, since mature endowment policy might not be enough to cover the capital cost of the house.
Flexible	You pay only interest and make your own arrangements for the capital payment.	You can pay off the capital as and when you like, in small or irregular amounts. You can also take payment holidays.	You must make arrangements for paying off the capital. Delaying this could make paying for the house difficult.
Pension	You pay only interest and pay the capital with your pension fund.	Lowest cost mortgage available for the self-employed.	You eat into your pension at the time you most need the money.

Locating a suitable mortgage lender

There are many places you can search on the internet to find a mortgage. These include:

- banks
- building societies
- estate agencies
- independent mortgage advisers
- insurance companies

They all vary in the quality of internet service they offer. Even now, many are still only offering 'informational' sites. Others, though, have application forms and some even have interactive sites so that you can manage your own mortgage. Remember though, the sophistication of the web site does not necessarily reflect the value of the mortgage being offered to you. Just because a mortgage company doesn't have interactive facilities on their web site, does not mean their offering is not suitable to you. In other words, fancy sites do not necessarily equate with the perfect mortgage. Always check the details of a mortgage and take into account your own personal circumstances before making a decision.

Moneynet
http://www.moneynet.co.uk/
One useful place to start your hunt for a mortgage on the internet is Moneynet. Although this site provides a range of other financial information, its search facility for mortgages is most impressive. The Moneynet site allows you to search for a mortgage that suits your specific needs. You enter a few basic details and then within seconds a list of mortgages appears; this list has a clear explanation of the costs you are likely to incur. You can then see details of each of the listed mortgages and even apply for further information to be sent to you.

▷ *Key benefits of the Moneynet mortgage site*

Quick and easy search for mortgages
Comprehensive information on each product

▷ *Disadvantages of the Moneynet mortgage site*

You may be bewildered by the sheer number of products available
Comparing like with like can be difficult

Using a bank for a mortgage

One of the benefits of using your own bank for a mortgage is that you can contain everything under 'one roof'. If you have an internet bank account and a flexible mortgage with a bank, or even a repayment one, you can pay regular or occasional lump sums into your mortgage account. This will help you reduce your liability and you will be able to manage your mortgage, even if the bank doesn't offer such management facilities in isolation. You can find information on bank mortgages at the following site:

Find
http://www.find.co.uk/
This is a list of sites in various financial categories (you can find out more about this site in Chapter 2). You will find a list of banks and you can go direct to their web sites simply by clicking on their names.

Abbey National
http://www.abbeynational.co.uk
The site includes details of a whole range of banking services, and

includes a really easy calculator. All you have to do is enter the amount you want to borrow. You are then given a list of all the different products available, together with the monthly cost and the APR (annualised percentage rate). You can click on the cost and you will be given the full details of what is being offered. This is an excellent way of finding out what you can afford. However, there is no online application form; you have to click on the 'Any More Questions' scrolling text and you are then provided with a form to fill in. Once you send this off, someone will be in touch by post or phone. Specific information on mortgages is available at:

http://www.abbeynational.co.uk/chile.cgi?id=3623565-5550&hr=
mortgage/index.hot

Bank of Scotland
http://www.bankofscotland.co.uk
The Bank of Scotland's web site is quite annoying. You have to click through several screens, or allow them to play on until you get to the real home page. Don't waste your time doing this; instead go straight to the following page where you will find mortgage information and details on how to apply:

http://www.bankofscotland.co.uk/newmortgages.html

Barclays
http://www.personal.barclays.co.uk/
The Barclays mortgage pages can be accessed by going to this web page and then selecting 'personal banking'. You will find a great deal of information about mortgages on the pages you are presented with. It is clear, well-written and easy to understand. However, you cannot apply online for a mortgage, you have to speak to someone. To save money on your phone bill, all you have to do is enter your phone number on the screen and Barclays will call you back within five minutes. This is a neat idea, but is virtually useless for web surfers who only have one telephone line – you would have to disconnect from the internet, wait for Barclays to call and then log on again. If you have two lines, there is no problem; you can carry on browsing. Otherwise, save the Barclays site until last when searching for a mortgage. Then you will be able to compare what they offer with everything else you have found.

Coutts
http://www.coutts.com/enhanced/index.htm
Coutts is the private banking arm of NatWest. As well as mortgages, Coutts offers a host of add-on extras, such as property searching. However, the web site is merely informational. You will need to be a individual with a high net worth or a very substantial income to open an account with this bank.

First Direct
http://www.firstdirect.co.uk
The First Direct site is mildly annoying in that you need to perform a lot

of clicks to get where you want, and some of the screens do not appear to be very clear on how you should proceed. Once you arrive at the mortgage section, you will find clear information that will help you decide, but if you want to apply, you have to resort to old-fashioned technology. Clicking on the button for applying leads you to a list of ways you can get in touch. The only recognition of new technology is the ability to send an email for further information to be posted to you.

Halifax
http://www.halifax.co.uk
The Halifax is one of the best banking sites on the internet. It is clear and the mortgage information is brief enough to be interesting but with enough detail to let you know what you want. You can access the mortgage pages at:

http://www.halifax.co.uk /mort/mort.html

The mortgage pages also let you calculate how much you can afford to borrow or how much you will pay for a given amount. In addition, you can apply online for your mortgage. The Halifax uses Adobe Acrobat Forms technology for your application. If you don't already have this useful software, you can obtain a free copy of it by downloading the following two items. You will need to go to both these sites so you can use Acrobat Forms from the Halifax. You will also find links to these items at the Halifax site itself:

http://www.adobe.com/prodindex/acrobat/readstep.html
http://www.adobe.com/supportservice/custsupport/LIBRARY/4de2.htm

Be warned, though. The Halifax mortgage form is 23 pages long. You may want to save the Acrobat file and fill it in while you are offline, to save telephone charges. As well as allowing you to apply for a mortgage online, the Halifax site also has some interesting and useful information about the house-buying process, particularly useful for first-time buyers.

Legal and General
http://www.landg.com
The Legal and General Bank is part of the Legal and General insurance conglomerate. As such, one of its main lines of business is providing mortgages, which can be found at:

http://www.landg.com/mortgage/mortgage1.html

Here you will find information on mortgages in general and a handy calculator to let you work out how much you can afford. The Legal and General web site allows holders of its popular flexible mortgage products to manage their mortgage over the internet. You can access the 'Inter Plan' area of this site and pay part of your mortgage off, arrange for sums to be borrowed again or see the impact of increasing or decreasing payments on the term and the interest you'll pay. This is an excellent example of how internet technology can really work to help you win greater control over your finances. If you don't have a Legal and General flexible mortgage, you can see how the Inter Plan site works by clicking on the 'mortgage demo' button. To run the demo you will need some well-known software called 'Shockwave'. If you don't already have this you can download a copy in a few minutes from Macromedia:

http://www.macromedia.com/shockwave/download/

The Legal and General mortgage site does not have an online application form, though. Like so many companies in the mortgage market, they want you to call them and speak to someone. This means that even though the Legal and General Bank is using the technology in a much more advanced way than most other banks on the internet, they still haven't yet gone the whole way. You can fill in an online form and send some basic information for a quote by post or phone, but this is not as advanced as the technology allows for at the moment.

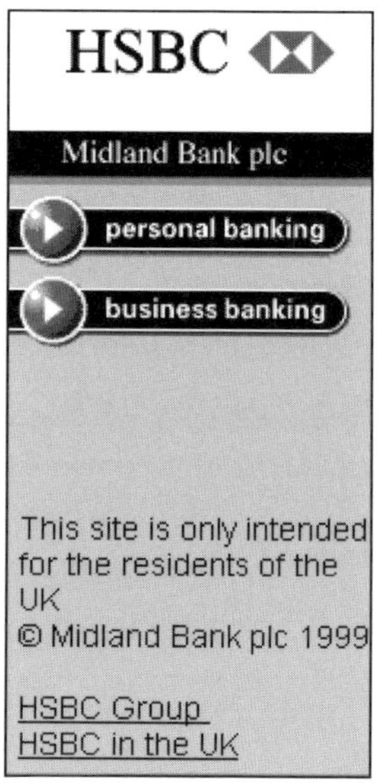

Midland
http://www.midlandbank.com
Midland is part of HSBC, a huge international financial organisation with its origins in the Far East. The information provided is minimal. There is no online calculator and the only action you can really take is to select from a list of booklets you would like to be sent in the post. You will find details of mortgages from HSBC/Midland at:

http://www.midlandbank.com/borrow/home/choose/choose.htm

NatWest
http://www.natwest.co.uk
The NatWest site is mostly informational. You can find details of home loans from NatWest, but be prepared for some work. The site contains tables of information that let you know how much mortgages from NatWest cost, but instead of offering some kind of calculation, the web site leaves that up to you. In other words, this site provides the detail, but makes it hard for you to work out the nitty gritty. Interestingly, though, there is a buildings insurance calculator that will work out the rebuilding costs of your home so that you can obtain the right level of insurance. Even though this is a novel use of internet technology, NatWest fails to provide a method of applying for a mortgage or even for more information. Instead, you have to speak to someone. The site does have a 'call back' facility, which allows you to enter your phone number so that someone can call you back; if you only have one phone line you will have to exit from the internet so that NatWest can call you. One good feature about the NatWest mortgage pages is the series of questions and answers about house-buying in general. These provide invaluable information on specific topics that are listed alphabetically.

Northern Rock
http://www.northernrock.co.uk
The Northern Rock bank provides some useful facilities and information

at its web site. Here you can use a calculator to work out how much you can afford. You can also complete an online application form for a mortgage quotation. If you fill in the 'quick quote' calculator, you are given a list of different mortgage products so that you can choose which one suits you best. All the charges are clearly shown on this site, together with answers to all the questions you might have about the small print. Its mortgage page is at:

http://www.northernrock.co.uk/html/mortgages/mortgages.htm

Royal Bank of Scotland
http://www.royalbankscot.co.uk
The site is an informational site, with no mortgage calculator and no means of application. There isn't even a form to fill in to get further information. Instead, it's back to the older technology of popping into a Royal Bank of Scotland branch, or contacting them by phone. This site, rather like the NatWest one, provides full details of the products available, including interest rates, but it isn't easy for you to work out exactly what you will pay. Other banking sites that offer mortgages do have clear methods of working out your repayments. The Royal Bank of Scotland has its mortgage pages at:

http://www.royalbankscot.co.uk/personal/buying/main.htm

Standard Life
http://www.standardlifebank.com
Standard Life is a new bank that was launched at the beginning of 1998. It has no branches and works by phone and internet. You only get brief information and to find out more you have to phone Standard Life. There is no mortgage calculator and no way of finding out your exact payments. There is no online application form and if, like many people, you are browsing the internet after the kids have gone to bed, you could well find the phone number you are encouraged to call is not answering. Unlike other telephone banking operations, Standard Life is not available 24 hours a day. You can access its mortgage pages at:

http://www.standardlifebank.com/mortgages.html

Virgin
http://www.virgin-direct.co.uk
The Virgin One account is an interesting concept. The idea is that you have a bank account that is also your mortgage, your car loan – in fact almost anything you want it to be. Confused? Basically, it is a flexible mortgage that allows you to pay in and out as though it were a bank account. Your only requirement is to make sure that the loan you are given to cover your house, car and credit card expenditure is paid off at the end of the agreed term. The attractive proposition is that you only have one interest rate for all your borrowing and that every time you pay in your salary, this reduces the interest you will be charged since it is calculated on a daily basis. The Virgin One site actually gives a very useful explanation of how its account works, but to watch it you will

need some extra software known as 'Flash', obtainable from the Macromedia site:

http://www.macromedia.com/shockwave/download

That said, though, the Virgin site is simply informational. As attractive and interesting as it is, you have to make a phone call to find out more or make an application. Further details are at:

http://www.virgin-direct.co.uk/one/html/body_home.html

Woolwich
http://www.woolwich.co.uk
The Woolwich converted from a building society to a bank in 1997. This page provides information about mortgages in general and about a product called 'Open Plan', that is very similar to Virgin One:

http://www.woolwich.co.uk/lending/index.htm

The Woolwich site is an informational site, and an annoying one in that you have to click through seven pages on the Open Plan mortgage to discover that it is a flexible mortgage. The number of words on each page is a mere handful. All of the information could have been put on one page, reducing your phone bill. This site has no mortgage calculator, which means you have to work out the payments yourself, from the information given in various tables, and there is no online application (you can complete a form asking for someone to contact you). However, if you go to the following page:

http://www.woolwich-direct.co.uk/index_mtg.htm

you can fill in a form to get an agreement in principle to your mortgage request. Woolwich Direct is the mortgage service offered to customers who do not want to visit a branch. This is not made very clear on the main mortgage web pages.

Finding out about building society mortgages

Many building societies are available on the internet and you can find out a great deal about mortgages from them. Since the opening up of the financial world a few years ago, which helped to increase competition, building societies have lost their stranglehold on the mortgage market. Even so, they are still a great place to start your search for a mortgage. They lend several billion pounds each year, so they must be offering something people want! You can start your search for a building society at:

Find
http://www.find.co.uk
Here you will find a list of all the major building societies that have web pages. Remember, too, that there are many local building societies that may not have an internet presence. These may be able to offer

excellent mortgage deals, so do not neglect them.

Alliance & Leicester
http://www.alliance-leicester.co.uk/
The Alliance & Leicester is one of Britain's biggest building societies. Here you will find a mortgage calculator to help you work out what you can afford. You can also apply online and receive a 'payment illustration', that will show you the exact details of the offer being made to you. If you need help in working out your payments, there is also an interactive budget planner on this site so that you can make sure you can afford to meet your commitments. Of course, the Alliance & Leicester offers a great deal more than mortgages and you can find details of all their other products at this site. Interestingly, the site also has a 'mortgage newsgroup'. Here, you can leave messages or discussion points about your Alliance & Leicester mortgage. The society will also post replies to the issues raised. This is an excellent and forward-thinking service that gives the Alliance & Leicester an edge over its competitors.

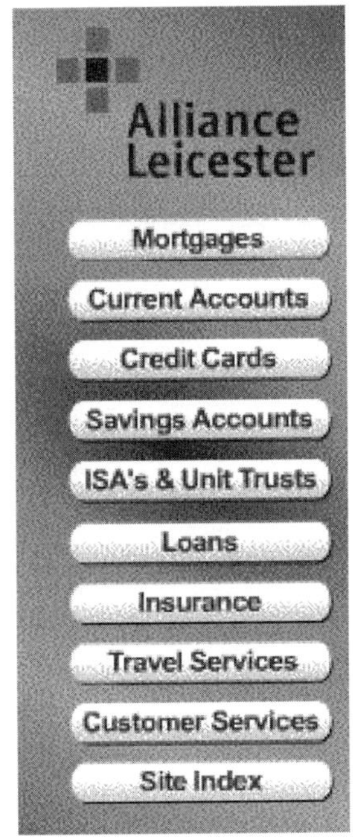

Bradford & Bingley
http://www.bradford-bingley.co.uk/home.htm
This is an information site with two sections on mortgages: one on 'home buying', the other on 'direct products'. However, they are not very direct. All you get is information and you then have to obtain further information by telephone, or arrange an appointment. You can submit a form asking for additional information but this is the only concession to new technology.

Bristol & West Building Society
http://www.bristol-west.co.uk
Apart from information about mortgages in general, and all the products available from Bristol & West, you can use an online borrowing calculator and repayment calculator. These allow you to work out how much you can afford to pay and how much you will pay back if you know what size of mortgage you want. While these are welcome items of interactivity, there is little else. Even though the site says, 'Don't go round the houses looking for a mortgage, stay at home', there will be some detours, because you can't apply online; you have to phone or send an email asking for an information pack to be put in the post. However, the Bristol & West does have an electronic mail list so that you can be kept notified of important developments such as new products that more closely match your needs. To do this you simply click on the 'register' button at the bottom of the page. The Bristol & West mortgage index is at:

http://www.bristol-west.co.uk/mortgage_hub.htm

Cheltenham and Gloucester
http://www.cheltglos.co.uk/
The C&G is now part of the Lloyds TSB group and is the place to which all Lloyds Bank or TSB mortgage enquiries are referred. This is a nice,

clean-looking site, but not without some cumbersome features. There is general information on mortgages plus a guide to the C&G products, and a useful mortgage calculator. The product pages tell you to contact C&G if you want to know more, but there is no way of finding out how you contact them at that point in the page. You have to click back to a previous page then click on 'enquiries' and then move to 'product enquiries', which is a bit awkward. Once you are there, though, you are initially encouraged to visit a branch or make a phone call, but you can complete an online form for more information to be sent to you.

Lambeth Building Society
http://www.lambeth.co.uk/
You can find out about each of the society's mortgage products. You can also use their calculator to work out what you can afford to borrow. In addition, you can make an online application for an agreement in principle. Simply fill in the form and the Lambeth will email back to you an offer of what they would be prepared to lend. This is an excellent example of internet technology being used well.

Leeds & Holbeck Building Society
http://www.leeds-holbeck.co.uk/frmmorts.htm
The Leeds & Holbeck Building Society is one of Britain's largest, but this site does not reflect its size. There is only basic information, which admittedly covers everything. But if you want to know more you have to visit a branch or complete a form so that they can mail you some information. The form for information is found on a sub-page of their feedback form, which is usually web parlance for sending back information to the web designer – hardly where you'd expect to find it. There is even a strange note on this form saying that you should bear in mind literature cannot at present be sent over email; yes it can, and you've been able to do that for several years!

Nationwide Building Society
http://www.nationwide.co.uk/
The Nationwide has adopted new internet technology to support its online banking but as yet doesn't appear to have gone so far with its mortgage products. There you will find full details of mortgages, as well as plenty of useful information and calculators to help you work out what you can afford. Even though there is an 'apply now' button, what you are really applying for is more information, not a mortgage. This site has an interesting guide to UK house prices at:

http://www.nationwide.co.uk/planning/default.htm

Newbury Building Society
http://www.newbury.co.uk/frame.htm
The Newbury Building Society is one of the south's largest lenders. Sadly, for such a large lender the web site has a distinctive small company feel about it. Some of the text is very small and hard to read. Only the most basic information is given about the products available and you are encouraged to go to a branch to find out more.

Skipton Building Society
http://www.skipton.co.uk/pp.htm
This is the entrance to the Skipton Building Society's web pages on mortgages. Here you can click on each mortgage product and find out more details. Within each product page there is also a calculator to help you work out what you will need to pay. However, if you go to the page listed below, you will find a great deal more useful information. Here there is general material on mortgages, advice for first-time buyers, a useful 'jargon buster', and a moving-home checklist that you can print out to make sure you haven't forgotten anything. This site does have an application form of sorts: essentially you provide basic information and then someone from the Skipton calls you to discuss the mortgage in detail.

http://www.skipton.co.uk

Other building societies
You can find details of other building societies at the following addresses:

Bath Building Society
http://www.bibs.co.uk/

Birmingham Midshires Building Society
http://www.worldserver.pipex.com/bmbs/mortgage/msummary.htm?

Cambridge Building Society
http://www.cambridge-building-society.co.uk/mortgage/mortgage.htm

Coventry Building Society
http://www.covbsoc.co.uk/mortgages/mtgframe.htm

Darlington Building Society
http://www.darlington.co.uk/mort.htm

Dunfermline Building Society
http://www.dunfermline-bs.co.uk/mortgage/index.html

Furness Building Society
http://www.furnessbs.co.uk/mortgages_menu.htm

Hinckley and Rugby Building Society
http://www.hrbs.co.uk/mortgage.html

Leek United Building Society
http://www.leek-united.co.uk

Mansfield Building Society
http://www.emnet.co.uk/mansfield-bs/

Market Harborough Building Society
http://www.mhbs.co.uk/mortgage.htm

Marsden Building Society
http://www.marsdenbs.co.uk/

National Counties Building Society
http://www.ncbs.co.uk/mortgage/mortgage.htm

Newcastle Building Society
http://www.newcastle.co.uk/resident/index.htm

Norwich and Peterborough Building Society
http://www.norwichandpeterborough.co.uk/

Nottingham Building Society
http://www.nottingham-bs.co.uk/mortgage/index.htm

Staffordshire Building Society
http://www.staffordshirebuildingsociety.co.uk/Hp-rm.htm

Stroud and Swindon Building Society
http://www.stroudandswindon.co.uk/mortgage.html

Teachers Building Society
http://www.teachersbs.co.uk/index.html

The Principality Building Society
http://www.principality.co.uk/front.html

Universal Building Society
http://www.ubs.uk.com/nav-mor.htm

West Bromwich Building Society
http://www.westbrom.co.uk/mort.htm

Yorkshire Building Society
http://www.ybs.co.uk/wel_mort.htm

Using a broker to find you a mortgage

If you don't want to do all the leg-work yourself, you can get an independent broker to help you find the right mortgage. Make sure that the broker is an independent financial adviser and that they are authorised by one of the regulatory authorities (see Chapter 2 for more details). Also check that they are part of the Council of Mortgage Lenders. Brokers vary in size from large multi-staffed companies to small independent firms, often run by a single individual. You should choose the company you want to use on the basis of the kind of service you want. For instance, some people like the solidity offered by a large company, whereas others prefer the individual service of a sole trader.

Choosing between brokers and mortgage companies

Broker	*Building Society*	*Bank*
Independent and can choose from a wide range of potential products	Limited to selling their own products	Usually limited to selling their own products
Open to influence from suppliers by commissions and special offers	No conflict of interest since no dependence on commission	No conflict of interest since no dependence on commission
Most brokers not very visible since they work from offices	Available on every high street	Available on every high street
Most brokers don't have web sites	Most building societies have web sites	All the major banks have web sites

Avoncourt
http://www.avoncourt.co.uk/
Avoncourt is a broker that allows you to apply online for a mortgage. There are application forms available for each different kind of mortgage that may be required. The site also has useful comparison tables showing the current best mortgage deals on offer, and there is a useful 'advice' centre that has the answers to a series of questions that you might ask about mortgages.

John Charcol
http://www.johncharcol.co.uk
The John Charcol company is one of Britain's main independent mortgage brokers and financial advice organisations. The amount of lending they organise ranks them alongside the top five building societies.[3] Here you will find a mortgage calculator and a guide to all the products on offer from the company. However, other than a form you can fill in to get someone to contact you, this is only an informational site. You are encouraged to phone in for specific advice. To find out about the mortgage service on offer go to:

http://www.johncharcol.co.uk/mortgages/

Other brokers
Ashton Thomas
http://www.internetlink.co.uk/ashton_thomas.htm

First Peoples Mortgage
http://www.first.co.uk/

Freedman and Co
http://www.moneysense.co.uk/

Homeloans Direct
http://www.homeloans.co.uk/

Mortgage Alliance
http://www.magreen.demon.co.uk/

Mortgage Clinic
http://uk.zarcrom.com/mortgages/

Mortgage Help Desk UK
http://www.mortgageman.u-net.com/

Mortgage Key
http://www.ftech.net/~mortgage/

Terry Smith Mortgages
http://www.net.dircon.co.uk/

Trustguard Homeloans
http://members.aol.com/trustguard/

Getting a specialist mortgage

Sometimes people need a specialist mortgage. For instance, you may want to buy a property to rent out, or you may want a second home for holidays. If you are only recently self-employed you may also have difficulty in getting a loan from traditional lenders. In such instances you may want to try one of the brokers who will have access to specialists within the lending companies who can help. 'Buying to let' is an increasingly common requirement as many people are investing in property. Hence a growing number of mainstream lenders, such as building societies, are now offering products in this area.

▷ *Case study* – Alan and Sheila are moving to a new area. They want to buy a new house so they have checked the internet already for what's available from the various builders. They have selected a suitable site and have even had a look round a 'virtual' example of their house. They are pretty sure they want the house, assuming the location is acceptable. Before they set off to look around the building site though, they have arranged their mortgage. They used a mortgage calculator program that Sheila downloaded from a shareware site and then they checked their figures in a couple of building society online calculators. They did some searches for a suitable mortgage company and made an online application. They have also found someone locally to do the conveyancing. In fact, the only time they needed to set off house-hunting was to visit the building site. Unlike many of their colleagues, who are also being moved to the new town, they did it without trudging round several unsuitable places.

Considering other factors in home buying

Arranging a mortgage is not the only activity you'll be involved in if you need to move house. You'll also need:

1. a surveyor
2. a conveyancing service
3. a removal company

You can, of course, find details of many of these on the internet. Here are just a selection of some of the key sites:

Surveyors
Whoever you choose, they should be professionally qualified and a member of the Royal Institute of Chartered Surveyors, with the letters ARICS or FRICS after the name. Most surveyors operate only locally so you may want to perform a search for:

"surveyor" AND "your region"

Conveyancing companies
Conveyancing Marketing Services
http://www.conveyancing-cms.co.uk/
A number of law firms have internet sites; you may like to check for one in your region. Remember too that laws relating to house purchase in Scotland are different from those in the rest of Great Britain, so if you are buying a house in Scotland make sure you get a conveyancer who understands Scottish home-buying. Whoever you choose should be a 'licensed conveyancer'.

Removal firms
Many removal companies are regional so you may wish to search for one in your area. Make sure that they are members of a professional association, such as the British Association of Removals.

A1 Removals
http://www.informationdesign.co.uk/a1moves/

Moves
http://www.moves.co.uk/

Essential tips for getting a mortgage on the internet

▷ Use the general information sites to find out about mortgages in general and the things you need to consider in your own case.

▷ Use a searching site, such as Moneynet, to help you locate a range of different products that meet your needs.

▷ Find out more about the products you locate by visiting the lender's own web site.

- ▷ If possible, complete an online application form.
- ▷ Some lenders, such as the Legal and General, offer online mortgage management services, so take advantage of these where possible.
- ▷ Make a diary note to re-check your mortgage on a regular basis so you can take advantage of better offers.
- ▷ If you use internet banking, set up a payment option so that you can pay off extra amounts on your mortgage.

Mortgage checklist

- ▷ Your mortgage is likely to be your biggest financial commitment, so choose it carefully.
- ▷ Seek professional advice so that you take into account all of the relevant factors in your own individual circumstances.
- ▷ Ensure you prepare a proper budget so you can check that you can afford any mortgage on offer.
- ▷ The earlier you can repay your mortgage, the less in total you will pay the lender, so making extra payments, if possible, should save you money in the long run.

References

[1] *Daily Telegraph*, 5 February 1999.

[2] *Sunday Times*, 21 February 1999. Or see: http://www.lineone.net/sundaytimes/99/02/21/money/money_news/stimonnws03013-d.fhtml

[3] See: http://www.johncharcol.co.uk/

6 Saving your money on the internet

In this chapter we will explore:

- *finding out about ways to save*
- *saving needs calculator*
- *making immediate savings with the internet*
- *hunting for bargains on the internet*
- *getting discounts on household bills via the internet*
- *saving money at the supermarket*
- *making savings using online auctions*
- *looking for short-term savings on the internet*
- *finding out about long-term savings*
- *a quick guide to long-term savings products*
- *looking for details about bonds*
- *tracking down information on endowments*
- *trading in your endowment policies*
- *finding out about friendly societies*
- *searching for material on investment trusts*
- *finding out more about ISAs*
- *looking up information on national savings*
- *locating information on notice accounts*
- *buying open-ended investments*
- *finding out about offshore accounts*
- *finding out about unit trusts*
- *saving money after your 50th birthday*
- *stumbling across old financial products*
- *essential tips for saving money on the internet*
- *saving money checklist*

We all like to save money. Whether it's for a rainy day, or for that special something you want to buy in the future, you'll need savings. Also, if you have an interest-only mortgage, you'll need savings to pay off the capital at the end of the term. Many of us also want to save money so that when we retire we have enough to live on, to top up our pensions. So, whatever your circumstances, you'll want to save money. The internet can come to the rescue here. Not only can you find out about various savings accounts and deposit services, there are other ways you can save money on the internet. For instance you can find the best deals on items you want to buy. You can even participate in online auctions, bidding for objects that sell for comparatively low prices.

Using the internet you can find the lowest price for almost anything you want to buy. You can then put the extra cash you have into an interest-bearing savings account, earning you even more. This surely must be a sensible way to proceed – only people who have tons of money to spare won't bother with the money-saving opportunities the internet provides. The internet can save you money in many other ways:

- ▷ cheap phone calls
- ▷ international communication at local call rates
- ▷ lower motoring costs, because you'll travel less

Clearly the internet has real value – you will almost certainly recoup the costs of using the internet through the extra savings you make by using the technology to its fullest potential.

Finding out about ways to save

In order to find out how you can save money you need to set some priorities; this will help you start using the search facilities to their best capability. Otherwise, if you simply look for anything to do with 'savings', you will be inundated; there will be several hundreds of thousands of web sites that could help! Generally, your savings are likely to fall into three main categories:

- ▷ immediate savings
- ▷ short- to medium-term savings
- ▷ long-term savings

Decide which of these are most important to you before you start thinking about setting off around the internet to find out more. There is so much information available on saving money that you could find yourself distracted if you haven't worked out what is most important to you at the moment. Once you have set your priorities you can start looking for items that are likely to be of interest. To help you work out your priorities, fill in this 'savings needs calculator'.

Your savings needs calculator

(A) Average monthly amount of money in your current accounts, plus cash etc.	....
(B) Average monthly expenditure	....
(C) Amount of money in short-term savings accounts	....
(D) Amount of money in notice accounts and other long-term savings plans	....

Now, work out the following:

A – B = X (excess current funds available)
D – C = Y (difference between long- and medium-term savings)

If X is greater than Y you have a far greater proportion of your money available immediately than you probably need. You are probably not getting the maximum return on your cash and could be losing out on favourable interest rates. Now do this calculation:

$$C - B = Z$$

Is Z a positive number? If so, you have more money available in short-term savings than you need to cover a month's outgoings. This means some of your excess saving is not reaping the rewards it might by being in a longer-term plan. Generally, you are unlikely ever to need more than a month's money available at immediate notice. Making these calculations can help you focus on where your financial priorities lie in terms of savings. If you have too much in short-term savings, you need to find information on long-term plans. Equally, if the differences you produce in the calculations are small, you need to find ways to cut your costs and worry about longer-term savings at a later date.

Making immediate savings with the internet

Even if you have plenty of short- or medium-term savings and you want to find out about long-term investments, you might want to investigate ways of cutting your costs and getting bargains. The internet has a myriad sites dealing with cost cutting but you might like to start at the following for a few tips:

BBC Watchdog
http://www.bbc.co.uk/watchdog/

Which?
http://www.which.net/upfront/contents.html

These two consumer sites are from leading organisations and can provide a whole host of useful tips on saving money. They will also help make sure you get the best service you can when buying products and services.

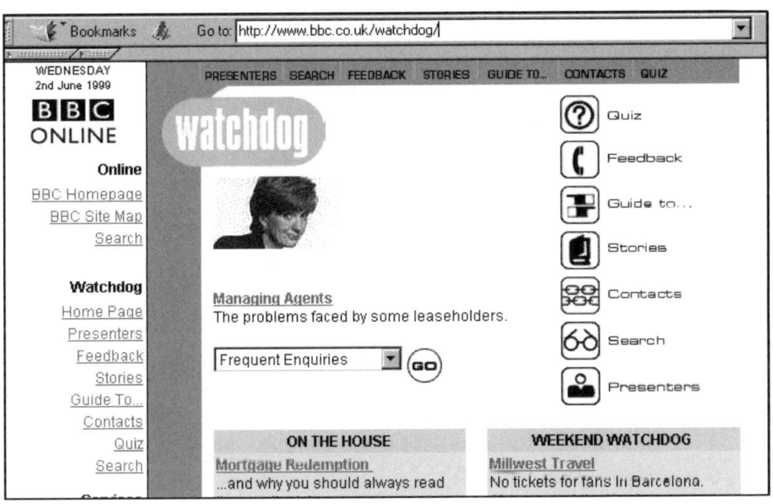

Fig. 64. The BBC doesn't only want you to tune in to *Watchdog* – it wants you to visit the TV show's web site, too.

Fig. 65. The Consumers Association has its own watchful and informative web site at Which.net.

If you want to find out how you can save money by using internet telephone calls, internet faxing or even internet video conferencing, go to:

http://www.ipxstream.com/
http://www.von.com/
http://www.virtual-voice.com/
http://www.savetz.com/fax-faq.html

By visiting these sites and others like them you will discover that you can save money by using the internet to reduce all your communications costs. Even now, you can send international faxes for the cost of the local call to your internet access provider. Equally, you can communicate using a simple video camera, across the oceans, simply by paying for a local phone call. You can also make telephone calls across the internet, to other people connected to the world wide web. In these three ways, you can cut out international call costs almost entirely. You can also use the internet telephony systems to communicate within the UK at local call rates.

Hunting for bargains on the internet

Another way you can use the internet to save money is to hunt for bargains. If you enter the word 'bargain' into your favourite search engine, you will find a huge list of shops and web sites that offer 'bargains' – how much of a bargain only you will be able to determine, but remember that internet shopping offers you the following advantages even if the prices are the same as on the high street:

1. no transport costs

2. no car parking costs
3. no need to buy shopping bags or wear out shoe leather!

In addition you'll benefit from buying over the internet in other ways:

1. no trudging up and down the high street
2. no getting wet!
3. no accepting a narrow range of supply.

To find bargains on the internet go to:

ShopGuide
http://www.shopguide.co.uk
Remember to investigate individual internet shops that deal in the specific products you want to buy. The beauty of the internet is that you can quickly compare prices from one supplier with those from another. This will save you time and money.

Fig. 66. The internet is very empowering for shoppers, because you can quickly locate millions of products and easily compare prices. ShopGuide is one of thousands of sites that can help you get value for money.

Getting discounts on household bills via the internet

For many of us, the regular household bills are a necessary evil. We simply have to pay for water, gas, electric, and so on. But we'd rather not! Reducing our household bills is therefore a great way of ensuring we have more cash to spend on the things we actually desire. To start your search for discounts on household bills go to:

Buy
http://www.buy.co.uk/
Here you will be able to enter details about your current household bills and be given a list of alternative suppliers and the amount you will save by switching to them. You could also try:

UK Power
http://www.ukpower.com/
This site has links to all the main suppliers of utilities, so you can find out

Fig. 67. The Buy.co.uk site will help you save on household bills. Don't let the big gas and electricity companies take you to the cleaners!

more about charges and work out who can save you money. Another way of getting discounts on household bills is to pay by direct debit. Many companies offer you discounts if you pay their bills by direct debit. To find out which companies offer such incentives go to:

Direct Debit
http://www.directdebit.co.uk/discounts.htm
At this site, you can fill in a form to arrange all the direct debits you want. You will then be sent the relevant documents to sign. However, don't follow the web site's link towards the application form, because it takes you through a series of pages, unless you happen to hit the right button first! A nice, fun idea, but a trifle time consuming. Instead, point your browser direct to the application form at:

http://www.directdebit.co.uk/action.htm

Saving money at the supermarket

It is also worth considering how you might save money by doing your weekly grocery shopping over the internet. Many supermarkets now offer this service and you will almost certainly save money. Even though they make a delivery charge, your own transport costs will be reduced, and you won't be tempted to add things to your trolley simply because they attract your eye; more importantly for families, you won't be put under pressure from your children to buy what has caught their eye either! To find out more about supermarket shopping over the internet try the following pages:

http://www.asda.co.uk/
http://www.groceries.org.uk/
http://www.sainsburys.co.uk/
http://www.somerfield.co.uk/
http://www.tesco.co.uk/

Making savings using online auctions

You can save money, if you take care, by purchasing items at online auctions. Often you will find that the prices bid for items are lower than you might pay in traditional auctions. Also, you can find auctions of items that are being offered at low prices anyway, such as items from bankrupt stock. To find out more about online auctions in general go to:

http://www.ebid.co.uk/
http://www.onlineauctions.co.uk/index.htm

These two sites deal with general items you might want but there are a number of more specialist sites. Use your favourite search engine to look for what you want. However, the 'e-bid' site is a good way to pick up some bargains. Even so, you need to check carefully what you are buying – unlike a real auction, you can't see what you are getting.

Looking for short-term savings on the internet

The most common form of short-term savings is a deposit account or a savings account. You can get such accounts from banks or building societies. A good place to start your search is:

Find
http://www.find.co.uk
This will give you a listing of banks and building societies so you can then select the ones you are interested in to find out more. You may also want to go to:

Moneynet
http://www.moneynet.co.uk
This site has a savings section so you can compare all the different rates

Fig. 68. All the major food chains now have web sites in various stages of development – this is Somerfield's. Online shopping is likely to be one of the biggest phenomena of the new millennium, with its value measured in hundreds of billions of dollars a year.

of interest available. You simply enter the kind of savings account you want and the Moneynet site works out what's available. You can then click on a button for more details on the accounts listed.

Times-Money
http://www.times-money.co.uk/
This is another site offering comparisons of rates.

Moneywise
http://www.readersdigest.co.uk/finance.htm
You can also get the latest savings rates at Moneywise. You will also find general material on savings at all of the information sites listed in Chapter 2.

Finding out about long-term savings

You can start your search for long-term savings in much the same way as you would for short-term savings. After all, many of the banks and building societies that provide instant access accounts also provide 'notice accounts'. These give you higher rates of interest, but you need to keep your money tied up for a longer period and give notice of any withdrawal. However, it is worth remembering that long-term savings products are much greater in scope than simple deposit accounts. You can also save your money for long periods in:

1. Bonds
2. Endowment policies
3. Friendly societies
4. Individual Savings Accounts (ISAs)
5. Investment trusts
6. National Savings
7. Notice accounts
8. Open Ended Investment Companies (Oeics)
9. Offshore accounts
10. Pension funds
11. Stocks and shares
12. Unit trusts

Because pensions and shares are such huge subjects in themselves, you will find more about them in Chapters 7 and 8. The remaining product areas will be covered in the rest of this chapter.

A quick guide to long-term savings products

Type of financial product	*Description*
Bonds	These are basically an IOU. You give the company a sum of money. They invest it to make even more and promise to return it to you with a share of the profits at a later date.

Endowment policy — This is a special form of life insurance policy that pays out after a set period of, say, 10 or 25 years. The policy can be a 'with profits' endowment – where extra cash comes your way; or the endowment can be 'unit linked', where it is invested in a specific fund. Most people choose a 'with profits' endowment.

Friendly societies — These offer 10-year investment plans in which you can invest a maximum amount, tax-free. These plans also offer life cover.

Investment trust — A publicly quoted company that invests in a range of other companies. You can buy shares in Investment Trusts as you would any other company, but its success depends upon the success of all the other companies it invests in.

ISA — A special form of 'investment savings account' that has interest provided free of tax. An ISA can include cash, stocks and shares, or life assurance. There are maximum amounts you can invest in order to remain tax free.

National Savings — There is a range of products available from the state run National Savings, including many that are tax free.

Notice account — A building society or bank savings account on which you have to give notice of intention of withdrawal in order to avoid loss of interest.

OEICs — Open Ended Investment Companies are expected to replace unit trusts in the long term.

Offshore accounts — Any kind of account where the money is kept outside of Britain, but usually taken to mean money invested in tax havens, such as the Channel Islands, the Isle of Man, etc.

Pension funds — A range of investments in a single fund, often including property, art treasures etc., as well as stocks, shares and so on.

Stocks and shares — In Britain, stocks are government bonds (in the USA they are shares). Shares are a purchase of a portion of the capital of a company. Shares can also be called equities.

Unit trusts — A fund that invests in a wide range of shares. Unlike an Investment Trust, this is not a public company.

Looking for details about bonds

There are many different kinds of bonds and many are offered by National Savings (see later in this chapter). However, other financial institutions offer bonds from time to time. You would usually buy a bond through an independent financial adviser or a life assurance company. Sometimes, though, building societies offer bonds. You can find a local independent financial adviser at:

MoneyWeb
http://www.seven.net/moneyweb/search/search.html

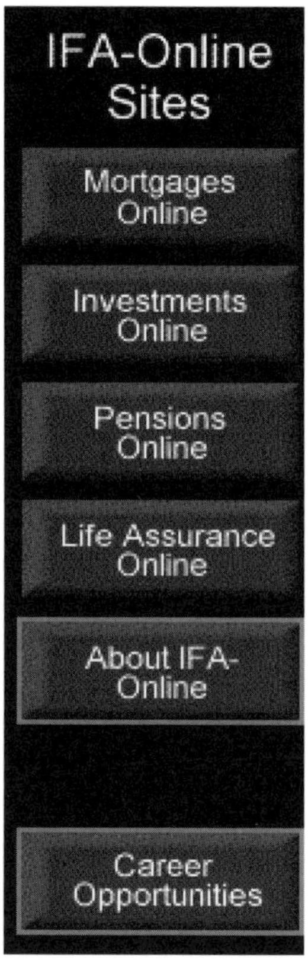

Investments Online
http://www.investments-online.co.uk/
For information about companies offering bonds try Investments Online. You should also look at the financial pages on the internet mentioned in Chapter 2. From time to time these advertise new bond offers.

Tracking down information on endowment policies

Generally you buy an endowment policy from a life assurance company. Essentially, the company invests your money and uses the profits to make payments to beneficiaries on the death of policyholders. Investments are made in a wide variety of financial items, including shares, bonds, property, art treasures and so on. You agree to let the insurance company have regular payments for a period of years, usually 10 or 25. Your money is then returned to you together with a share of the profits it has made. (This is the most common form of endowment policy. A variety called 'unit linked' invests only in specific equity funds and therefore carries greater risks.) To find out about endowment policies on the internet, you need to visit life insurance companies, rather than banks or building societies. You can find a list of suitable companies at:

Find
http://www.find.co.uk

Information on specific endowment policies can also be found at the following sites:

Legal and General
http://www.legalandgeneral.co.uk

Norwich Union
http://www.norwich-union.co.uk/index.htm

Royal Liver Assurance
http://www.royal-liver.com/royaliver/fram.htm

Scottish Friendly
http://www.scottishfriendly.co.uk/find/inxleaf.htm

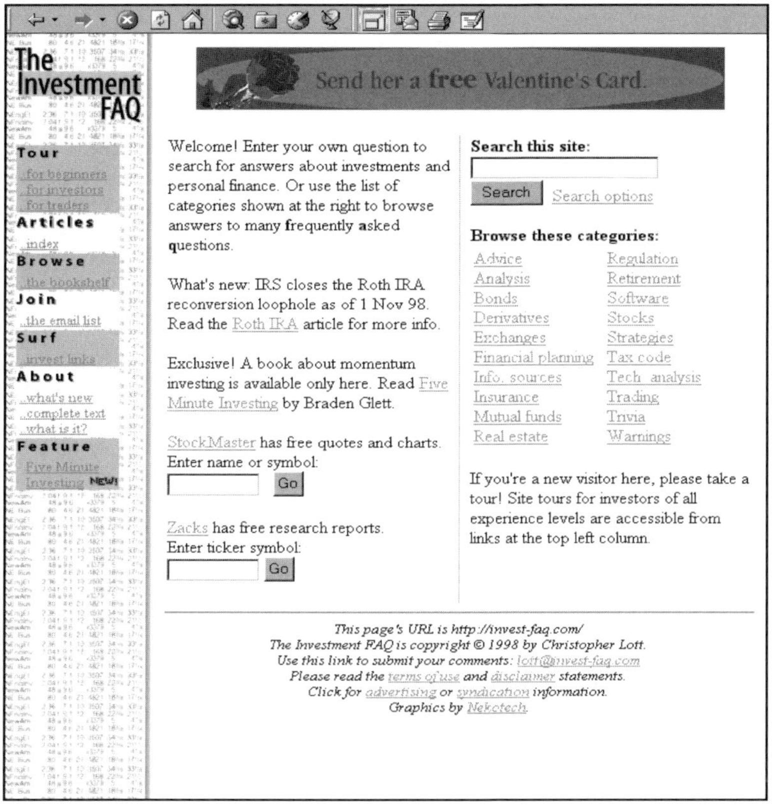

Fig. 69. Investment FAQs (frequently asked questions – and answers, of course!). FAQs have become a very common and welcome feature of most well-known web sites today.

Standard Life
http://www.standardlife.co.uk/products/savings.html

Trading in your endowment policies

You can trade in your endowment policies, selling them on for an immediate income now, sometimes at a higher rate than you would get if you simply cashed in early. You can find out about 'traded endowments' at the following sites:

Absolute Assigned Policies
http://www.aap.co.uk/main.htm

Beale and Dobie
http://www.bealedobie.co.uk/home.htm

Policy Plus
http://www.policyplus.com/main.html

SEP Marketing
http://www.zynet.co.uk/childs/sepm.htm

Surrenda Link
http://www.surrendalink.u-net.com/

Traded Endowments
http://www.endowments.com/

Finding out about Friendly Societies

Friendly Societies are mutual organisations that offer investment plans for a long period, usually ten years. You can invest in one Friendly Society plan tax-free. The following web sites contain information about Friendly Societies:

Holloway Friendly
http://www.holloway.co.uk/main.htm

Homeowners Friendly Society
http://www.homeowners.co.uk/home.htm

Scottish Friendly
http://www.scottishfriendly.co.uk/find/mcone.htm

Searching for material on investment trusts

Investment trusts are companies in which you buy shares. The company then makes its money, of which you gain a proportion, by buying and selling shares in other public companies. That's all it does. There are many investment trust companies operating in the UK and you can buy shares in them in just the same way as you would any other public company (see Chapter 7). However, most of the investment trust companies offer regular savings plans, so you can increase your shareholding on a planned basis. To find companies that offer such facilities you could try:

Find
http://www.find.co.uk
This site will point you in the direction of investment trust companies.

Association of Investment Trust Companies
http://www.aitc.co.uk
You may also want to go to the Association of Investment Trust Companies. This site includes a links page to all of the companies that offer savings products based on investment trust companies. You may also want to visit:

TrustNet
http://www.trustnet.co.uk/f
This site provides up to date performance tables of hundreds of different investment trust companies, enabling you to make an informed choice or keep an eye on how your funds are doing. Investment trust companies on the web include:

Flemings
http://www.flemings.co.uk/fitm/homepage/

Herald Investment Trust
http://www.heralduk.com/herald98/himl/default/Default.htm

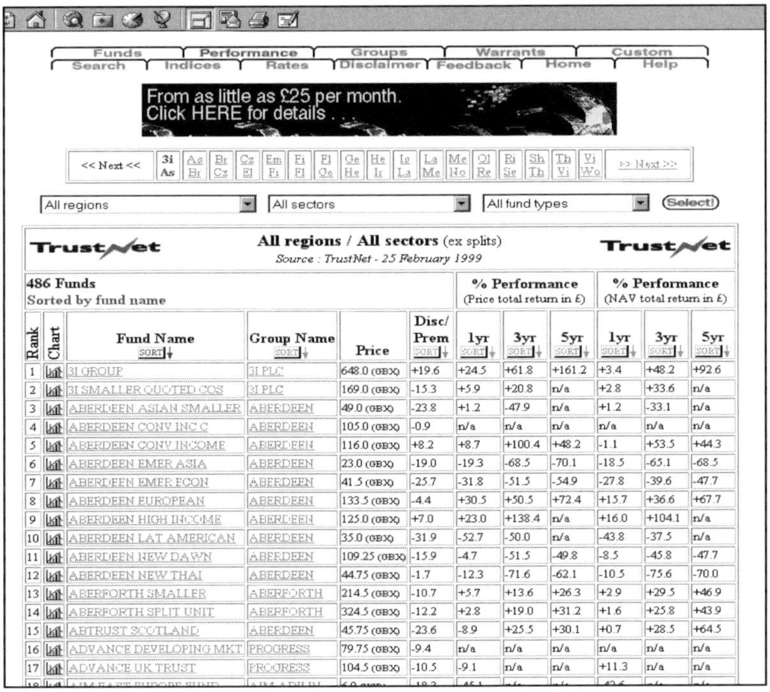

486 Funds Sorted by fund name						% Performance (Price total return in £)			% Performance (NAV total return in £)		
Rank	Chart	Fund Name	Group Name	Price	Disc/ Prem	1yr	3yr	5yr	1yr	3yr	5yr
1		3I GROUP	3I PLC	648.0 (GBX)	+19.6	+24.5	+61.8	+161.2	+3.4	+48.2	+92.6
2		3I SMALLER QUOTED COS	3I PLC	169.0 (GBX)	-15.3	+5.9	+20.8	n/a	+2.8	+33.6	n/a
3		ABERDEEN ASIAN SMALLER	ABERDEEN	49.0 (GBX)	-23.8	+1.2	-47.9	n/a	+1.2	-33.1	n/a
4		ABERDEEN CONV INC C	ABERDEEN	105.0 (GBX)	-0.9	n/a	n/a	n/a	n/a	n/a	n/a
5		ABERDEEN CONV INCOME	ABERDEEN	116.0 (GBX)	+8.2	+8.7	+100.4	+48.2	-1.1	+53.5	+44.3
6		ABERDEEN EMER ASIA	ABERDEEN	23.0 (GBX)	-19.0	-19.3	-68.5	-70.1	-18.5	-65.1	-68.5
7		ABERDEEN EMER ECON	ABERDEEN	41.5 (GBX)	-25.7	-31.8	-51.5	-54.9	-27.8	-39.6	-47.7
8		ABERDEEN EUROPEAN	ABERDEEN	133.5 (GBX)	-4.4	+30.5	+50.5	+72.4	+15.7	+36.6	+67.7
9		ABERDEEN HIGH INCOME	ABERDEEN	125.0 (GBX)	+7.0	+23.0	+138.4	n/a	+16.0	+104.1	n/a
10		ABERDEEN LAT AMERICAN	ABERDEEN	35.0 (GBX)	-31.9	-52.7	-50.0	n/a	-43.8	-37.5	n/a
11		ABERDEEN NEW DAWN	ABERDEEN	109.25 (GBX)	-15.9	-4.7	-51.5	-49.8	-8.5	-45.8	-47.7
12		ABERDEEN NEW THAI	ABERDEEN	44.75 (GBX)	-1.7	-12.3	-71.6	-62.1	-10.5	-75.6	-70.0
13		ABERFORTH SMALLER	ABERFORTH	214.5 (GBX)	-10.7	+5.7	+13.6	+26.3	+2.9	+29.5	+46.9
14		ABERFORTH SPLIT UNIT	ABERFORTH	324.5 (GBX)	-12.2	+2.8	+19.0	+31.2	+1.6	+25.8	+43.9
15		ABTRUST SCOTLAND	ABERDEEN	45.75 (GBX)	-23.6	-8.9	+25.5	+30.1	+0.7	+28.5	+64.5
16		ADVANCE DEVELOPING MKT	PROGRESS	79.75 (GBX)	-9.4	n/a	n/a	n/a	n/a	n/a	n/a
17		ADVANCE UK TRUST	PROGRESS	104.5 (GBX)	-10.5	-9.1	n/a	n/a	+11.3	n/a	n/a

Fig. 70. Share price information online from TrustNet, one of many web sites offering such data at your fingertips.

Hill Samuel
http://www.hillsamuel.co.uk/

Martin Currie
http://www.martincurrie.com/i-trusts-infof.html

Mercury Asset Management
http://www.mam.com/frameset.htm

Scottish Investment Trust
http://www.sit.co.uk/

Finding out more about ISAs

Because ISAs are new financial products, you will find a great deal of information on them at personal finance news and magazine sites such as:

Financial Times
http://www.ft.com

Moneywise
http://www.readersdigest.co.uk/finance.htm

Times-Money
http://www.times-money.co.uk

MoneyWorld
http://www.moneyworld.co.uk/faqs/isafaq3.htm
You will also find an excellent guide to ISAs at the MoneyWorld site. In

addition to these sites, many of the banks' and building societies' own web sites will include information on ISA products.

Looking up information on National Savings

National Savings
http://www.nationalsavings.co.uk/
This is an excellent site, with clear design and in easy-to-understand language. You will need a program called 'Shockwave' to use it (see Chapter 5 for information on how to get this program). In addition to being well designed, the National Savings site answers all the questions you are likely to have on their products and services. Clicking on the 'toolbox' icon takes you to a handy calculator and glossary. You can even see application forms on screen and fill them in. However, you have to then print them out and put them in the post together with your cheque – online processing using a credit or debit card would have been nice. Even with this limitation, though, the National Savings site is probably going to have everything you need to know about the organisation's long-term savings options.

▷ *Key benefits of the National Savings site*

Comprehensive coverage
Easy to understand

▷ *Disadvantages of the National Savings web site*

You can't make online applications for products
You don't always see what you are looking for, since it may be in a drop-down menu

Locating information on notice accounts

You will find information on notice accounts at the general information sites as well as individual bank and building society sites. A guide to the latest notice accounts can be found on the savings pages of:

Moneynet
http://www.moneynet.co.uk
At this site you will be able to see all the details of various accounts, including the latest interest rates. The site is updated daily so you can be sure you are getting the most recent information.

Buying open-ended investments

An Open Ended Investment Company (OEIC) is a relatively new form of savings. It is expected to replace unit trusts in the longer term. However, because they are so recent, there is a distinct lack of information about them on the internet. You can find basic guides in the usual general information sites, but finding any details is at present difficult. The best route is to search through the various companies that offer OEICs. You can find OEIC products at the following sites:

Fidelity Investments
http://www.fidelity.co.uk

Friends Provident
http://www.friendsprovident.co.uk

M&G
http://www.mandg.co.uk/

Templeton
http://www.templeton.co.uk/

Finding out about offshore accounts

Putting your money away in some far-off land and avoiding tax sounds a nice idea. However, think carefully before putting money in some offshore tax haven. For a start, if you are a UK resident you are likely to be liable for tax if you bring the money back into the UK, so you may have to spend it where it is; you may not find that easy if it is in the Cayman Islands, for instance. You really do need professional advice that takes into account your own tax circumstances. If you have so much money that you are considering storing it offshore you can afford to pay for an accountant! You can find one by going to the professional bodies:

Institute of Chartered Accountants in England and Wales
http://www.icaew.co.uk/

Institute of Chartered Accountants of Scotland
http://www.icas.org.uk/

Institute of Chartered Accountants in Ireland
http://www.icai.ie/

MoneyWeb
http://www.seven.net/moneyweb/search/search.html
Also, check with your personal financial adviser, if you have one. If not, you can find one in your local area by going to this MoneyWeb page.

Once you are satisfied that offshore investing is in your interests, you may want to explore the following sites, all of which contain details of offshore products. Remember, too, that the general personal finance information sites will all contain some material on investing offshore.

Bank of Wales
http://www.bankofwales.co.uk/jersey/index.htm
The Bank of Wales has a Jersey office offering a range of offshore services. This site provides an online brochure and a form you can complete to obtain further information.

Barclays Offshore Banking
http://www.offshorebanking.barclays.com/
Here you will find details of all the offshore services provided by

Barclays. You can view the various brochures online, but you cannot apply for an account; you will need to call Barclays on the number given.

Bermuda Offshore Investment Services
http://www.offshoreinvesting.com/
This is a simple information site, but you can submit your details so that further information can be sent to you.

Chartered Trust
http://www.chartered-tci.com/
This site only gives information – the sole interactive feature is an email button. However, it does contain a clear guide to the products and services.

Flemings
http://www.flemings.com/
Flemings is a private bank offering a range of services on an international basis. You can find out more about its offshore services by visiting its web site which details all the products offered by the bank; you can complete an enquiry form for further details.

Heritage
http://www.heritage-capital.co.uk/
This is a company whose offices in Guernsey can provide specialist offshore investment advice. Here you can see the latest economic review, subscribe to a quarterly newsletter and check your fund prices.

Fig. 71. Interactive Offshore. The internet makes it easy to discover all kinds of offshore investment opportunities.

Interactive Offshore
http://www.offshore.net/
This is a site that provides you with a wide range of information on offshore savings. On this site you'll even find an 'offshore forum' so you can discuss your views about investing offshore with others like you. The site also has a useful page of links to companies that provide offshore accounts.

Jersey Trust and Finance Companies
http://www.jersey-mail.co.uk/finance/index.htm
Here you can find a list of companies offering offshore finance facilities in Jersey.

Northern Rock
http://www.northernrock-guernsey.co.gg/index.htm
Northern Rock is a British bank with considerable offshore interests. You can view all the details of the products and services available and enter your details in an online form for further information. There is a lot of text on this web site and much of it is small, so you'll need to adjust the font size (see Chapter 2 for details of how to do this).

Perpetual
http://www.perpetual-offshore.com/home.nsf/offshore
The Perpetual Fund Management Company has a strong reputation in offshore services. At this site you can find out details about the services on offer and make a request for literature to be sent to you.

Finding out about unit trusts

There is a vast array of unit trusts and there are many companies that can offer advice. As always, you might like to start by checking with your personal financial adviser or your accountant. If you don't have such professional support, you should seriously consider it. Unit trusts carry a measure of risk – their value can fall as well as rise, since they are dependent upon the stock market. Investing in unit trusts without much knowledge of the market could result in losing money, so take advice. However, you don't have to believe what you are told. That is one of the great features of the internet; you can actually check what you are told by advisers and see if they are telling the truth.

For instance, suppose an adviser tells you a particular unit trust is doing well and that you should invest in it. You could visit the fund's web site and some of the independent information sites, to check up on what you have been told. Also, remember that financial advisers are fallible. Many newspapers and financial magazines now run competitions for amateur financiers; you can predict how particular companies or funds will perform. Frequently, the 'amateurs' taking part in the competitions make better predictions than the professionals do. Indeed, one winning amateur, Jayesh Manek, turned professional because he was so good at predicting the market in the *Sunday Times* 'Fantasy Fund Manager' competition. Nevertheless, the unit trust market is huge and you will need to consider proper advice. You can find general information on the unit trust sector at:

The Association of Unit Trust and Investment Funds
http://www.autif.co.uk/

The Internet Investors Journal
http://www.discover.co.uk/~iij/
This web site will provide you with up-to-date information on a wide range of unit trusts. There are also comparison tables so you can see how well a particular fund is performing. You may also want to perform a search for a local stockbroker, as many of these offer services in purchasing unit trusts. Companies that offer unit trust products include:

Aberdeen Prolific
http://www.iii.co.uk/aberdeen-prolific/

Baillie Gifford
http://www.bailliegifford.co.uk/home.html

Cazenove
http://www.cazenove.co.uk/cc/1home.htm

Fidelity
http://www.fidelity.co.uk/direct/index.html

Friends Provident
http://www.friendsprovident.co.uk

Garrison Discount Investments
http://www.garrison.co.uk/

Hill Samuel
http://www.hillsamuel.co.uk

Investec
http://www.investecguinnessflight.com/uk/ukframe.htm

Martin Currie
http://www.martincurrie.com/u-trustinfof.html

Mercury Asset Management
http://www.mam.com/frameset.htm

M&G
http://mandg.iii.co.uk/html/top_home.htm

Save & Prosper
http://www.prosper.co.uk/entry/content.html

Saving money after your 50th birthday

If you have reached half a century, you might find that SAGA can provide savings products more targeted towards your age group's needs. To find out if there is anything of use, visit SAGA's investment web site:

SAGA
http://www.saga.co.uk/investment/index.html
Here you can find details of the products aimed specifically at the over 50s, together with the telephone number that you need to call for further information.

Stumbling across old financial products

In your travels around the internet you will be certain to find pages that refer to Personal Equity Plans (PEPs) and Tax Exempt Special Savings Accounts (TESSAs); these financial products, which were tax free, were abolished by the British Government on 5 April 1999. However, if you bought a PEP or TESSA before that date, you are still entitled to the tax-free benefits. Since a TESSA must be held for at least five years from the date you bought it and PEPs are best left as long-term investments, you will still find information on both these products right up until at least 2004, but the material you see on various web pages will only be of practical value to those people who already own these kinds of accounts. If you want tax-free investments, you should check out ISAs or National Savings products. If you already have a PEP or TESSA and wish to find out more about it or keep track of its progress, you should go to the web site of the relevant company.

▷ *Case study* – Sandra is about to retire. She knows she will get a lump sum of about £50,000 from her pension fund. She is also due a pension of about £8,000 a year. Sandra wants to invest the lump sum to generate some income and build up extra savings she can pass on to her grandchildren. She is rather hoping that, aged 63, she'll be around for another 20 years or so. This means she wants the money to last and is prepared to invest it for a long time. She has spoken to a financial adviser, but she found his name in the phone book, so she's not sure if his advice is sound. Sandra uses the internet to communicate with friends in Canada, so she started off looking around the world wide web for information. Happily, she discovered that the advice she had been given was sound – she checked the company's performance in some league tables on one of the information sites. She also discovered that Friendly Societies have special savings plans for children, so she has decided to put some of her cash there for her grandchildren. Without the internet she might have tied her money up in long-term savings before finding out about the children's accounts.

Essential tips for saving money on the internet

▷ Remember that the internet can save you money by allowing cheaper phone calls, faxes etc.

▷ The internet offers a huge number and variety of bargains for online shoppers, so take advantage of them.

Savings checklist

- ▷ By shopping online you can eliminate travel costs and avoid unnecessary expenditure.
- ▷ Use the general information sites to check the latest savings rates on a wide range of accounts.
- ▷ Remember that many organisations offering savings accounts and services are local, such as regional building societies. Use sophisticated searches in web search engines to locate local deals.
- ▷ Join one of the mailing lists or newsletters offered by some of the general sites so you can be kept up to date with savings offers.

Your savings checklist

- ▷ Set out your savings priorities before you buy any products or services.
- ▷ Work out how much you need for the short term – the rest can usually be invested over a longer period.
- ▷ Don't keep too much cash in current accounts or instant access accounts or you will lose extra interest you could gain by moving the money to longer notice accounts.
- ▷ It is wise to spread your risks by having a mix of investments from a number of different companies.
- ▷ Make saving a habit. Just one pound a day adds up to £22,000 over the average adult's lifetime – even without interest!

7 Buying stocks and shares on the internet

In this chapter we will explore:

- *internet share dealing*
- *avoiding confusion about internet shares*
- *finding out about share dealing on the internet*
- *finding out about share dealing in the USA*
- *getting information from stock exchanges*
- *using brokers to buy shares*
- *using banks to buy shares*
- *buying your shares on line*
- *tracking your investments*
- *finding the best tracking web sites*
- *following shares in Britain*
- *using accounts software to track your investments*
- *using specialist investment software*
- *essential tips for buying shares on the internet*
- *share buying checklist*

In the recent past there have been two main newspaper stories on internet stocks and shares. Firstly, financiers and industry commentators have said that the shares of internet companies are too highly priced. Indeed, we have seen a great deal of speculation that the rapid rises in internet company stocks and shares can only be reversed, with massive losses for some and huge gains for others. The second story concerned the fact that you can now trade on your own on the internet. You no longer have to be one of the financial élite – everyone can buy stocks and shares, instantly, on the world wide web.

This second story is by far the more interesting and important for society as a whole. The fact that a handful of companies may be overvalued in market terms is only of real importance to the firms themselves and their investors. Since every one of us can buy and sell shares over the internet, this means that in society there is a substantial change taking place that is going almost unreported. Before too long, banks and other high street share-dealing outlets will not need to offer their service. After all, why would you trudge out in the rain, spending money on transport, to queue in a banking hall, just to sell £200 worth of utility shares so you can have some holiday spending money? Wouldn't it be much better to log on to the internet, sell your shares and have the cash paid straight into your bank account – all within a few minutes? That is a reality, today. It is not a dream about some distant future. You can do this right now.

Personal share-dealing is now a possibility and is going to have substantial ramifications for the way stockmarkets work. The buzz of excitement about internet stocks is largely because the investors in large American technology companies are not the usual stockmarket players. They don't have the same rules or the same cultural heritage. Their 'overvaluing' of internet stocks is upsetting the traditional players – they don't fully understand what's been going on. Traditionally, the institutional investors can make large gains by trading in shares every day. They see the shares in particular companies rise in value and they sell to make a profit, buying shares in other firms who are at a comparatively low value. They then just repeat this cycle day in, day out, and are only interested in the value of companies now and the profits they are making now. This is reflected in the American trend of companies reporting their financial results every three months.

Individual investors – the bulk of people buying internet stocks – are different. We don't want to buy and sell every day. Instead, we want to keep our shares so that we can sell them in the future for a profit. In other words, we value a company on its potential future price, rather than its present worth. This is not playing by the rules and has been upsetting the markets. Even though this minor tremor is not that significant to stockmarkets as a whole, it does convey an important message for the future: individual investors are going to be much more important than ever before, largely because we can buy and sell shares at will; until internet share-dealing became a reality this was too cumbersome for us to do.

Back in the 1950s, most shares in companies were owned by individuals. By the late 1980s the proportion of individual shareholders had fallen dramatically and most public companies were owned by a handful of institutions.[1] Nowadays that trend is reversing and one in five people owns shares in a public company.[2] In 1997, for instance, when four major building societies became public companies, they distributed shares to 20 million people.[3] Control is gradually shifting back towards individuals and that is one of the reasons for the so-called concerns about the equity market at the moment.

Don't be put off by such bleating. The stockmarket is a great place for individuals to find financial success. If you had invested £100 in a building society in 1980 it would have grown to £171 by 1995 (happily well ahead of inflation).[4] Had you invested £100 in the stockmarket, your money would have grown to a whopping £1,185. There is no contest, is there?

Understanding internet share dealing

Internet share-dealing is only an extension of what stockbrokers do. For several years now, in stockmarkets throughout the world, brokers and dealers have been using their computers to buy and sell shares. Until fairly recently we had to call in to these dealers (or get our bank to do that for us), tell them what we wanted to buy and they used their computers to do the purchase. Now, instead of having to go through two or three intermediate stages, we can arrange the purchase ourselves using our own computers; the popularity of doing this is immense. Indeed, the first ever online trade by a non-broker was made by a doctor in Michigan, USA, back in 1983[5] before the internet.

Since the launch of internet trading in 1996, the popularity of 'do-it-yourself' share-dealing has risen dramatically. Indeed, at the beginning of 1999, it was estimated that five million people were trading stocks and shares via the internet.[6] Internet share-dealing is therefore not difficult, anyone can do it and, with the right care, you can make money out of it; there is little to 'understand' about share-dealing on the internet, it is just like making any other online purchase: you find a supplier you like (one of the online traders) and you buy from them. It is as simple as that. Indeed, this simplicity is obviously appealing; in a survey conducted by the financial information group Bloomberg, researchers found that, although only 3 per cent of people currently buy shares on the internet, 52 per cent of people who were asked said they would surf the web to purchase shares.[7]

Avoiding confusion about internet shares

It is easy to become confused about share-dealing over the internet because there are a number of different words that mean the same thing. For instance in the UK we buy 'shares' on the 'stock' market. But in the USA, you buy 'stocks' at an 'exchange'. In the UK we have only two 'stock exchanges', London and Edinburgh, but in the USA there are exchanges all over the nation – including a number in the New York financial district, Wall Street. Try not to get submerged in all the confusion. Just remember the following basic points:

1. In the UK you buy 'shares' in companies.

2. In the USA you buy 'stocks' in companies.

Finding out about share-dealing on the internet

There is a wealth of information on share-dealing on the internet, naturally enough on the world wide web. You can find out everything you ever wanted to know about shares, and dealing in them, at a whole host of internet sites. Your first port of call should be your favourite general financial information site. If you haven't already discovered one, try the following, which all have good general information on buying stocks and shares on the internet.

Financial Times
http://www.ft.com

Moneywise Magazine
http://ww.readersdigest.co.uk/finance.htm

Motley Fool
http://www.fool.co.uk

Quicken
http://www.quicken.co.uk

Times-Money
http://www.times-money.co.uk

This Is Money
http://www.thisismoney.com

You will also find a page of useful links to investment sites at:

UK Portfolio
http://www.ukportfolio.freeserve.co.uk/

Finding out about share-dealing in the USA

It is possible to buy shares in American companies, via the internet. However, you should be aware that many British companies do not offer this service, because they feel they cannot keep up to date with what is happening in the US markets. Added to this, there are many more markets in the USA and economic conditions are different from those here in the UK. Hence, entering the American equity market is something you may do without much support. As always, get proper advice before entering any transactions. You can find more details about the American equity situation at any of the following sites:

Bloomberg
http://www.bloomberg.com/welcome.html
The Bloomberg financial site is brimming with information. Many people watch Bloomberg TV (via satellite or digital television) in Europe; you can even watch the programmes on the Bloomberg web site. Once at the site you will find a host of information about stockmarkets, the latest prices and the latest financial news. You can look at the pages of a personal finance magazine and read general information about investing in the USA; you can also hear Bloomberg Radio if you want. To get the audio feed of this or any other internet radio station, you will need Real Player software, obtainable from:

http://www.realaudio.com/

▷ *Key benefits of the Bloomberg web site*

All-round view of the financial scene in the USA
Excellent use of internet technology incorporating, text, audio and video

▷ *Disadvantages of the Bloomberg web site*

Large amount of content can confuse
Can take a long time to move around (it is very popular – you won't be the only person on the site!)

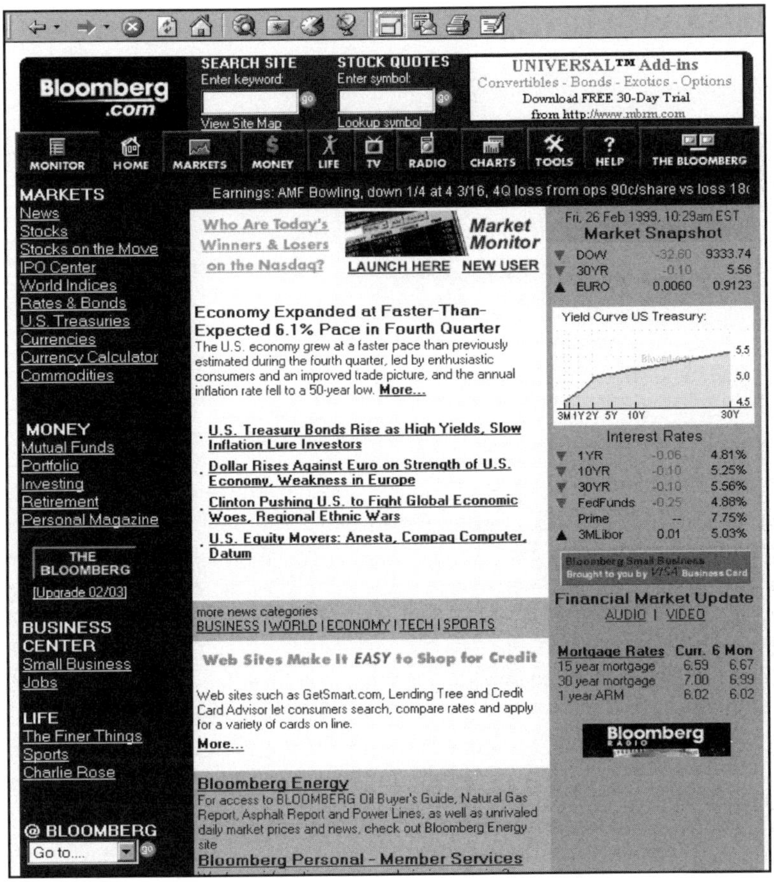

Fig. 72. Bloomberg is one of the leading (US-owned) providers of share information and services.

Individual Investor
http://www.iionline.com/
This is another busy American site. Here you can keep up to date on all the latest stock prices, read up-to-date market news and read various opinion columns on financial matters. It's a good site to keep up on the latest news in the stock exchanges, plus you can look up your own 'portfolio' to see how that's doing.

▷ *Key benefits of the Individual Investor web site*

Comprehensive USA coverage
Useful columns with helpful information

▷ *Disadvantages of the Individual Investor web site*

Some US financial jargon is used

Money Magazine
http://www.pathfinder.com/money/plus?page=index.oft
This is a really jazzy site with plenty of information about the US markets. There's even a live graph of how the markets are faring. There is also plenty of financial news and a whole host of articles on various aspects of finances and investing in the stockmarket, as well as a handy range of tools that you can use to work out how you'll meet the various 'goals' in your financial life.

▷ *Key benefits of the Money Magazine web site*

Comprehensive coverage and up to date information
Handy set of financial tools

▷ *Disadvantages of the Money Magazine site*

Lots of text to work your way through
Some of the text is quite small

SmartMoney
http://www.smartmoney.com/
SmartMoney is a highly popular American magazine on investing and personal finance; it now has a highly sophisticated web site to accompany the magazine. If you are interested, *SmartMoney* magazine is also imported into the UK and your newsagent should be able to order a copy for you. Meanwhile, the web site should give you plenty to look at – it is exceedingly busy, full of news and information about getting the best out of the US stockmarket. The site includes various 'trackers' so you can see how well a particular market is performing. There are also various sophisticated searches you can perform to find out exactly what you want about the US stock situation, and the site comes with a range of tools that help you plan your finances.

Key benefits of the SmartMoney site

Excellent financial search capabilities
Good range of news and information

Disadvantages of the SmartMoney site

It is huge and you could be here for hours!
There is so much to choose from you might be put off using it

Fig. 73. The web site of SmartMoney, the *Wall Street Journal* internet magazine of personal business. It features an impressive array of share listings, price charts, stock-market trackers, analysis and comment.

Getting information from stock exchanges

Many of the world's stock exchanges have web sites. If you are interested in some of the minor markets, or have financial interests outside the UK or USA, you will be able to find a web site for a local exchange. Mostly, the stock exchange sites are informational, though they do have some useful extras. Remember, though, that the exchanges are merely the places where stocks and shares are bought and sold. They also regulate the dealing industry. They do not provide financial advice. Nevertheless, you may find their sites useful since they can link you to other sites where you can get the support you need.

Fig. 74. The London Stock Exchange web site.

London Stock Exchange
http://www.londonstockex.co.uk/
Although the London Stock Exchange is one of the world's main markets, its web site is rather like those produced by small businesses. It is basic, but helpful. It has no real interactivity, though there is a form you can complete to request publications on various aspects of shares and dealing. The site has a drawback in that there are few links to take you back to where you started; instead you need to use your browser's 'back' button to turn backwards. This problem aside, there is plenty of useful information at this site: an extensive glossary, detailing all the terms you need explaining (plus plenty you'd never heard of); a question and answer section on share ownership; and if you are thinking of launching a public company, you'll also find the information here. There is a link to the separate site for the FTSE indices of share prices at:

FTSE (Financial Times Stock Exchange index)
http://www.ftse.com/
This site explains how the FTSE works and gives you the latest valuations of all its indices.

▷ *Key benefits of the London Stock Exchange web site*

Provides useful, authoritative, background information
Quick and responsive

▷ *Disadvantages of the London Stock Exchange web site*

Comparatively poor implementation of web technology
Few links to other useful sites

American Stock Exchange (AMEX)
http://www.amex.com/cgi-bin/WebObjects/AmexWeb
The AMEX is operated by the largest securities group in the USA. Its web site is clearly aimed much more at dealers and those in the finance industry – there is not a great deal of consumer information at this site. Even the glossary makes it clear that it is aimed at financial professionals. However, of interest is its live video link to the trading floor at the exchange itself. By going to the following page you can see the AMEX in action!

http://www.internetbroadcast.com/amex

EASDAQ
http://www.easdaq.be/pb/enb_00.asp
This is a pan-European stockmarket, the European Association of Securities Dealers Automated Quotation, to give it its proper title! This is a nice clear site that provides plenty of information on European trading and also gives a guide to the terminology used. There are pages of the latest price information and you can even download a Microsoft Excel spreadsheet of the day's closing prices on all shares traded through EASDAQ. The site also has a useful 'portfolio' application where you can select your own favourite shares traded at EASDAQ and have a table appear that gives you the data on these shares only. However, to access this table you will need the most recent browser applications. If you haven't got Microsoft Internet Explorer Version 4.0

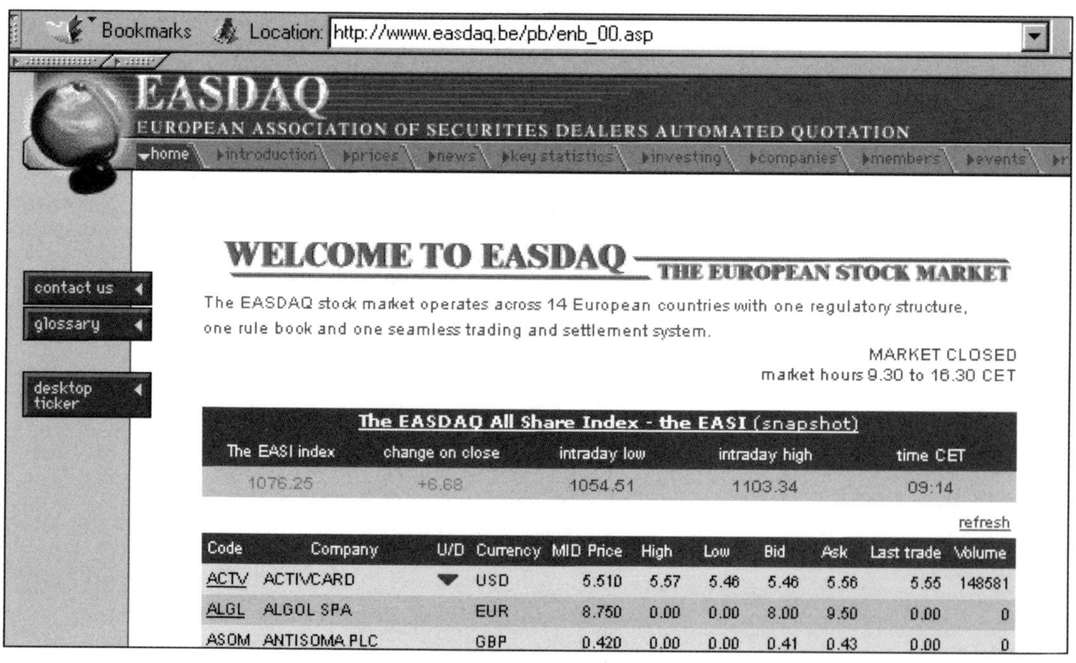

Fig. 75. EASDAQ is the leading European stockmarket. It operates across 14 different countries, but under a unified dealing and regulatory system.

or above or Netscape 3.02 or above, you will need to upgrade your browser. You can do this at:

Microsoft
http://www.microsoft.com/

Netscape
http://www.netscape.com/

NASDAQ
http://www.nasdaq.com/
This is the real success story of stock exchanges. The shares traded on NASDAQ have outperformed all others, by a long way. NASDAQ – the National Association of Securities Dealers Automated Quotes – deals mostly with new technology shares. However, its electronic trading system and its success has attracted many other companies and now NASDAQ is set on a path to make this the first, real international stock exchange. Indeed, NASDAQ has run television adverts in the UK, saying just that. Here you will find the latest prices, the ability to search for prices on individual companies, up-to-the-minute links to financial news stories from organisations such as Reuters, and a handy, quick guide to investing in stocks and shares, as well as tips on selecting brokers. There is a special UK NASDAQ site as well:

UK NASDAQ
http://www.nasdaq-uk.com/
This contains an excellent guide to how people in Britain can invest in American equities. There is also a useful question and answer page, helping provide more information. A useful guide to NASDAQ can also be found at the following page:

http://www.nasdaq-uk.com/services/Guide.pdf

(You will need Adobe Acrobat installed to receive this guidebook – see next entry.)

Adobe
http://www.adobe.com/prodindex/acrobat/readstep.html#reader

New York Stock Exchange
http://www.nyse.com
This is a very businesslike site where you can find out about share ownership in general and read the latest news and information in a downloadable monthly newsletter. There are also plenty of useful guides and background articles on share ownership in general. Naturally, you can find the latest NYSE prices and information about dealing. Interestingly, you can also buy NYSE merchandise, such as clothing, gifts, and toys, all emblazoned with the NYSE logo.

New York Stock Exchange – UK site
https://www.nyse.com/public/intview/4-1/4-1-5/415fm.htm#United
Many British companies also trade at the NYSE, so there is a UK site.

Be warned, though, the NYSE site has lots of graphics, so at busy times on the internet it can be slow to arrive.

Tradepoint
http://www.tradepoint.co.uk/
Tradepoint is a new all-electronic stock exchange based in London. Sadly, there is little information of use to consumers here, though you can see some demonstration pages of what happens. The idea is that the web site will provide stockbrokers and dealers with an easier way of buying and selling shares on your behalf.

Other stock exchanges
The following stock exchanges also have web sites, as do many smaller exchanges. To find what you want, use your favourite search engine.

Australian Stock Exchange	http://www.asx.xom.au/
Frankfurt Stock Exchange	http://www.exchange.de/fwb/fwb.html
Johannesburg Stock Exchange	http://www.jse.co.za/
Montreal Stock Exchange	http://www.me.org/
Tokyo Stock Exchange	http://www.tse.or.jp/eindex.html

Using brokers to buy shares

Even though you can trade direct yourself, many people still prefer to use a broker, but the costs of doing it yourself are often far lower. Even the high street banks' instant share-dealing services can work out more expensive than trading on your own on the internet. Nevertheless, some people still feel more secure using a broker. Naturally enough, there are stockbrokers who run web sites and can give you all the support you need. Brokers on the world wide web include:

Charles Stanley	http://www.charles-stanley.co.uk/
Durlacher and Co	http://www.durlacher.co.uk/
Ellis and Partners	http://www.ellisandpartners.co.uk/
Kyte Securities	http://www.kytesecurities.com/
Pilling and Co	http://www.pilling.co.uk/

If you want to know more about stockbrokers you can order a book (*The Good Stockbroker Guide*) from the following site:

The Good Stockbroker Guide
http://www.mb2000.com/Good.htm
You can also use this site to find a local stockbroker.

The Association of Professional Client Investment Managers and Stockbrokers
http://www.apcims.org/find.html
Here you can find a searchable listing of members of the professional body representing the stockbroking industry.

Using banks to buy shares

All the major banks and some building societies offer share-dealing services. However, only Barclays offers online share-dealing through the internet. All the other banks require you to call in at a branch.

Barclays Stockbrokers
http://www.barclays-stockbrokers.co.uk/
You need to register and Barclays will conduct credit checks before you get your online access. However, once you are registered, you can buy and sell shares using your account as often as you like. But remember there are commission charges – these are clearly laid out in this easy-to-use site.

Buying your shares online

Over the next few years, buying and selling shares online will become the norm. Many financial institutions are investigating internet share-dealing services, which could reduce their costs dramatically. Imagine having to train several thousand branch-based staff in share-dealing as well as having the technology at every one of your 2,000 branches. That's a costly operation. What if you were in charge at one of these high-street outlets? Wouldn't you rather run a share-selling operation which can reach more people than trudge up and down the high street, which can provide a greater level of expertise than even the best bank clerk, and which can be run by a team of a mere dozen or so? For cost-conscious directors, there's not a lot of competition. Internet share-dealing is here to stay and it is going to become remarkably successful.

Charles Schwab & Co
http://www.schwab-worldwide.com/europe
An indication of the likely success comes from Charles Schwab & Co, one of the pioneers of internet share dealing. Their web site had a threefold increase in visitors within the first month of setting up a dealing service.[8] This was during the time in which Schwab hadn't even advertised the new service! Currently, economic forecasters

Fig. 76. This is the Charles Schwab Corporation web site. Charles Schwab has emerged as one of the world's leading stock-brokers, and their impressive web site reflects their position.

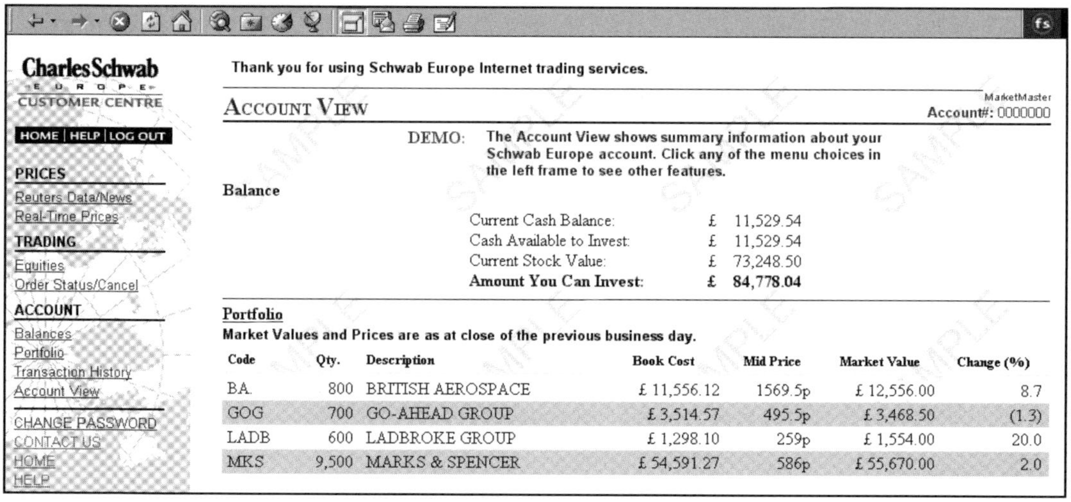

Fig. 77. A typical Charles Schwab trading statement, showing full details of each transaction made by the customer.

predict that almost US$700 billion will be traded annually on the internet by 2002.[9] That is equivalent to almost two years of British Government spending. With more of us owning shares and more shares being sold via the internet, you need to get to grips with online trading!

Schwab's excellent dealing service sets standards for others to follow. At this site you will find an online demonstration of how the service works, showing some dummy data, and an application form so you can register for the service. To do this, you will be sent an information pack in the post, which contains all the security forms you need to complete. Once these are back at Charles Schwab you will be issued with a password (which you can change) and an account number. You can then start trading on the internet. You can transfer funds into your Charles Schwab account by standing order or by making occasional contributions by cheque. Your money will earn interest while it is not used buying shares. If you want to buy shares, you log on to the service, select the shares you want and then arrange for the purchase, using the money in your account. You can later sell shares and return the money to your account or withdraw the profits.

All your shares at Charles Schwab are held in a 'nominee account'. This means that, although you receive the benefits of being a shareholder, the shares themselves are held on your behalf in a central account owned by Charles Schwab. This can have practical implications. For instance, shareholders whose holding is in a nominee account don't usually get annual reports (though you can get them by other means). Nor, usually, do you receive perks such as favourable discounts with the company whose shares you own. These problems aside, the Charles Schwab web site allows you to get the latest valuation on your holding and see the latest prices of your own shares and others you might want to buy. You are given a clear indication of the costs involved. You also receive a quarterly statement of your position. The downside is that you can only deal at specified times. The site does not operate 24 hours a day. This may be a problem if you travel to other time zones and want to sell or buy shares in a hurry.

▷ *Key benefits of the Charles Schwab web site*

Ability to buy and sell online
Easy accounting system with clear explanation of costs and profits

▷ *Disadvantages of Charles Schwab web site*

Not available 24 hours a day
Sometimes a little slow to respond

Share Centre
http://www.share.co.uk/
Here you will find general information on share trading and an application form for an account. The concept is very similar to the Charles Schwab way of dealing. You set up an account, gain a password and invest a sum using a cheque. You can then use this money to buy and sell shares. The site also has a useful background guide to investing in stocks and shares.

Stocktrade
http://www.stocktrade.co.uk/
Stocktrade offers an internet share-dealing service to registered members. You can register at this site and once you receive your password and log-in ID you can start using the service. You have to keep the shares in a nominee account, but if you want the share certificates yourself, you cannot sell your holding until you send the certificates back to Stocktrade. The site does provide you with real-time prices of shares and also lets you place orders. There is some general information about share dealing, but it is not as extensive as many other

Fig. 78. UK-based Stocktrade has a share-dealing demonstration on its web site.

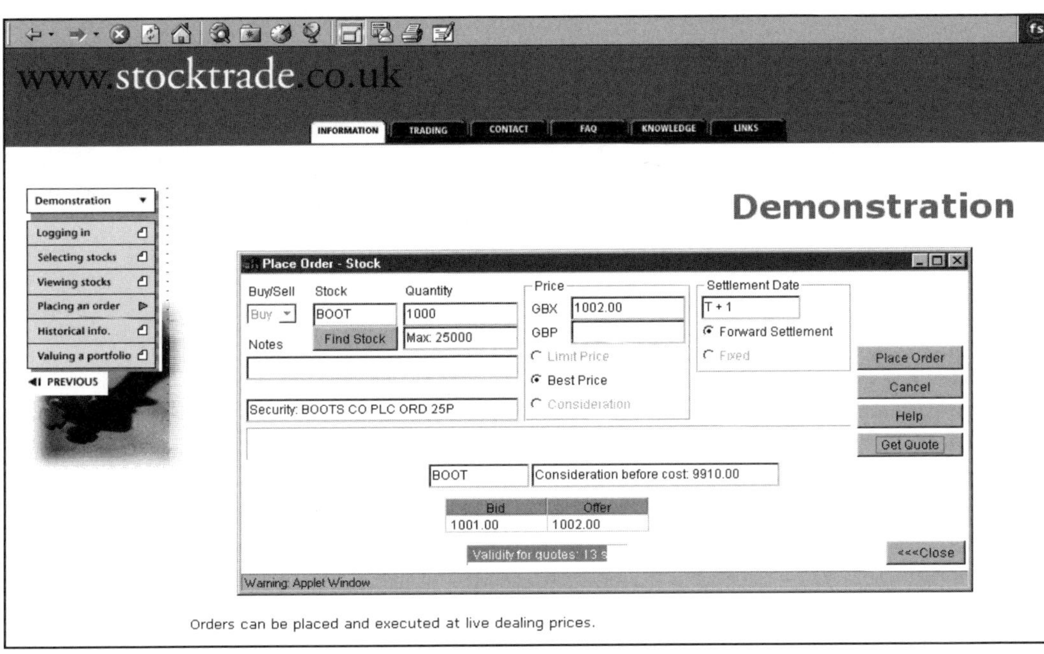

Orders can be placed and executed at live dealing prices.

sites. This site is clearly aimed at those who want to deal; the way an account works is similar to the Charles Schwab system.

Xest
http://www.xest.com
This is an online share-dealing service that allows you to buy and sell online as well as check the latest share prices. There is a comprehensive help section and almost everything you want to ask is answered there. In addition, all the charges are clearly laid out; your account works in much the same way as the Charles Schwab site. Strangely, though, this site has a 'lifestyles' section, linking you to showbiz news, horoscopes, and sporting news, amongst others! More importantly, you'll find the latest financial news and a bookshop where you can buy financial titles.

Fig. 79. The Xest share trading system. The name stands for 'execution only share trading'. The service comes complete with charts, graphs, financial news, specialist bookshop and more.

Tracking your investments

Once you have shares, you'll want to know how they are getting on. You'll also want to keep up to date with developments in the company you have invested in, as well as the industry sector. The dealing site you have used should be able to keep you up to date with the progress of your shares and the latest stock-market information. There are a number of other ways you can track your shares and keep an eye on progress in the market, helping you to work out when to buy or sell. The three principal ways are:

1. Tracking web sites
2. Accounts software
3. Specialist investment software

Finding the best tracking web sites

Providing the latest stock-market information and tracking your portfolio (real or mythical!) is a major activity on the internet. There are numerous sites that can help you do this and most, of course, follow the American markets. For a general overview of how each of the main international markets are faring go to:

CNNFN
http://cnnfn.com/markets/world_markets.html

If you invest in US shares, try the following sites:

Free Real Time
http://www.freerealtime.com/
You need to register if you want to obtain real time prices, but registration is free. However, you need to complete various agreement forms that contain whole pages of small print. You cannot successfully log in unless you have confirmed your agreement to each of these pages.

Quote.com
http://www.quote.com
This site provides quotes without registration plus there is a great deal of general information on the US markets. There is a useful 'symbol

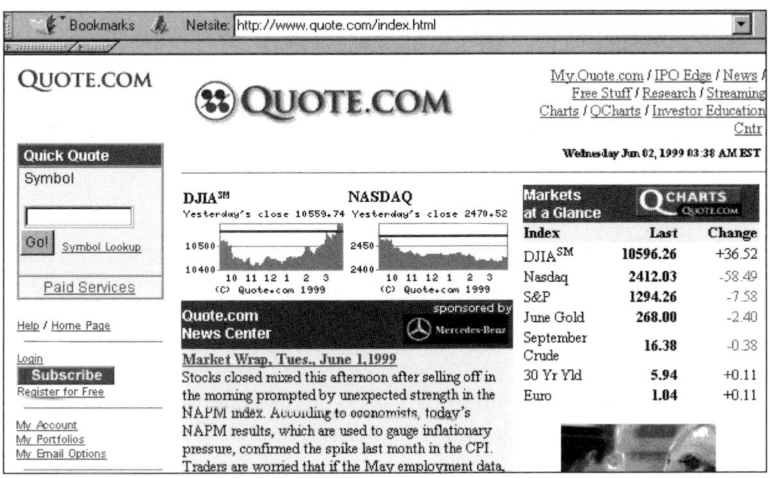

Fig. 80. You can check global prices and manage your portfolio at Quote.com, another challenger in the fiercely competitive internet-based share-dealing business.

lookup' button at this site – all quotes are provided on company symbol, rather than on name. If you don't know the symbol for the company you are interested in, use this site.

Don't forget that general financial information sites also keep you up to date on stock-market positions, so you may want to explore these as well. Many are listed in Chapter 2. Whenever you look at American share prices, remember they are quoted in dollars and fractions of dollars. British prices are in the decimal system.

▷ *Case study* – Barry and June are both successful executives in a large computer firm. They are given shares in their company as part of their annual bonus scheme. Each year the company provides a statement of what the shares are worth, but Barry and June would rather keep more up to date. Also, they might like to trade in some of the shares and buy equities in another firm that they know is likely to do very well in the future. Because they are both computer managers, they are internet fans. So they dial up and discover they can trade their shares online. They sign up for one of the share-dealing services and transfer their shareholding into the nominee account set up for them. In this way they can sell their existing shares online if they wish. They also sign up for a tracking service so they can keep up to date with their share values. Barry also joins an industry newsletter and gets a weekly email with all the latest snippets of news, which helps him decide whether or not to trade. So far, they have seen the value of their shares rise by 22%.

Following share prices in Britain

Even though the world wide web is swarming with sites on American stockmarkets, you can still find a great deal of information about the British scene. Your favourite general information site could contain stockmarket information, so check there. The best place to start for a complete picture of finances in Britain, though, is the *Financial Times*:

The Financial Times
http://www.ft.com
This site has all the latest news and access to all the pricing information you might need. However, it is very busy and full site, aimed at those in the City, so you might like to try something more consumer-oriented:

Carol
http://www.carol.co.uk
This stands for 'Company Annual Reports On Line' and does just that, very well. You can check the latest annual report of the companies you have invested in, or look up details of those you'd like to buy shares in. This is an excellent site and for serious investors should be a regular place to visit.

Fig. 81. ESI offers continuous market briefs geared to the UK stock-market.

Electronic Share Information
http://ww.esi.co.uk
This is an in-depth site that contains a whole host of share information. You need to register, but registration is free. The site allows you to create your own 'stockwatch' of up to three shares, so that you can keep up to date with specific investments. You can also subscribe to services, for a fee, which provide even more in-depth information. This is an excellent site offering serious investors an excellent tool.

UK Equities Direct
http://www.hemscott.com/EQUITIES/
This Hemmington-Scott site provides basic share information as well as access to the latest company reports.

Using accounts software to track your investments

You can use personal finance and accounts software to track your investments quite easily. Both Microsoft Money and Quicken allow you to track your investments and will both produce charts of how your shares are performing. Essentially, you enter your share purchases in the accounts program and then ask it to update the prices. The program then dials up the internet, downloads the latest information on your selected shares and updates your accounts program data. This is an excellent way of maintaining a clear idea of the value of your investments. It is easy to do and does not require any in-depth financial knowledge on your part. Both programs can also provide you with access to the latest financial headlines at their own web sites, as well as provide a host of other monetary information. If you own a few shares and are not really so serious an investor that you want to trawl the internet for information, these programs are an excellent tool. You can keep a close eye on your investment progress, without having to do a great deal of work yourself.

Using specialist investment software

In addition to the main accounts programs that track investments, there are plenty of specific pieces of software you can buy, or you can develop your own spreadsheet models to follow your shares – if you want to spend the time working out what to do. However, there are many ready-made programs and plenty of free or shareware spreadsheets available. To look up free or cheap spreadsheets go to:

Softseek http://www.softseek.com
ZDNet http://www.zdnet.com

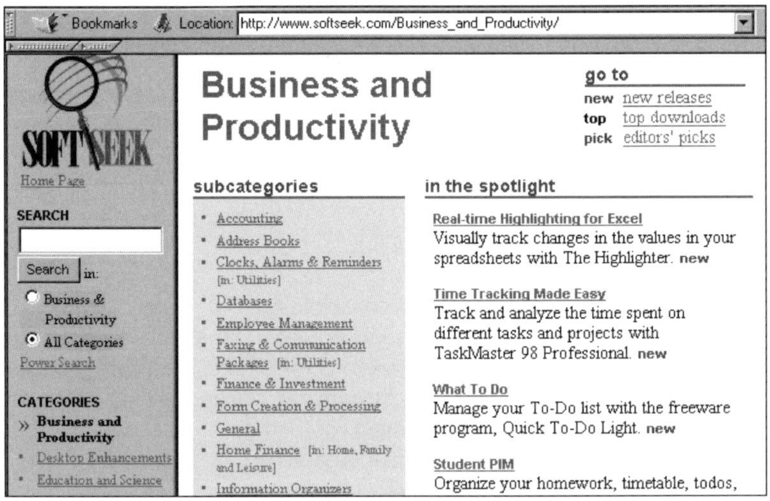

Fig. 82. Visit the SoftSeek web site if you want to track down specialist investment software to help you manage your portfolio.

Commercial programs that help you track your shares vary widely in price. What you choose will, of course, depend on your own circumstances and your seriousness in equity investing.

FairShares
http://www.fairshares.com/
This program can help you track a range of investments, from shares to PEPs and TESSAs. Interestingly, you can obtain pricing updates for the program from Teletext and a range of other data providers.

Indexia
http://www.indexia.co.uk/indexia-intro.html
Information for the casual or novice investor can be found here. Indexia make a number of different share-tracking programs which can produce a whole host of charts and information tables based on your share-price information.

Stockmarket
http://www.meridian-software.co.uk/programs.htm
A range of programs with the common title Stockmarket are produced by Meridian Software. These programs can help you manage your portfolio of shares by providing various charts and graphs to illustrate how well your investments are performing.

Updata
http://www.updata.co.uk/welcome
Using Updata you can download share price information and then incorporate it into your files. You can also link the Updata information to a Microsoft Excel spreadsheet so that you can perform sophisticated analysis.

Essential tips for buying shares on the internet

- ▷ Find out as much as you can about shares and stockmarkets using the general information sites.
- ▷ Keep up to date with your investments using a tracking service.
- ▷ Use an online company reports service to follow the activity of the companies you invest in.
- ▷ Consider buying and selling your shares using an internet-based dealer; this can be cheaper than traditional routes.

Share-buying checklist

- ▷ Remember that share prices can fall as well as rise.
- ▷ Investing in shares should be viewed as a long-term activity, measured in years rather than days or weeks.
- ▷ Always get advice before investing in companies.
- ▷ Track your investments to make sure you are getting the best return you can.
- ▷ Don't invest in shares simply for any perks offered. While these are nice to have, your investment decision should be based on how well the company itself will perform.
- ▷ Always check the share-dealing prices from a range of suppliers. Gains can quickly be lost in commission and fees.
- ▷ Any gains you make on share selling could affect your tax position. Check your situation with an accountant or tax adviser.

References

[1] *Running The Country*, David Coates, Hodder & Stoughton, 1995, p. 115.
[2] *Social Trends 28*, HMSO, 1998, p. 105.
[3] *Moneywise Guide to Planning Your Finances*, Isabel Berwick and Caroline Laws, Prentice Hall Europe, 1998, p. 176.
[4] *The Armchair Investor*, Bernice Cohen, Orion, 1997, p. 2.
[5] *Daily Telegraph*, 16 January 1999.
[6] *Daily Telegraph*, 16 January 1999.
[7] *Bloomberg Money*, February 1999, p. 6.
[8] *Banking and Finance on the Internet*, Ed. Mary J. Cronin, John Wiley & Sons, 1998, p. 247.
[9] *Net Future*, Chuck Martin, McGraw Hill, 1999, p. 27.

8 Buying pensions and insurance over the internet

In this chapter we will explore:

- *finding out about pensions on the internet*
- *types of pensions available*
- *looking up details of pensions information*
- *using an adviser or broker to find a pension*
- *pension buying checklist*
- *buying life assurance*
- *finding out about life assurance on the internet*
- *making a will*
- *considering critical illness cover*
- *considering permanent health insurance*
- *deciding on medical insurance*
- *accepting that accidents can happen*
- *buying household insurance*
- *finding out about car insurance*
- *deciding whether or not to have special insurance plans*
- *special advice for the over 50s*
- *essential tips for buying pensions and insurance on the internet*
- *checklist for insurance and pensions*

Financial protection is an important subject, yet for many people it is one that is an afterthought. How often have you heard retired people say they wish they had paid more attention to pension planning in their 20s? Or what about the number of people who wished they had taken out the right insurance? Once you are retired, or once a crisis has hit you, it will be too late and you will regret not having paid into schemes earlier on in life. Like it or not, protecting your financial status now for the future is important.

For most people, the main financial protection required is a pension. Everyone who has paid National Insurance contributions during a working life will be entitled to some form of state pension, but many will only get a small amount that is not enough to live on. Even if you have paid National Insurance for 40 years or more, you will still only get the maximum entitlement which in 1999 is £64.70 a week – just enough for the basics. To find out more about National Insurance and pensions go to:

Department of Social Services
http://www.dss.gov.uk/ca/
Here you will find all the latest information from the Contributions Agency, and be able to download many government leaflets on

pensions issues. If you want to know how much your state pension will be, go to this next page:

http://www.dss.gov.uk/ba/htgarpf.htm
Here you can apply for a form that will give you a forecast, based on your National Insurance contributions to date. You may also like to visit:

http://www.dss.gov.uk/pen/index.htm
This is the Social Security Department's web site on pension issues and is full of useful information about the state pension. You can download all the leaflets, or just the text (to avoid wasting time on the pictures). In Northern Ireland go to:

http://ssa.nics.gov.uk/

Even though all these sites demonstrate the billions of pounds that are being spent in benefits and pensions, for individuals the amounts are tiny. It is therefore of fundamental importance that you seek additional pension arrangements – otherwise your retirement will be spent on the breadline. The figures that the government makes available are at:

http://www.dss.gov.uk/hq/index.htm

These figures also reveal the funds that are paid out in circumstances where people have no financial protection of their own. For instance, in 1998 the government paid out £38m to 47,000 families who had no cover for funeral expenses.[1] It is clear therefore, that we all need to think about the future, however difficult that may be, and buying some financial protection now, when you can afford it, is much better than having to live on a tiny income sometime in the future. There are several key areas you will need to consider:

1. retirement pension
2. life assurance
3. critical illness insurance
4. permanent health insurance
5. medical insurance
6. accident insurance
7. household insurance.

Depending on your circumstances you might also need to think about:

8. car insurance
9. long-term care insurance
10. pet insurance
11. school fees insurance
12. specialist sports insurance
13. travel insurance

You can find information about all these areas of financial protection, and even purchase many of them, over the internet.

Finding out about pensions on the internet

Some of the key places you might like to start your search are the general information sites, mentioned in Chapter 2. In particular, there is plenty of useful background information at:

Times-Money
http://www.times-money.co.uk
You need to scroll down until you see the 'pensions' link; once there, you will find a number of articles dealing with all aspects of retirement planning.

This Is Money
http://www.thisismoney.com/pensions.html
Here you will find the latest retirement planning news, plus general background on pensions.

MoneyWorld
http://www.moneyworld.co.uk/faqs/penfaq3.htm
This site has a useful questions and answers guide to pensions.

Types of pensions available

There are various forms of pension available, depending on your personal circumstances. Broadly they fall into three categories (see facing page):

1. Employment pensions.
2. Top-up pensions (additional voluntary contributions or AVCs).
3. Personal pensions.

Looking up detailed pensions information

Once you have found some general background information on pensions you will probably want to find out more about the various products that are available. To do this you will need to visit the sites of the companies that provide pension plans. Some companies do sell pensions plans direct to individuals; others will only go through an independent financial adviser. Even if you are confident of making the selection yourself you may also want to discuss your choice with a professional adviser. Nevertheless, you may want to visit the following sites for information.

Allied Dunbar
http://www.allieddunbar.co.uk
This site gives you background information on the products available from the company. However, Allied Dunbar sells only through its financial advisers. You can find a local adviser by entering your postcode. You are then given the name, address and phone number of whom to contact. It's a shame there isn't an email facility or a call-back service, as offered by most banks.

	Employment	*Top-up*	*Personal*
Contributions	Made by employer on your behalf (or deducted from your salary).	Paid by you to employers scheme or into a 'free standing' scheme.	Paid by you into any plan of your choice.
Benefits	Depends on type of scheme used by employer and the frequency with which you change jobs. Also the Inland Revenue limits the final amounts paid to you.	Final amounts depend upon your salary since the State limits you to paying in no more than 15% of your income.	You can have as many pension plans as you like. Providing you pay in no more than specified limits (the lowest is 17.5% of salary) you can reap the rewards – there is no maximum for the amount that can be paid to you.
Tax position	Contributions for employees do not gain tax relief. You are limited to a final lump sum of £126,000.	You can get tax relief on contributions paid to top up pension plans.	All contributions are eligible for tax relief. You can take up to 25% of the fund's final value as a lump sum.
Disadvantages	You get little or no choice on the scheme being used.	Relatively inflexible way to save for retirement.	Completely flexible, but you have to pay the entire contributions.
Limitations	Only available to employees.	Only available to employees.	Only available to the self-employed and those without a company pension scheme.

Edinburgh Fund Managers
http://www.edfd.com/
At this site you can find out about the investment trust pensions on offer, as well as see the latest prices of all the funds in which Edinburgh invests. You can send in a request for further information.

Equitable Life
http://www.equitable.co.uk
This company has a site packed with information, helpful advice, a very useful pensions planning guide, and the facility to alter details of your pension online. From the opening page you can reach a demo of the interactive capabilities of this site. In addition there are some handy personal financial planning calculators. The site also allows you to apply for more information so that you can purchase a pension direct.

Legal and General
http://www.landg.com/pensions/pensions1.html
Here you can find out about the pension plans that Legal and General

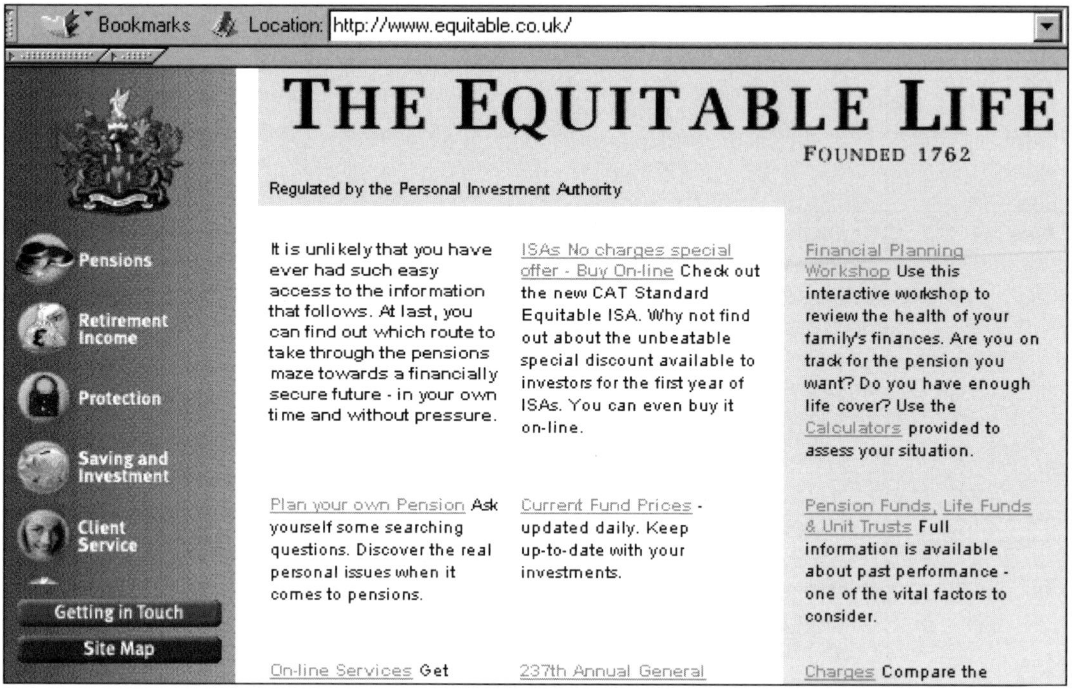

Fig. 83. The home page of Equitable Life, one of the longest established UK pension funds, founded in 1762. Plan your pension, check out ISAs and more.

sell direct. There is a clear guide to what is available, what it will cost and how you can get it. You can either use the telephone numbers provided, to obtain a quotation, or fill in a 'quickquote' form and submit this via the web site. You will also find a useful 'jargon buster' at the Legal and General site.

Marks and Spencer
https://www.marks-and-spencer.co.uk/financial-services/
For a number of years, M&S has been heavily involved in personal

Fig. 84. An example of an online pension plan statement, showing a typical customer's monthly contributions and premiums (Equitable Life).

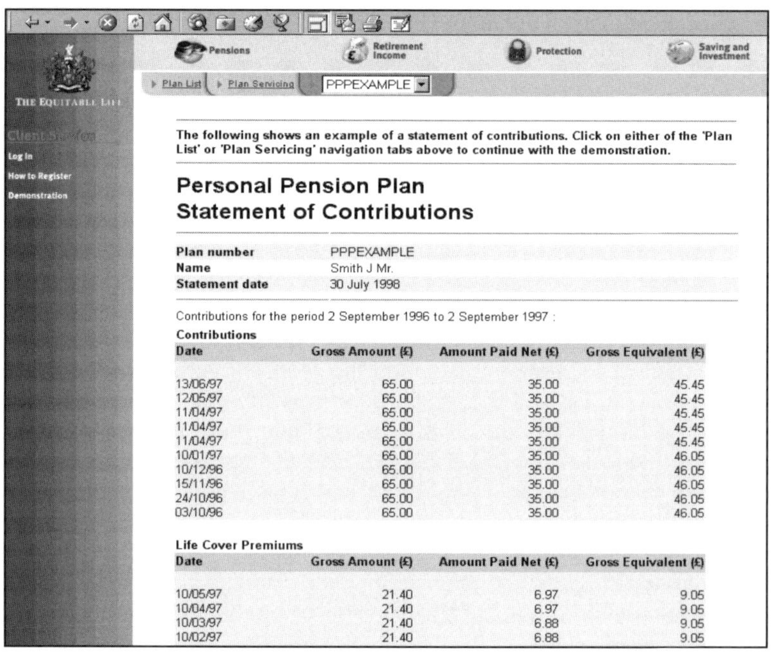

financial services. You can find details of their pensions at this secure web site, together with calculation tools to help you work out what you can afford. In addition you can apply for a quotation using an online form and they will send you a brochure and an illustration of a pension in the post.

Merchant Investors
http://test.merchant-investors.co.uk/
At this site there is a calculator to work out how much you need to invest as well as a regular magazine on personal finance, *In Touch*. You can view the pension products on offer as well as send an email for further information.

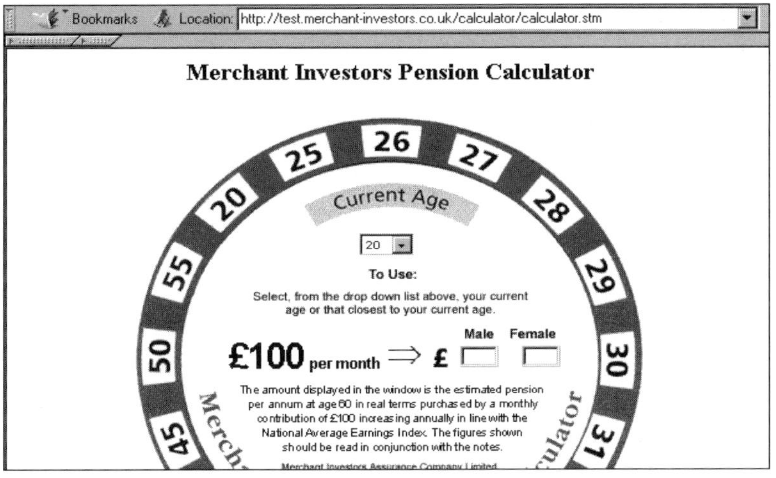

Fig. 85. Merchant Investors offer an easy to use pensions calculator, so you can estimate what your pension is likely to be, depending on your age and contributions.

Norwich Union
http://www.norwich-union.co.uk/homepage.htm
Although clearly laid out, this site is a bit confusing. To find pensions you need to select 'fund prices' from the opening page, then a button marked 'pensions'. To find out more, scroll down to the bottom of this page, click on 'seek professional advice' and scroll down to the bottom of that page to find a button to contact Norwich Union Direct. Finally, you need to scroll down to the bottom of this page to find an email button. This site is crammed full of information, but as yet there are no interactive features.

Prudential
http://www.pru.co.uk/
The 'Pru' is one of the largest financial institutions in Britain, but its site does not appear to reflect this. Essentially, it is nothing more than a listing of all the company's financial products. There is almost no interactivity. You are limited to submitting a form telling them what you think of their web site, or performing a search for a phone number which will give information on the product you are interested in.

Royal Liver
http://www.royal-liver.com/
This is a purely informational site with details of all the products available from this established institution; to find out more you need to call the number provided or fill in a form requesting their brochure.

Scottish Amicable
http://www.scottishamicable.com/products/index.html
The material at this site is classified into three categories: for basic pension information, select the appropriate symbol; if you want some detail, click on another symbol; and if you want the full works, use the third symbol. This is an excellent idea as it allows you to choose what you want to see. You can complete an online form requesting more information – and you can even take part in a 'spot the ball' competition!

Scottish Life
http://www.scottishlife.co.uk/Scottish%20Life/products/pensions.htm
Here you will find a complete listing of all the products available, with some details about each. Your only choice for further information is to click on a button to find your nearest branch.

Scottish Widows
http://www.scottishwidows.co.uk/
This is a large provider of pensions. Its web site has a useful 'personal pension planner' that helps you work out what you need to save now for the future. It shows you a graph comparing what you are likely to get with what you want to achieve – very revealing! There are few product details on the site so you will need to obtain extra information. You can do this by submitting an email with the date and time you want someone to call you.

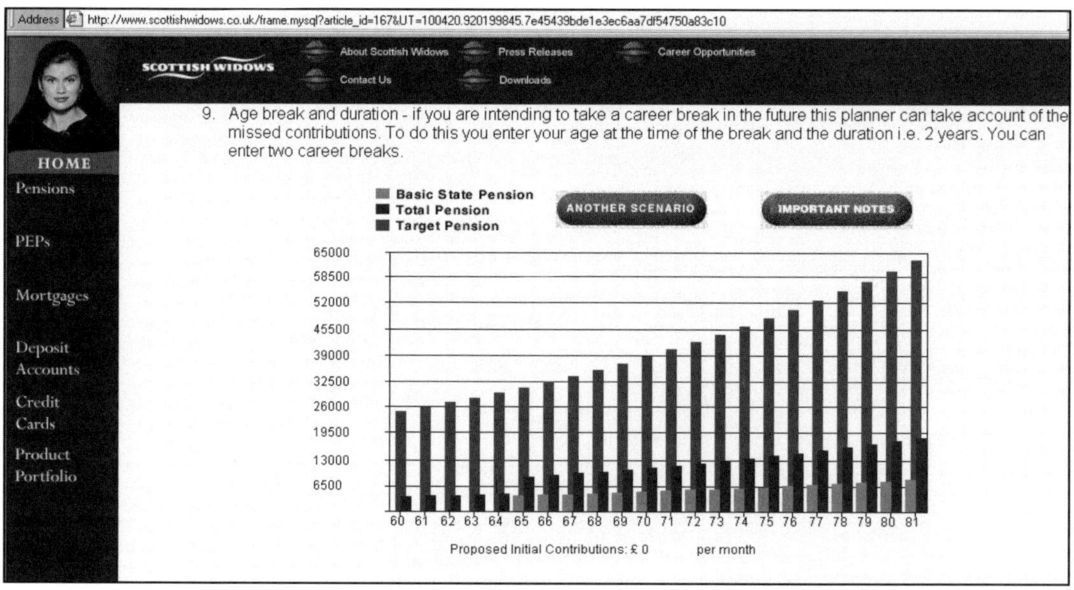

Fig. 86. The Scottish Widows web site. You can find out about mortgages, deposits, credit cards and more.

Standard Life
http://www.standardlife.co.uk/products/pensions.html
At this site you will be able to see brief details of the pensions products available and submit a form asking for further information to be sent to you. If you are interested in the company's philosophy over the investment decisions it makes, you can find out more at:

http://www.standardlifeinvestments.co.uk/investing/

Sun Life
http://www.slocpensions.co.uk/index.html
This is where Sun Life of Canada has its pensions web site. You can read details of each product available and some general background information on pensions, and complete a form requesting further information.

Using an adviser or broker to find a pension

Instead of searching for a pension yourself, you may want a financial adviser to do all the legwork for you. There are now many pensions advisers with their own web sites, and the following is a list of the major companies. However, you may want to perform a search using your favourite web search engine to track down professional advisers in your own locality. Alternatively, you can find a local financial adviser at:

MoneyWeb
http://www.seven.net/moneyweb/search/search.html

Independent pensions advisers include:

AssureNet
http://www.assurenet.sonnet.co.uk/

Consultant Insurance Brokers
http://www.consultant-insurance.co.uk/

Garrison and Co
http://www.garrison.co.uk/

IFA Direct
http://www.ifadirect.co.uk/

Independent Advice
http://www.independent-advice.co.uk/

Pace
http://www.paceltd.co.uk/

Winterthur Life
http://www.winterthur-life.co.uk/

You can also find a local broker by visiting:

British Insurance & Investment Broker Association (BIIBA)
http://www.biiba.org.uk/brokingonline.html

Retire Early
http://home.earthlink.net/~intercst/reindex.html
If you can't wait to get your pension because you want to retire early, the online magazine 'Retire Early' is for you!

Pension-buying checklist

Check out the following when buying a pension:

- ▷ Can you change the amounts you pay in without penalty?
- ▷ Can you take payment holidays in times of financial trouble without penalty?
- ▷ Can you convert the pension plan should you change your employment?
- ▷ Can you choose when to pay – monthly, quarterly or annually?
- ▷ What will you be charged for the pension?
- ▷ When will the charges be incurred?
- ▷ What is the past performance of the pension company when compared with that of other pension companies?
- ▷ How often will you be kept up to date with statements?
- ▷ Can you manage your pension yourself via a web site?
- ▷ Can you get a discount from the pension company if you also buy life assurance from them?

Buying life assurance

It is said that there are only two certainties in life – taxes and death. You can't escape either of them. Difficult as it is to come to terms with your own mortality, your death will lead to financial problems for those left behind if you don't plan now. The very least you should do is plan to insure yourself so that your relatives can at least clear up your debts when you go. Even a basic funeral will cost more than £600. There are two main categories of life assurance: term assurance, and whole life assurance.

- ▷ *Term policies* run for a specified period. Usually, if they are linked to a pension plan they run up to your retirement date. If you die during the term of the policy, your estate receives the money. If you live beyond the term of the policy you receive nothing. Term assurance is the cheapest form of insurance around.

- ▷ *Whole life assurance* runs for the whole of your life. No matter when you die, the policy pays out. Whole life policies are the most expensive kind of life assurance.

Between whole life and term assurance, there is a broad band of products which are largely convertible. You can elect to convert your term policy into a whole life policy, once the term has expired, for instance. These policies tend to be mid-priced and can offer the degree of flexibility many people require. Remember though, other factors contribute to the cost of life assurance. Principally, these are:

(a) your age
(b) your health
(c) your gender.

Finding out about life assurance on the internet

There are many sites on the internet that deal with life assurance. Almost every major financial institution sells life assurance, so you may want to start with your own bank or building society. Many pensions can also have life assurance linked to them, so if you are searching for a pension you may want to incorporate a life policy as well. In addition, every independent financial adviser will be able to deal in life assurance. If you want to find out more about the products on offer from various companies try the following selected sites, where you can at least apply for further information easily or obtain a quote online.

AXA Equity and Law
http://www.axaassurance.co.uk

Co-operative
http://www.cis.co.uk/products/life.html

Direct Line
http://www.directline.com/Life/index.htm

Guardian
http://www.guardianfs.co.uk/public/html/lifetitle.html

Legal and General
http://www.landg.com/lifeass/family/protfamily.html

Marks & Spencer
https://www.marks-and-spencer.co.uk/financial-services/

Norwich Union
http://www.norwich-union.co.uk/life_menu.htm

Royal & SunAlliance
http://www.royalsunalliance.co.uk/direct/life/index.htm

Royal Liver
http://www.royal-liver.com/royaliver/lifeassu.htm

Scottish Amicable
http://www.scottishamicable.com/products/index.html

Standard Life
http://www.standardlife.co.uk/products/lifeassurance.html

Making a will

An important aspect of dealing with the inevitable is making a will. Many people die without having drawn up this essential legal document, without which your financial affairs could take two years to settle – bringing extra problems for your relatives when they least need it. Also, without a will your wishes may not be met. If you really wanted your art collection to be sold in favour of the cats' home, you need to specify it in a proper will; without a will, your art collection might find its way into the hands of that naughty nephew you despise! You do not need to go to the expense of using a solicitor, but if your affairs are complex or you want to make some special provisions, hiring a solicitor could be money well spent. You can find local solicitors at:

Law Guide
http://www.lawguide.co.uk/

If you do not want to use a solicitor, you can use a specialist will-writing service, or you can buy some computer software that will do the job for you. To find out more about will-writing go to:

The Society of Will Writers
http://freespace.virgin.net/society.willwriters/

You can find experienced will-writers at a number of sites, for example:

Bequest Wills
http://dspace.dial.pipex.com/bequest/index.htm

County Wills
http://members.aol.com/countywill/index.htm

C J Erwood
http://www.atlantica.co.uk/personal/cjlegacy.html

Lawnet
http://qvartnadecet.mkn.co.uk/HELP/LAW/WILLINFO

Professional Will Writing Company
http://www.pwc.ndirect.co.uk/

Quicken Family Lawyer
http://www.parsonstech.com/software/famlaw.html

Willmaker
http://www.nolo.com/item/wd7.html

These sites are American; you may find British versions of the software available in computer stores or via mail order in a computer magazine.

Willwriters
Software for will writing is at:
http://www.willwriters.co.uk/

Considering critical illness cover

Critical illness insurance is a special form of life assurance that pays out if you develop a life-threatening condition such as serious heart disease or cancer. Once you are diagnosed, the policy pays out. However, you do not then get any payments upon death. You do, though, receive money if you die before the end of the policy term and you haven't made a claim for serious illness. Most of the companies that offer life assurance also offer critical illness cover, so look at the web sites listed earlier in this chapter. An insurance company that specialises in critical illness cover is:

The Permanent
http://www.permanent.co.uk/
This web site provides basic information about critical illness cover and has a map to help you locate one of the professional advisers who can discuss your requirements in more detail.

Considering permanent health insurance

Permanent health insurance (PHI) is a strange name for what this product does. It pays out when you are permanently ill (the only 'permanent' thing about it is the premiums!). The concept is that you pay a monthly premium, then if you fall ill for a long period you are provided with an income. Sometimes this kind of insurance is called 'income protection' as well (though you can get income protection

Fig. 87. The British Insurance and Investment Brokers' Association. Make sure the firm or individual you deal with is a member.

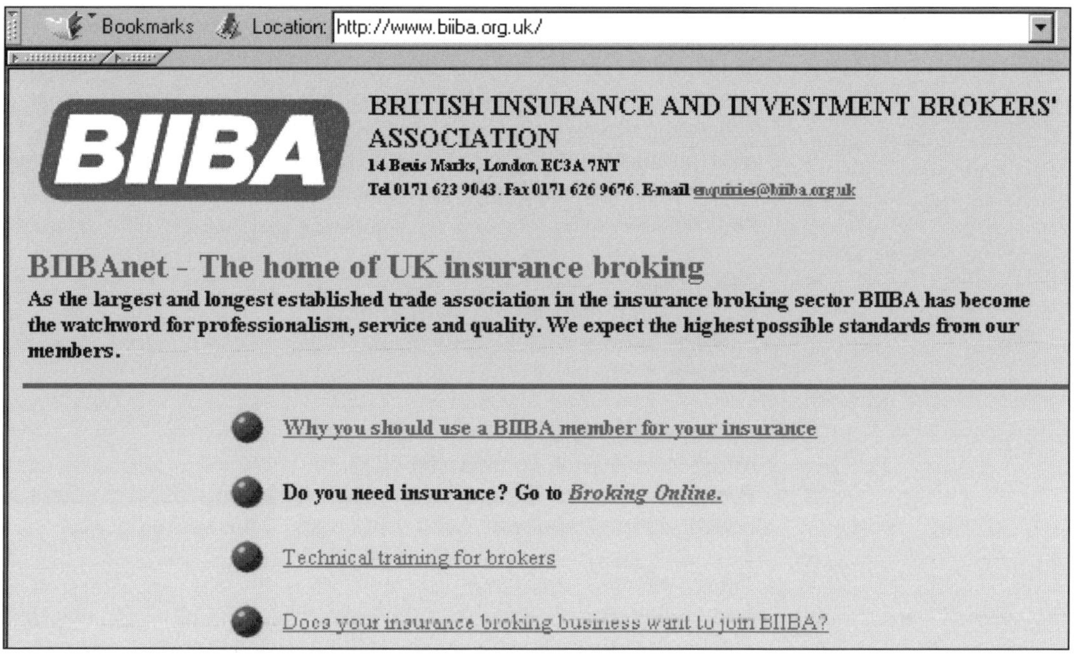

policies to cover you for other eventualities besides illness). PHI policies are offered by many insurance companies, especially by those that offer life cover. You might also like to try the following site where PHI is discussed.

Medical Sickness
http://www.medical-sickness.co.uk

Deciding on medical insurance

Whether or not you buy medical insurance is often a political decision. If you believe the NHS should provide an all-round service because you pay taxes, you are unlikely to opt for private medical cover. Equally, if you believe you can get more immediate attention by 'going private', you are likely to want to buy medical insurance. Private medical insurance offers a wide scope, from 'hospital cash benefits' where you receive an amount of money for each day you are in hospital, to the complete payment of everything at one of the country's top private hospitals. What you receive will depend upon what you pay into the scheme. A number of specialist brokers in the healthcare sector can help you find the best deal. These include:

1st Medical Healthplans
http://www.1stmedical.co.uk/
1st Medical Healthplans Ltd is an independent insurance adviser, specialising in cover for private medical insurance for UK residents and expatriates of the UK. An independent intermediary acts on your behalf to find the best deal on the market, and this page aims to help you make the right decision with the minimum fuss.

Medibroker
http://www.medibroker.co.uk/main.html
Medibroker has negotiated discounts with about 15 UK insurance providers and may be able to save you money by transferring an existing policy, should you be covered already. It researches the market place for new products and for competitive, comprehensive, value-for-money healthcare plans and schemes available, keeping its clients informed of its findings.

Mediquote
http://www.mediquote.co.uk/main.htm
The site includes a nationwide directory of independent specialist advisers.

Private Health Associates
http://www.demon.co.uk/dayco/pha.html
Based in Sidcup, Kent, Private Health Associates are specialist healthcare intermediaries, with more than 30 insurance agencies.

Private Health Partnership
http://www.php.co.uk/php/
The Private Health Partnership is a UK-based independent consultancy

providing information and advice on the full range of private medical and dental insurance schemes for companies and individuals.

You can also investigate private medical insurers' web sites at:

BUPA	http://www.bupa.com
Norwich Union	http://www.norwichunion.co.uk
PPP HEALTHCARE	http://www.ppphealthcare.co.uk/
Prime Health	http://www.primehealth.co.uk
Western Provident	http://www.wpahealth.co.uk

Accepting that accidents can happen

What would you do if you fell and broke both wrists? How would you drive? How would you be able to use your computer at work? What would happen if the damage were permanent? Thankfully you can buy accident insurance to cover such eventualities. Even so, few web sites appear to cover accident insurance, even those of main insurers. You can find out about accident insurance from the following brokers:

Butcher Robinson and Staples
http://www.brasil.co.uk/

Buying household insurance

You are required to insure your property if you have a mortgage on it. If you are lucky enough to have dispensed with your mortgage, whether you insure the building is up to you. Also, there is no compulsion to have your contents insured at any time – but what would you do in the event of fire or theft? Household insurance is considerably cheaper than having to buy an entire house and its contents again! This type of insurance is very popular and you can find links to all the relevant companies on the world wide web by going to:

Find
http://www.find.co.uk

Screentrade
http://www.screentrade.com/
Here you will be able to complete an online form and get an instant quote for your insurance.

Finding out about car insurance

The motor insurance market is huge and there are literally hundreds of companies offering policies for your car. Remember, car insurance is compulsory – so use the internet to search for the best deal. To start your search go to:

Screentrade
http://www.screentrade.com/
At this web site you can fill in an application form and receive an instant

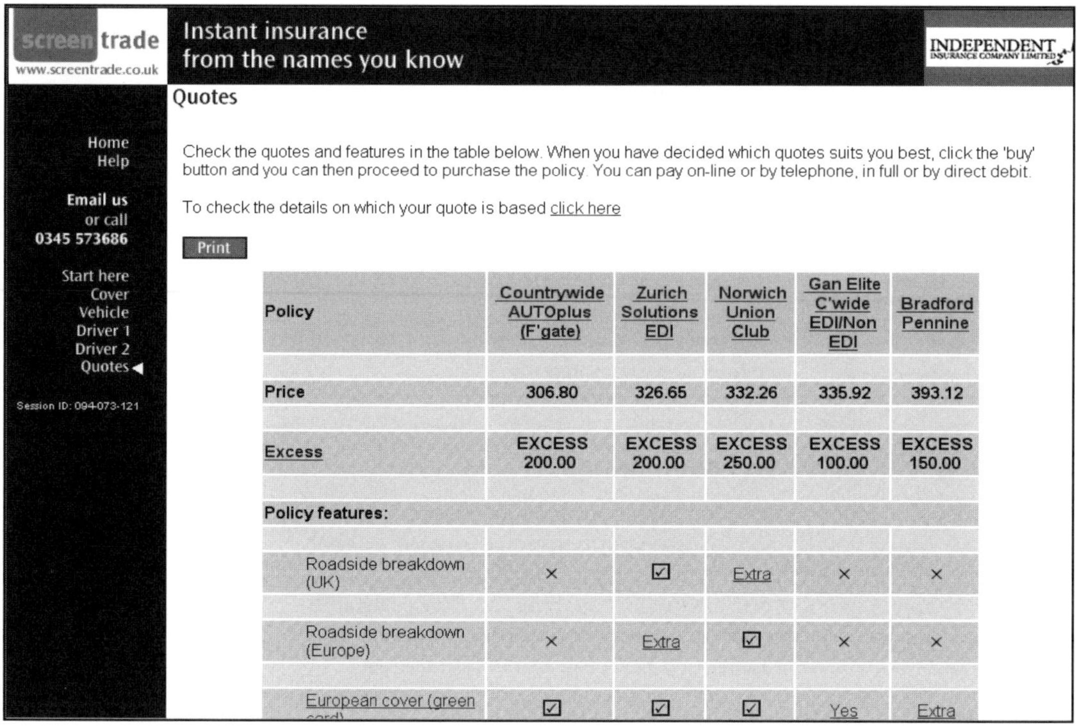

Fig. 88. You can use Screentrade to compare quotations from several different insurers for the same insurance cover. The example here shows a range of competitive quotes for motor insurance.

quote for your car, together with comparisons. It takes about five minutes to complete the form and is much quicker than ringing round brokers, waiting for them to call you back, or even wandering down the high street to potential insurance agents. You could also visit:

Car Quote
http://www.carquote.co.uk/
Here you complete a form, but a quote is emailed back to you.

Car Source
http://www.carsource.co.uk/
This offers a service similar to Car Quote.

St Christopher Driver Plan
http://www.st-christopher.com/
Another insurance you might like to obtain is cover for losing your licence – how would you pay for taxis, or chauffeurs? The St Christopher Driver Plan can support you if you lose your licence.

Deciding whether or not to have special insurance plans

There is a whole host of specialist insurance plans on offer to cover everything, from your cat to your holiday and your sky-diving hobby! Only you can decide whether or not you need or want such insurance, since in most instances they are not compulsory. You can find lists of specialist insurances at:

Find
http://www.find.co.uk

Shop-Yell
http://www.shopyell.co.uk/aquote/defaultnew.asp
You can also get online quotes for a range of insurances at Shop-Yell.

British Insurance and Investment Brokers Association
http://www.biiba.org.uk/brokingonline.html
A visit to BIIBA should also help you locate specialist insurance.

Longtermcare
http://www.longtermcare.co.uk
With many more people entering residential or nursing homes, paying for their care is becoming an expense that needs to be considered. If you are nearing retirement you might like to consider how you might pay for your accommodation if you had to move into a residential home. You can find out more about long-term care insurance at this site.

Veterinary fees can soon mount up, especially if your animal falls ill enough to require surgery. You can now get a range of animal health insurances and the following web sites have further information.

E&L Insurance	http://fido.k9.co.uk/e&l/index.htm
Exotic Direct	http://www.exoticdirect.co.uk
Healthy Pets	http://www.healthy-pets.co.uk/
Pet Healthcare	http://www.pethealthcare.co.uk/
Pet Plan	http://www.petplan.co.uk/
Pet Shield	http://www.petproducts.co.uk/
Pet Wise	http://www.swireblanch.co.uk/petwise/
Woolwich Pet Guard	http://www.woolwich.co.uk/petguard/petad.htm

If you plan to send your youngster off to private school you may want to set up an insurance plan now that pays out lumps sums to help you cover the fees. Essentially, such products are like endowment policies.

British Insurance and Investment Brokers Association (BIIBA)
http://www.biiba.org.uk
Your bank or personal financial adviser will be able to give you specialist help, but you might also like to look at the BIIBA site. You should be able to locate a broker near you who can help.

If you go skiing, sky-diving or mountain climbing you may want to consider specialist insurance. Although brokers can help you, you may find the following web sites useful as they specialise in unusual sports insurance.

Fogg Travel
http://www.itsnet.co.uk/insure/fogg/
Fogg Travel Insurance Services Ltd specialise in skiing, snowboarding and other winter sports, and cover all the British ski teams from alpine to freestyle.

Snowcard
http://www.ski.co.uk/snowcard/
They offer eight-day cover for such activities as abseiling, scrambling, trekking, alpine walking, hill walking, glacier walking, orienteering, marathon running, fell running, cross country running, white water rafting, sea kayaking, non-coastal yachting, rock climbing, mountaineering, pot-holing, caving, hang-gliding, paragliding, ski racing and ski mountaineering.

The travel insurance market is enormous. In 1998 the Monopolies and Mergers Commission halted the linking of holiday offers to specific insurance policies. That has opened up the market considerably and now hundreds of insurers provide travel policies. You can get a variety of policies including:

1. individual travel cover for a specific holiday
2. annual personal cover
3. annual family cover
4. European only cover
5. worldwide cover

You can find travel insurance offers at a whole host of web sites, from banks to building societies to travel agencies. However, you might like to try the following sites, which specialise in travel insurance:

Assured Travel Insurance	http://www.britsurf.org/dial-direct/assured.html
Insurance Connections	http://www.demon.co.uk/dayco/phatrav.html
Nomad Travel Insurance	http://www.nomad-insurance.co.uk/
Travel Insurance Agency	http://www.travelinsurers.com/
Travel Insurance Club	http://www.travelinsuranceclub.co.uk/
World Wide Travel Insurance	http://www.wwtis.co.uk/
World Cover Direct	http://www.worldcover.co.uk/

Special advice for the over 50s

If you are over 50 you might like to see what special deals are on offer. No matter what insurance you are looking for, the insurance industry often gives discounts to this age group. You can find out more by visiting the SAGA insurance site at:

SAGA Insurance
http://www.saga.co.uk/insurance/index.html

▷ *Case study* – Diana is a single mother in her late 30s. Her husband died last year and left her with two small children. He had no will and Diana has been clearing up the financial problems he left behind. So that her children don't have to go through the same trauma, Diana hunted through the internet until she found a will-writing service. She has now completed her will and it is stored safely. During her trawl round the world wide web, Diana realised there were plenty of other things she ought to do to protect her children. For a start, her life insurance was insignificant, so she found a web site that could provide her with an instant quotation. She also discovered a company that offered income protection insurance, so she has sent off for more details of that. Without using the internet Diana might not have thought of the other areas of her life that needed protection, so that her children were cared for in the future.

Essential tips for buying pensions and insurance on the internet

▷ Find out as much information as you can about the specific area that you want to investigate. You can do this at one of the general information sites.

▷ Work out how much pension income you will need in the future. You can do this using the handy calculators on some of the pensions web sites.

▷ If your pensions provider has a web site, check whether you can manage your pension using it. Some companies offer this service, allowing you control and flexibility.

▷ Visit the relevant government web sites to make sure you don't miss out on what the state can offer.

▷ Use online quotation systems from insurance providers as this will get you rapid estimates of what you will need to pay.

▷ If you get a better quote from one company but prefer another's service, email them your lowest quote to see if they'll reduce their fees.

Checklist for insurance and pensions

▷ Pensions and insurance are financial protection systems. Consider all the areas of your life that need protection and rank them in order of priority.

▷ Start a pension early. The more you pay in, the more you'll get out.

▷ Contribute as much as you can afford into a pension plan, but don't go over the relevant limits.

▷ Make sure you enter personal pension details on your tax return, as you could be entitled to tax relief.

▷ Always get a range of quotes for all insurances. Prices and benefits vary so you'll need to make some careful comparisons.

▷ Keep a diary of when your insurances need renewing. Then a month in advance you can gain competitive quotes, rather than simply renewing with a company that may be more expensive than others.

- ▷ Make sure you have written a will – you can save your family a great deal of sorrow, guilt, heartache and financial difficulty.
- ▷ If you buy term life assurance, consider how you will insure your life once the term is over.

Reference

[1] See: http://www.saif.org.uk/public/aboutfunerals.htm#claiming

9 Checking your taxes on the internet

In this chapter we will explore:

- ▶ *searching for information on tax*
- ▶ *finding information on tax from independent sources*
- ▶ *using tax calculation software*
- ▶ *using online tax calculators*
- ▶ *using accountants and tax professionals*
- ▶ *finding out about capital gains and inheritance tax*
- ▶ *finding out about council taxes*
- ▶ *essential tips for tax planning on the internet*
- ▶ *tax checklist*

Like it or not, as UK residents we are all liable to pay tax. UK residents pay a range of different taxes. These include:

- ▷ Capital Gains Tax
- ▷ Council Tax
- ▷ Customs and Excise Duties
- ▷ Income Tax
- ▷ Inheritance Tax
- ▷ National Insurance
- ▷ Stamp Duty
- ▷ Value Added Tax (VAT)

Each of these taxes contributes to the Government's finances and pays for schools, hospitals, transport and other services. Every year the Government takes around £70 billion from us in income tax alone.[1] The cost of running the country is more than £300 billion per year.[2] Hence, taxation is vital and everyone is expected to pay their fair share. Those, of course, are the important words aren't they? What is a fair share? This is the question that exercises many of our politicians. Whatever your fair share is, you certainly should not pay any more than you need to. Equally, you'll want to make sure that you pay what is required – the penalties for underpayment of taxes of all kinds are increasingly draconian. Ideally, you should pay just the amount of tax you are required to – no more, no less.

Ascertaining your tax liabilities is not always an easy matter. As we have seen, there are several different taxes all administered by different departments of the state. For instance, income tax is collected by the Inland Revenue, VAT by HM Customs and Excise and National Insurance by the Department of Social Security. Checking on your tax affairs and making sure you pay just the amount you need can be a complicated and time-consuming task. Thankfully, the internet can

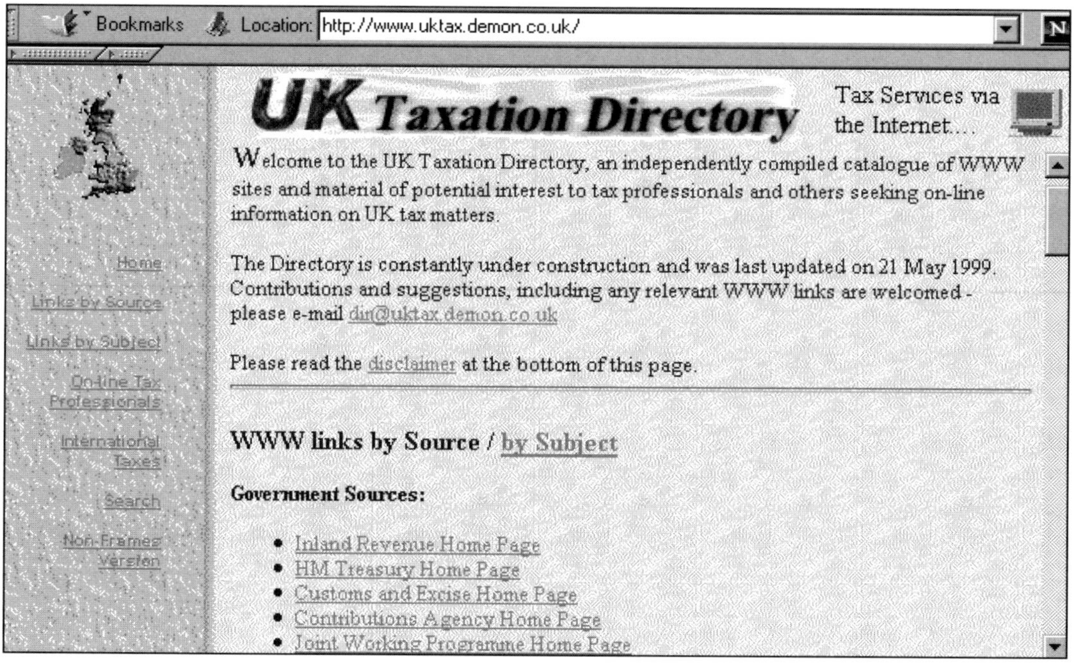

Fig. 89. The UK Taxation Directory is a user-friendly resource. It contains most of the links you need to key taxation web sites. You can even find out about international taxation.

point you towards some resources that will help reduce the amount of effort you need to make.

Searching for information on tax

UK Tax
http://www.uktax.demon.co.uk
This is a useful place to start because of its helpful index of tax links. However, if you are minded to visit specific government tax-related sites the following should all be added to your list of favourites.

The Contributions Agency	http://www.dss.gov.uk/ca/index.htm
HM Customs and Excise	http://www.hmce.gov.uk/
The Inland Revenue	http://www.inlandrevenue.gov.uk
The Treasury	http://www.hm-treasury.gov.uk/

At each of these sites you will find information on the services provided by the relevant department, together with access to various leaflets on offer and press releases that have been issued. For most people the Inland Revenue web site will be of most relevance.

The Inland Revenue site is packed with information and is clearly laid out with plenty of question and answers to help you find the material you require. The personal taxation area will be the most relevant to the majority of people. You can to go straight to this by selecting a drop-down menu at the top of the page and choosing 'Tax for Individuals'. In this list you will see other areas of the web site which may be of interest, but if you want to go straight to the personal taxation site, go to:

http://www.inlandrevenue.gov.uk/p_index.htm

At the Tax for Individuals page you will find a list of each of the subsequent pages, together with brief details. For instance, there is a special section on self-assessment, and one on technical documentation. At each of these sub-pages you will find a host of material, including various Inland Revenue leaflets that give even more detail. It is also possible to download a whole range of tax forms, which saves having to go to the local tax office to collect them. If you do want to go, though, the site also has the address of your local office. Overall, this is a very clear and helpful site and although there is a great deal of text, the use of white space means it doesn't appear too unapproachable.

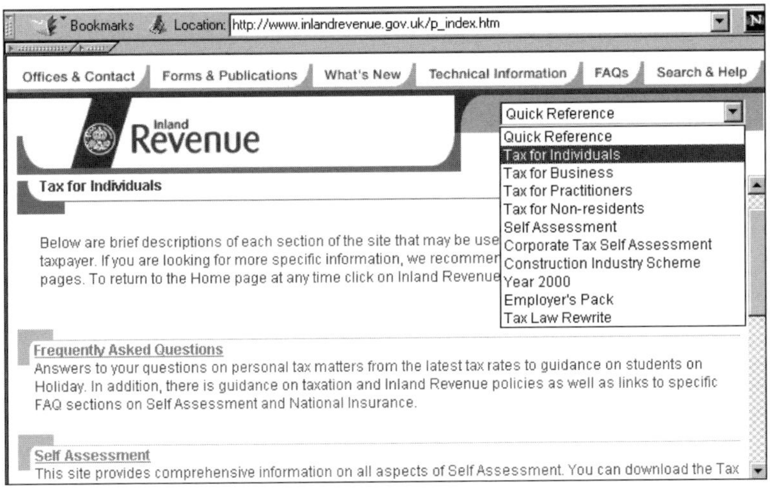

Fig. 90. This is the official Inland Revenue web site. They want to persuade tax-payers to start submitting their tax returns online.

▷ *Key benefits of the Inland Revenue site*

Comprehensive and authoritative coverage
Ability to download forms and leaflets

▷ *Disadvantages of the Inland Revenue site*

Large amount of text
Sometimes slow to respond

Finding information on tax from independent sources

There are many web sites that will help you save tax. Most of the general information sites mentioned in Chapter 2 include tips on saving tax. So too do the accountancy sites such as those run by Microsoft Money and Quicken. If you are prepared to pay a small subscription you can also get tax-saving information from the Consumers Association.

The Consumers Association
http://www.which.net
There is an in-depth guide to taxation in their members-only section. You can gain access to this material only if you subscribe, though a free 30-day trial is available. The site is crammed with useful information and is laid out in a clear and understandable way. It is well worth investigating.

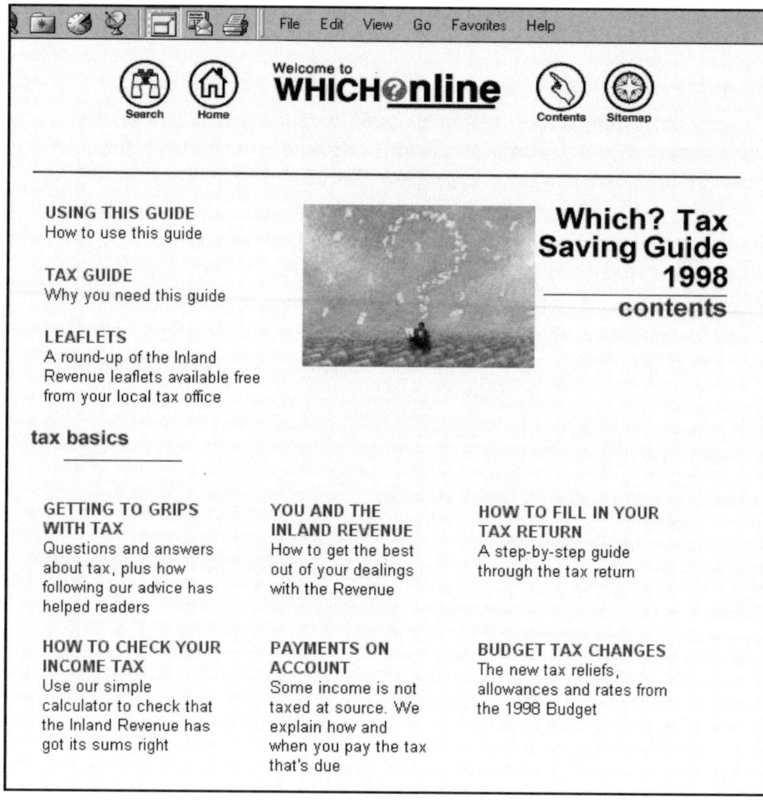

Fig. 91. Which? Online. This web site of the Consumers Association will help you sort out your tax affairs and keep you up to date with budget changes.

The Chartered Institute of Taxation
http://www.tax.org.uk/
This site, with lots of useful information, is run by the Chartered Institute of Taxation, the professional body of those working in the field of taxation. Here you can access 'beginner' level information or material for the expert. There is a great deal of useful background material, and a handy guide to selecting a professional tax adviser.

LineOne
http://www.lineone.net/clubs/money/tax/
The LineOne network also offers independent taxation information as part of its 'tax club'.

Using tax calculation software

The easiest way to make sure that you do not pay too much or too little tax is to get a computer program to work out your liabilities for you. There are several such programs available on the market and you can find out more about them via the internet. They include:

Microsoft Money
http://www.eu.microsoft.com/uk/products/prodref/699_ov.htm
This program has basic tax calculation facilities, but it can export all your financial information into a separate tax-calculating program if you want more detail. An advantage of Microsoft Money is that it includes a great deal of information and background on taxation.

QuickTax
http://www.intuit.co.uk/marketing/quicken/features.htm#quicktax
This page is part of Quicken Deluxe, a widely available and leading personal finance package. QuickTax works out your tax liability and completes your tax return for you! You can find out more about this product and even place an order online here.

Taxsoft
http://www.taxsoft.co.uk/
Taxsoft is another program that helps you complete your tax return, making sure you only pay what is due. Taxsoft provide other taxation software that may help if you have complicated financial affairs or if you are in business.

Which? TaxCalc
http://www.idp.co.uk/tcw98set.htm
The TaxCalc program will help analyse your tax position and complete your tax return. It also provides a host of tax-saving tips.

Financial Software
http://www.financialsoftware.co.uk/
This is a good place to come for specialist information on calculating capital gains tax. Remember, too, that all the leading accounts packages, such as Sage, QuickBooks and TAS Books, can help you calculate your tax liabilities.

Using online tax calculators

If you do not want to invest in computer software for tax calculation, you can do the job online. There are a number of sites offering internet-based tax computation. They include:

The Consumers Association
http://www.which.net
You will find an online tax calculator in the financial pages of the Which? site run by the Consumers Association. To access this calculator you will need to register with the association and pay a membership fee. However, you can get a 30-day trial.

MoneyWorld
http://www.moneyworld.co.uk/cgi-bin/taxcal98/tax_calc
This general information site has a tax calculator at this page. You enter your information and the results are shown on screen. It also has the latest budget information and some tax-saving tips.

Quicken
http://www.quicken.co.uk
Another online tax calculation service is offered free at the Quicken online tax centre. Here you will be able to enter your financial information and have an estimate of your tax position calculated.

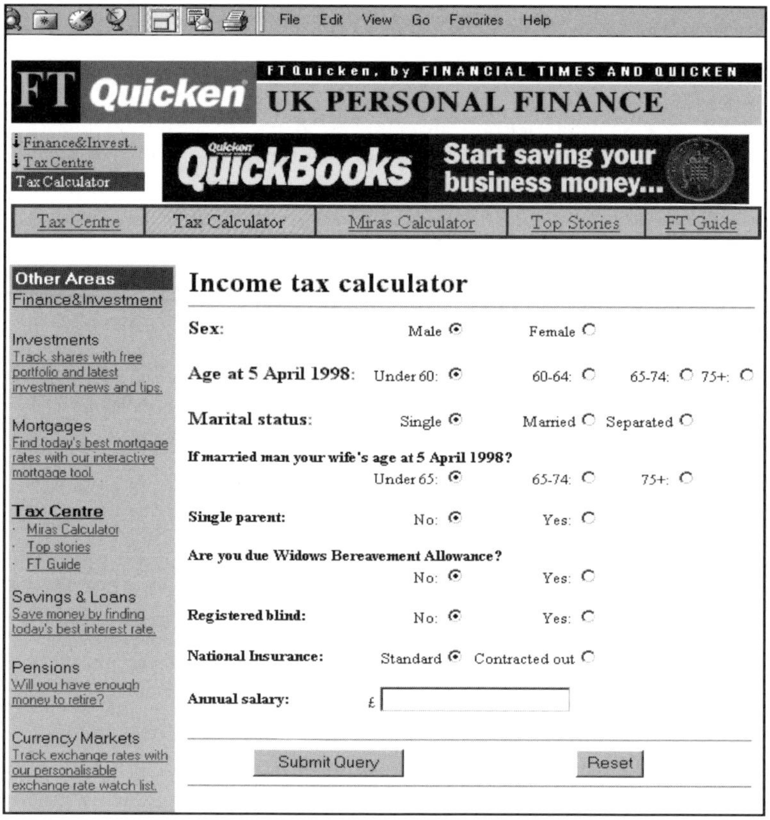

Fig. 92. The Quicken Tax Calculator aims to make it easy to calculate your tax liability.

Using accountants and tax professionals

There is an index of UK tax professionals at this web site:

UK Tax
http://www.uktax.demon.co.uk/uktaxpro/index.htm

Chartered Accountants
http://www.icaewfirms.co.uk/
You can also find a list of local accountants by visiting this site, which contains details of members of the Institute of Chartered Accountants in England & Wales.

Tax.org
http://www.tax.org.uk/
More useful advice on choosing a tax adviser can be found here.

Remember, whoever you choose to advise you, personal recommendation is usually best. If you don't know anyone who can recommend an accountant or an adviser, ask your local Chamber of Commerce. Also, make sure you ask for precise quotations of costs. Taxation advice is often the most expensive part of an accountant's work since it can take a great deal of time. Don't just accept the first local tax adviser – they all make different charges; find one that you think suits you best and at the right price. Most will charge an hourly rate, often between £50 and £100.

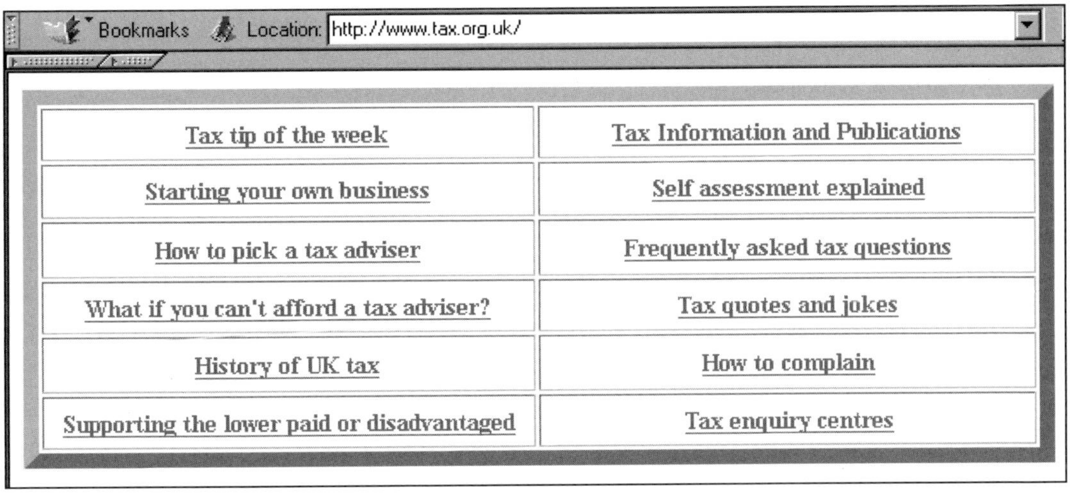

Fig. 93. Tax.org is the web site of the Chartered Institute of Taxation. This independent professional body offers authoritative guidance on all aspects of personal taxation.

Finding out about capital gains and inheritance tax

Times-Money
http://www.times-money.co.uk
A hefty 40 per cent capital gains tax (CGT) will become due for payment if you make substantial gains after selling a capital item (except your main home). Inheritance tax at the same rate will be levied on your estate after you die, assuming your assets are worth over a certain amount and are being transferred to someone other than your spouse. There is some excellent information on both these kinds of taxes available at the Times-Money site.

Finding out about council taxes

Every home in Britain is subject to council tax. This is levied at varied rates by different local authority councils and relates to the value of the property. Use your favourite search engine to locate your local council in order to check your tax liability. A quick guide to the rates of local council tax, and the chance to compare taxation in different parts of the United Kingdom, can be found at the following well-presented web site:

Up My Street
http://www.upmystreet.com/

Essential tips for tax planning on the internet

▷ Get as many tax saving tips as you can from the general financial sites and the specialist tax sites.

▷ Use an online calculator to arrive at a quick guide to your tax liability.

▷ Check the online calculations in a specialist tax calculation program.

▷ Keep up to date on taxation matters by downloading leaflets from the Inland Revenue's site.

Your tax checklist

- ▷ Make sure you pay the tax you are liable for, no more no less.
- ▷ Always check the calculations made by taxation authorities. They can make mistakes.
- ▷ Predict your tax liabilities each year and put into a deposit account any money you will need to pay, earning you some extra cash in the meantime.
- ▷ Make sure you use all your tax allowances and reliefs. Obtain specialist advice if you are not sure of your entitlement. What you save could more than cover the fees.
- ▷ Use as many tax-free methods of income generation as you can, such as ISAs and National Savings.
- ▷ Make sure you have a properly written will so that your heirs can avoid paying excessive inheritance tax.
- ▷ You can donate to charity and claim tax relief on your contribution. Check with your employer about the scheme called Give As You Earn.

References

1 *Social Trends 28*, HMSO, 1998, p97.

2 *Government Spending: The Facts*, Richard Cocks and Roger Bentley, Databooks, 1996.

Fig. 94. Fed up with crippling taxes and the rat race? If you want to drop out of the system, visit the web site of Escape Artist. This unmissable site contains an impressive 4,000 pages of information and guidance for expats and would-be tax exiles everywhere.

10 Considering all the angles

In this chapter we will explore:

- *online gambling*
- *swapping assets*
- *running an international business*
- *working online*
- *predicting the future*

So far, this book has looked at the traditional aspects of personal finance, though there have been one or two hints how the internet itself can help save you money. This final brief chapter covers a few of the other aspects of finance that are increasingly being dealt with across the internet. These include:

1. gambling
2. swapping assets
3. running an international business
4. working via the internet

Each of these, combined with the traditional financial transactions now being conducted over the internet, are laying the foundations for a whole new way of earning money, making the most of it and using it. Before too long, you will be able to work online from home, either in your own business, or for someone else; that business is likely to be new, dynamic and pioneering and setting tough competition for the traditional operators who will find it difficult to survive against the technologically aware youngsters behind such firms; your earnings will be paid into your online bank account and you will do much of your shopping through the internet; you won't have a car, because you won't need one to get to work; you'll meet people in online pubs (yes they do exist) and visit the horse races online and even place your bets through your computer, with your winnings automatically going into your internet bank account; as soon as you have amassed a valuable stamp collection, you'll find a more valuable book collection via the internet and swap, thus improving your overall financial picture. Does this sound strange or utopian? Well, no, this is the real world. You can do all of this, now. Let's take a look at some of these internet money-making schemes so that you can take a glimpse at what could well be your own future.

Gambling online

Interbet
http://www.inter-bet.com/
If you want, you can have a flutter online, and maybe make a profit. One of the first online gambling services was Interbet, where you can gamble on a wide range of sporting events world wide – you simply

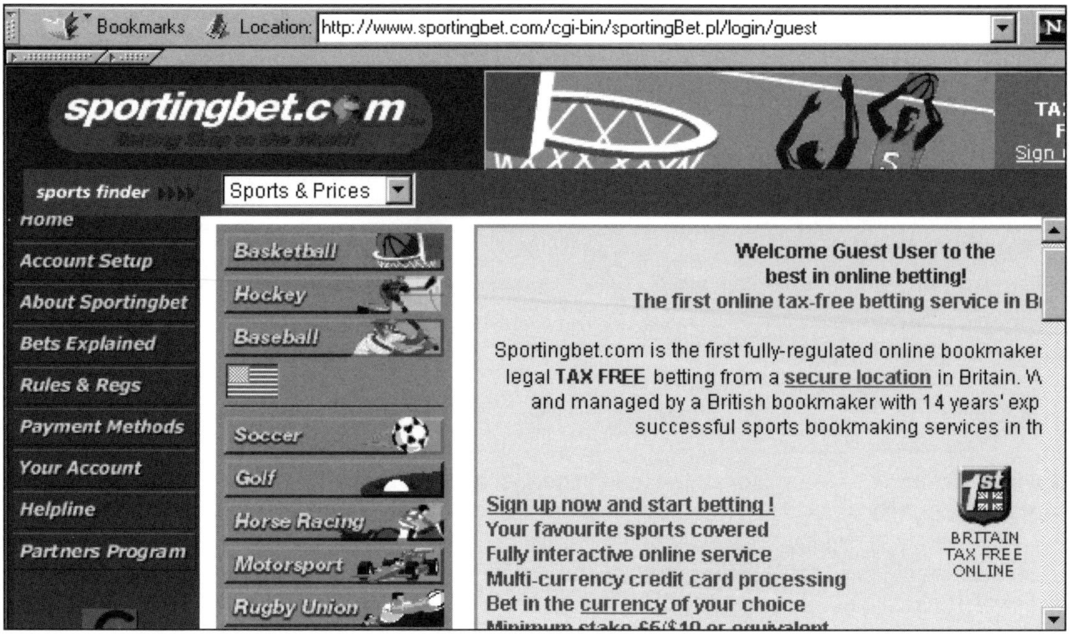

Fig. 95. Sportingbet says it is the first online tax-free betting service in the UK. It is an example of a cyber company which reduces its costs by being based offshore in Alderney. It supports a campaign for keeping Britain Tax-Free Online.

register for the service and bet using your credit card. There are some other online bookmakers:

Sportingbet	http://www.sportingbet.com/
Sports World	http://www.betting-syndicates.co.uk/
UK Betting	http://www.ukbetting.com/

With all these services you open an account using a credit card and you can then bet on a wide range of sporting events. However, you don't have to limit yourself to betting on the horses. There are plenty of other ways of gambling online. You can find a list of links to gambling and casino sites at these web sites:

Gambling Links	http://www.gambling-links.com/
Casino Links	http://www.casinolinks.com/

There are even online lotteries to explore:

Irish Lottery	http://www.irish-lottery.com/
Lottery	http://www.lottery.com/
Plus Lotto	http://www.pluslotto.com/
World Lotto 2000	http://www.worldlotto2000.com/

If you want to improve your chances of winning the UK National Lottery you can find a way of selecting your numbers at:

http://www.lottogenie.com/

Swapping assets

The internet is littered with sites where you can barter various items, from computer games to old football programmes. You might want to use your favourite search engine to find exactly what you are looking for. Remember, though, that you will need to look for 'swop' as well as 'swap'. Be prepared for a shock, though: your search is likely to come up with pages for wife-swapping as well! If you don't want to risk this, there is a central site you can visit:

Swap & Shop
http://swapandshop.com/

Fig. 96. Swap & Shop offers you the chance to buy, trade and bid at online auctions. Sites like this are becoming hugely popular with people all over the world.

Running an international business

Because anyone in the world can access a web site, you can reach potential customers worldwide. This is opening up whole new areas of business that were unthought of until the advent of the internet. For instance, you could set up a specialist property agency that provides a home-finding service to people emigrating to the UK. You offer a service over the internet and they complete a form with all their details, offering you their credit card number for payment. You find them some suitable properties and email the details to them. They choose and you introduce them to the seller or selling agents. Without the internet you would have needed staff, probably an office in the USA, and expensive advertising and brochures to attract potential clients. With the internet you can keep your costs down and make more money.

The internet also allows you to experiment. For the price of a web domain, you can set up shop and see what happens. If you don't get any takers, or you don't make a great deal of cash, you can easily close down. You will have lost a few hundred pounds at the most. Traditionally, people have been put off starting a business because of the large amount of capital required. The internet dispenses with the need for much of the initial outlay, thus making setting up business a realistic proposition for many people. Indeed, you could run a profitable international business part-time, perhaps in the evenings or at the weekend

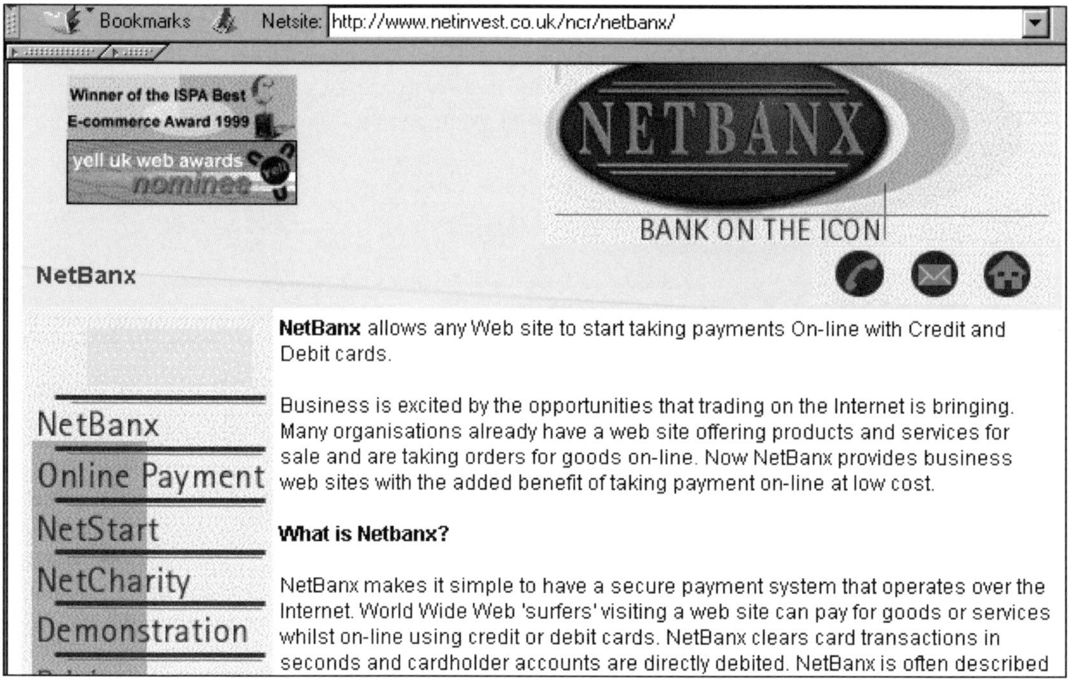

Fig. 97. Is your UK clearing bank helping you put your business online cheaply and fast? If not, NetBanx offers a streamlined service for businesses to accept credit and debit cards online.

You can arrange for people to pay you with a credit card without having to become a credit card 'merchant'. Indeed, you'd be unlikely to gain merchant status with the banks unless you could produce an in-depth business plan with a three-year cash flow forecast. If your proposed internet business is a 'suck it and see' idea, you wouldn't get the means of accepting payments from around the world. Happily a new internet business has come to the rescue:

NetBanx
http://www.netbanx.com
NetBanx will accept the credit card payment on your behalf and then pay you once they receive payment from the credit card company.

Working online

Imagine, for a moment, that you work for a bank. You are a financial adviser providing up-to-date information on your company's products and services to a wide range of personal customers. You usually visit them in their home to discuss their requirements. The only reason you go to the office is to deal with the paperwork. Working online you'd be able to do so much more. You would be able to have all the paperwork dealt with automatically, for example using online forms. These could be sent back to headquarters using state-of-the-art encryption for security purposes. The head office could also email you the latest brochures, pricing structure and other information, as well as memos and other communications. Working online you would also be able to communicate more easily with customers using email, even video conferencing. You would find life less stressful as your job involves fewer hours on the road. Your company would reduce its costs and be able to dispense with expensive office space. If you were lucky, they may even pass on some of their savings to you in bonuses!

Working online has attractions for both employer and employee. More and more people are working online nowadays, and experience much less stress since they can be more flexible about how, where and when the work is done. There is even an online organisation you can join:

The Association of Online Professionals
http://www.aop.org/

Predicting the future

Throughout this book we have indicated what is already possible and what might be coming our way. The internet is growing so rapidly, and so many new ways of using it are being developed, that it is hard to say what will happen in years to come. The internet is changing the world dramatically. It is having dramatic effects on society in ways that no one could have foreseen even five years ago. The internet is sure to continue growing and will become as commonplace as the telephone is now – the phone in the hall is an everyday piece of technology for everyone from eight to eighty, yet thirty years ago many homes didn't have a telephone, relying instead on the local call-box. Now we have extensions in the bedroom and individual ringing patterns for different members of the family, and mobile phones everywhere.

The humble phone has become accepted as normal, and so too will the internet; yet, because it can do so much more than the phone, it is certain to have a much greater impact. In the world of finance, individuals are already regaining control from institutions – the internet is cutting out the middleman everywhere: more and more customers and suppliers are getting in direct touch with each other. We are seeing big business being seriously threatened by people working from home, and we are seeing money being replaced by electronic cash.

A huge financial revolution is under way that will change all our lives – and that revolution is around the corner. Much of what we can see in the future is already happening. So don't be surprised if you soon discover that you are working from home, using a computer as your main communications tool rather than a telephone. You will be paid in a new international currency of electronic funds paid directly into your internet bank account. That account – which could exist anywhere in the world – will be securely run by a new, lean, dynamic bank that has shaken off the competition of the major institutions, now long consigned to the scrap heap of history. You will be routinely doing your shopping online and investing your electronic funds online.

Taxes, too, will change out of all recognition owing to increasing globalisation and the rapid erosion of traditional national boundaries. It is likely that tax burdens will start to fall as it becomes increasingly difficult for governments to prove where transactions are taking place in cyberspace. The internet is heralding an extraordinary new 'borderless world'. Personal and business finances are going to change beyond all recognition, and sooner rather than later. And it's all coming about as a result of this extraordinary and explosive new technology – the internet.

Appendix: What you need to get on the internet

In this chapter we will explore:

- *hardware requirements*
- *processor*
- *memory*
- *storage space*
- *fast disks*
- *monitor*
- *modem*
- *software requirements*
- *internet service provider*
- *telephone line*
- *BT highway and ISDN*
- *other information*

This book assumes that you already have the necessary equipment to gain access to the Internet. If not, this brief guide will help you set things up so that you can enjoy the benefits of all the sites mentioned in this book. For a complete guide you can refer to another of my books on the internet, *Using the Internet*, by Graham Jones, published by How To Books Ltd, 3rd edition, 1999.

Hardware requirements

To gain access to the internet you will need a computer. For access to the full benefits of financial sites you will need a standard IBM compatible personal computer (PC). An Apple Macintosh can be used to access the internet, but few of the financial or accounting programs that work with the information you can gain from the world wide web work on the Macintosh. For instance, none of the direct access online banking services mentioned in this book is available for the Macintosh.

Your PC should be the most expensive you can afford. Don't try and skimp on this. Computers are almost always falling in price. For example, the cost of a mid-range machine fell by 50% in the six months from September 1998 to February 1999.[1] On the whole, you always get much more for your money each year. Hence, there is no 'right time' to buy. If you wait, you will get more for your money, but the month after you buy, you could have got more again. No matter when you buy a computer, the next month will always bring a better deal. You simply have to accept that and buy the most expensive you can afford at the time.

Essentially what you should be buying is:

- ▷ the fastest processor you can afford
- ▷ the largest amount of memory you can afford
- ▷ the greatest amount of disk storage space you can afford
- ▷ the fastest disks you can afford
- ▷ the biggest monitor (screen) you can afford
- ▷ the fastest modem you can afford.

In other words, go for the biggest and the fastest of everything and you won't go far wrong.

Processor

The processor is the heart of your computer and performs all the necessary work to make your machine do what you want it to do. There is a wide range of available processors, including those from Intel and from AMD. The choice is not that important for most users, but speed is. These days it would be unwise to opt for a processor that runs at anything less than 350MHz.

Memory

The memory capacity of your computer will be quoted in megabytes. Most computers these days are sold with 32Mb or 64Mb as standard. Ideally, you should upgrade these minimum amounts to 128Mb or more. The extra cost will be repaid many times over in greater functionality and reduced chances of computer failure (crashes).

Storage space

The storage space on your computer will be quoted in terms of the size of a hard disk. This will be measured in gigabytes (one gigabyte is a thousand megabytes). Go for the maximum you can get. Don't be fooled into thinking you won't use the space; you can never have enough computer storage space! The new software being developed today devours ever more and more hard disk space.

Fast disks

The disks that require fast access times are the hard disk and the CD-ROM player. Your hard disk should have a fast access time. If you are buying an off-the-shelf computer you should ask for an upgrade to a fast access time hard disk. This will improve your work on the internet. Also, make sure your CD-ROM player is the fastest you can get. The speeds are quoted as '24x' or '32x' for instance. Simply don't accept access speeds for CD-ROMs less than 24x. Get an upgrade if necessary since this will allow you to install software, such as accounts packages, much more quickly. If possible get a fast CD Writer/Re-Writer which will allow you to make your own CD-ROMs as backups – this could be quite useful if you end up downloading a great deal of information from the world wide web.

Equipment and software

Monitor

The monitor or screen is what you will stare at when you access the internet. Make sure it is large. Most computers these days come with a 15-inch monitor (as measured diagonally). However, this is quite limiting and upgrading to 17 or 19-inch monitors will help considerably. Another important aspect of a monitor is its 'refresh' rate – the speed at which it updates the picture. The faster the refresh rate, the better. When choosing a monitor you should look for speeds of 85MHz and upwards.

Modem

Your modem connects your computer via the telephone line to the internet. To get the maximum benefit from the internet, get the fastest modem you can afford. They are quoted in speeds of 'Kbps' (kilobits per second), or more simply 'K'. Many computers are sold with internal modems; if this is the case, make sure you upgrade to a 56K modem. Some modems are quoted as being V90 compatible. A V90 will help boost your connection to the internet, but only if the computer that you connect to at the other end of your phone line is also V90 compatible. This means that V90 is not particularly important, though if you can afford such a modem, it will help improve reliability.

Software requirements

Browsers
In order to 'surf' the world wide web you will need some 'browser' software. The two main browser programs are:

- ▷ Microsoft Internet Explorer
- ▷ Netscape Communicator

Both are widely supplied free of charge, though add-on services will cost. The usual places to obtain the software are:

1. cover-mounted disks on computer magazines
2. internet service providers (ISPs)
3. downloaded direct from the web sites of Microsoft or Netscape

Email software
You may also want separate email software since the facilities available in the web browser programs are limited. Popular email 'clients', as such programs are called, include:

Eudora	http://www.eudora.com/
Outlook Express	http://www.microsoft.com/ie/ie40/oe/?/ie/ie40/oe/main.htm
Pegasus Mail	http://www.pegasus.usa.com/

These programs are available via the web, as above, or from PC retailers.

Other software
You may also want an accounts program so that you can integrate your

banking details with your financial information. The banks support a range of accounts packages, including:

Microsoft Money http://microsoft.com/money/
Quicken http://www.quicken.co.uk
Sage http://www.sage.com/home/

Each of these programs can be purchased by mail order or from PC retailers. You can get more information on each program from their following web sites as shown above.

Internet service provider

In addition to the hardware and software you will need an internet service provider (ISP). This is the company that provides you with access to all the computers on the internet. Essentially they provide you with a gateway to the world wide web or email or usenet. There is a wide range of ISPs available – more than 200 in the UK and more than 10,000 worldwide. Some charge (such as America OnLine and CompuServe), but a growing number of others are free (such as FreeServe and Virgin Net). They are all advertised in popular internet magazines such as:

Internet
Internet Business
Net

These magazines list full details of each provider. You should choose a provider that has the following attributes:

- ▷ local call rate access
- ▷ full access to the world wide web and usenet
- ▷ email facilities
- ▷ 56K access
- ▷ a high number of modems to user ratio
- ▷ 24 hour technical support
- ▷ membership of the Internet Service Providers Association (http://www.ispa.org.uk/)

You can then decide whether to use someone who charges or provides free access.

Benefits of charged services	*Benefits of free access*
Free technical support	No access charges
Flexible email options	Large companies (such as Dixons with Freeserve) behind the service
Large amount of your own web space	
Fewer users, so easier access	

Some of the problems of free services include:

(a) payment for technical support (which could be 50p or £1 a minute)
(b) intrusive advertising on home web pages
(c) addition to a mailing list as a requirement of sign-up

Most people decide either to put up with these restrictions for free access, or are prepared to pay to avoid these restrictions. Choose your internet service provider after you have carefully considered all the different ways in which you are likely to want to use the internet, how much technical support you might need, and so on. You can also try out most service providers using 30-day free access from cover-mounted disks on PC and internet magazines. However, you will need to enter your credit card details; you will then be charged if you do not end the 30-day trial in writing. So, it is important to note the date you started the trial and then cancel it three weeks later if you are unhappy with the service you receive.

▷ *Tip* – If you want to try a completely free service, you can get a disk from any branch of Dixons or PC World for the company's 'Freeserve' ISP. Freeserve has recently overtaken America OnLine as the top internet access provider in the UK, with more than a million users. Other retailers seeking to compete include Tesco and WH Smith.

Telephone line

You will need a telephone line to access the internet. Ideally, have a separate line installed. This has two advantages:

1. You can access the internet whenever you want, without waiting for other members of the family to hang up and without interfering with their use of the telephone.

2. You can get your telephone line supplier to alter the 'gain' of the line so that it is set up for data, rather than voice. This improves connection speeds and reduces likely problems.

You can get telephone lines from:

British Telecom
Eurobell (in certain regions)
Cable and Wireless
Cable TV operators

You do not need to use your existing supplier of telephone lines if you can get a better deal for internet access lines. For instance, some cable operators provide you with a line and access to the internet for a single charge.

BT Highway and ISDN

You can get even faster access to the internet using BT Highway or ISDN lines (which you can get from a range of suppliers other than British Telecom). These services provide internet access at faster rates – up to almost three times faster than the fastest modem. However, the lines cost more to install, they have different line rental structures and you will need to replace your modem with another device specifically produced for ISDN lines, called a 'terminal adapter'. These are available from PC retailers and cost about the same as a modem, for basic models. If you use the internet a great deal – more than a few times a week – going the ISDN route could be useful.

Other information

You can gather a host of information on what you need for internet access from the popular PC and internet magazines. Also, you might have an 'internet café' locally which can provide information and allow you to test out the internet for yourself. Internet cafés are just what they seem – cafés that provide you with a coffee and a sandwich, but they also have computers that are connected to the internet. You can have a coffee, get a bite to eat and check your finances all at the same time. This is a very effective way of gaining occasional internet access or to try out what is available, typically for around £5 an hour. The staff are also very helpful in most internet cafés and can give you advice on what equipment and software to buy. For an internet café near you look up:

'Internet Providers and Services' in *Yellow Pages*
'Internet Services' in your *Thomson Local* directory

The future

Access to the internet is increasing all the time. You can already buy television set-top boxes to access the internet on your TV screen – avoiding the need to buy a computer. Digital television has the capability to allow access to the internet, but this is not a priority for the providers of digital services, so it will be a while before this becomes commonplace. Internet services, though, are being added to telephone technology with the use of 'web phones' and email on mobile phones. This is already established in the USA and set to become popular in Europe. If you wish to wait for new technology to deliver your ideal solution, you can be sure that it will not be too far into the future.

The benefits of access to the internet now are already so great that using a standard computer and accepting the limitations of the current technology is still the best way to go. You will gain so much control over your finances that you'll wonder how you ever managed before!

Reference

1 *See* http://www.zdnet.co.uk/pcdir/content/1999/marketwatch/desktops_price.html

Further Information

Internet Access

Call the following numbers for information on accessing the internet:

AOL	0800 376 5432	Global Internet	0870 909 8042
BT Internet	0800 800 001	LineOne	0845 601 0374
ClaraNet	0845 355 1000	Netcom	0800 980 9116
CompuServe	0870 600 0806	NetDirect	0800 731 3311
Demon Internet	020 8371 1234	Netkonekt	020 7345 7777
EasyNet	0800 053 0533	UUNet	0500 567 000
Force9	0800 073 7880	Virgin Net	0500 558 800
Free Online	0870 706 0510	X-Stream	0870 730 6466
Freeserve	0990 500 049		

Internet magazines

You can get the following magazines at your local newsagent: *.Net, Internet, Internet Access, Internet Business* and *Internet Works.*

Useful books

The following books should help you with the internet or with financial matters:

A-Z of Investment, Caroline Sefton, Pitman Publishing, 1996.
Banking and Finance on the Internet, Ed: Mary J Cronin, John Wiley & Sons, 1998.
Doing Business on the Internet, Graham Jones, How To Books, 1998.
Find It on the Internet, Kye Valongo, Internet Handbooks, 1999
Going Digital, The Economist, Profile Books, 1998.
Homes and Property on the Internet, Philip Harrison, Internet Handbooks, 1999.
How to Choose Stockmarket Winners, Raymond Caley, Piatkus, 1994.
Moneywise Guide to Planning Your Finances, Isabel Berwick and Caroline Laws, Prentice Hall Europe, 1998.
Net Future, Chuck Martin, McGraw Hill, 1999.
The Armchair Investor, Bernice Cohen, Orion Books, 1997.
Using the Internet, Graham Jones, How To Books, 3rd edition, 1999.

Correspondence course

If you want more detail about personal finances, there is a long-established correspondence course available called 'Successful Personal Investing'. You can find out more from: Independent Research Service, 5-7 Bridge Street, Abingdon, Oxfordshire OX14 3HN.

Internet Handbooks

Check out the latest titles in the Internet Handbooks series at:

http://www.internet-handbooks.co.uk

Glossary of internet terms

Access provider – The company that provides your access to the internet. This may be an independent provider or a large international organisation such as AOL or CompuServe. Sometimes also called a Service Provider.

Adobe Acrobat – A program that allows documents to be opened on a computer even if you do not have the program that created them.

Address book – A directory in a web browser where you can store people's email addresses. This saves having to type them out each time you want to email someone.

AltaVista – A popular internet search engine used to find pages relating to specific keywords entered.

AOL – America Online, the world's biggest internet service provider, with more than fifteen million subscribers. It has given away hundreds of thousands of free CDs with the popular computer magazines to build its customer base.

Agent – This is a search tool that acts on your behalf to find information throughout the internet. An agent is usually a separate programme, such as WebFerret.

Ask Jeeves – A popular internet search engine. Rather than just typing in a few key words for your search, you can type in a whole question or instruction, such as 'Find me everything about online investment.'

Attachment – A file sent with an email message. The attached file may be a word-processed document, a database, spreadsheet, graphic, or even a sound or video file. For example you could email someone birthday greetings, and attach a sound track, or photograph of yourself.

Bandwidth – The width of the electronic highway that gives you access to the internet. The higher the bandwidth, the wider this highway, and the faster the traffic can flow.

Banner ad – This is a band of text and graphics, usually situated at the top of a web page. A banner acts like a title, telling the user what the content of the page is about. It invites the visitor to click on it to visit that site.

Barclaycoin – A form of electronic cash from Barclays Bank.

Baud rate – The data transmission speed of a modem, measured in bps (bits per second).

BBS – Bulletin board service.

Blue Ribbon Campaign – A widely supported campaign supporting free speech and opposing censorship of the internet by national governments or other agencies.

Bookmark – A file of URLs of your favourite internet sites. Bookmarks are very easily created by bookmarking (mouse-clicking) any internet page you like the look of.

Boolean search – A search in which you type in words such as AND and OR to refine your search. The words are called 'Boolean operators'. The concept is named after George Boole, a nineteenth century English mathematician.

Glossary

Browser – This is the program that you use to access the world wide web. The two most common browsers are Microsoft Internet Explorer and its rival Netscape Communicator.

Bulletin board – A computer service that provides an email service and a file archive.

Cache – A file storage area on a computer. Your web browser will normally cache (copy to your hard drive) each web page you visit. When you revisit that page on the web, you may in fact be looking at the page originally cached on your computer. To be sure you are viewing the current page, press **reload** or **refresh** on your browser toolbar. You can empty your cache from time to time, and the computer will do so automatically whenever the cache is full.

Certificate – A computer file that identifies a person or organisation on the internet.

Client – This is the term given to the program that you use to access the internet. Your web browser is a web client; your email program is an email client.

Closed areas – Those areas of a web site that only registered users can enter.

Community – The internet is often described as a net community. This refers to the fact that many people like the feeling of belonging to a group of like minded individuals.

Compression – Computer files can be electronically compressed, so that they can be uploaded or downloaded more quickly across the internet, saving time and money. If an image file is compressed too much, there may be a loss of quality.

Crash – What happens when a computer program malfunctions. The operating system of your PC may perform incorrectly or come to a complete stop ('freeze'), forcing you to shut down and restart. A crash is more likely to happen when you have several windows open on screen and several software programs running simultaneously.

Credit scoring – When you apply for a loan or a credit card, information about you and your financial status is given a score. This helps financial institutions quickly assess the level of risk they are taking on.

Cybercash – This is a trademark, but is also often used as a broad term to describe the use of small payments made over the internet using a new form of electronic account that is loaded up with cash. You can send this money to the companies offering such cash facilities by cheque, or by credit card.

Cyberspace – Popular term for the intangible 'place' where you go to surf – the ethereal and borderless world of computers and telecommunications on the internet.

Deja – An online community providing news and information on a host of topics.

Dial in account – This allows you to connect your computer to your internet provider's computer remotely.

Digicash – A brand of electronic cash (see also Cybercash).

Digital – Based on the two binary digits, 1 and 0. The operation of all computers is based on this amazingly simple concept. All forms of information are capable of being digitalised – numbers, words, sounds and images – and then transmitted over the internet.

Digital certificate – A computer file that confirms you are who you say you are, when dealing or buying online.

Domain – A domain is a specific area on the internet and identifies to the computers on the rest of the internet where to access particular information. The domain for Internet Handbooks for instance is: www.internet-handbooks.co.uk

Download – You 'download' something by copying it from one computer on the internet to your own computer. You perform this task by clicking on a button that links you to the appropriate file. It is an automatic process, except you have to accept the download and give it a file name.

E-cash – See cybercash.

Email – Electronic mail – anything you send from your computer to another computer using your 'email client' program (such as Eudora or Microsoft Outlook).

Encryption – Encoding. Email and other data can easily be encrypted using the freely available software PGP and similar programs. Modern encryption is so powerful that to all intents and purposes it is uncrackable.

Excite

A popular internet directory and search engine used to find pages relating to specific keywords which you enter. See also Yahoo!.

E-zines – Magazines and newsletters published on the internet.

FAQ – Frequently Asked Questions. You will see 'FAQ' everywhere you go on the internet. If you are ever doubtful about anything check the FAQ page, if the site has one, and you will find the answers to your queries.

Favorites – The rather coy term for **bookmarks** used by Internet Explorer, and by America Online.

File – A file is a body of data such as a word-processed document, a spreadsheet, a database file, a graphics file, video or sound file.

Firewall – A firewall is special software designed to stop the flow of certain files into and out of a computer network.

Form – A means of collecting data on web pages, using text boxes and buttons.

Forums – These are similar to usenet groups and allow you to read, post and reply to messages.

Frames – A web design feature in which web pages can be divided into several areas or panels, each containing separate information. A typical set of frames in a page includes an index frame (with navigation links), a banner frame (for a heading), and a body frame (for text matter).

FTP – File transfer protocol – the method the internet uses to send files back and forth between computers. Your browser will automatically select this method, for instance, when you want to download your bank statements to reconcile your accounts.

Hacker – Someone who makes or seeks to make an unauthorised entry into someone else's computer system or network.

History list – A record of visited web pages. Your browser probably includes a history list. It is a handy way of revisiting sites whose addresses you have forgotten to bookmark – just click on the item you want in the history list. You can normally delete all or part of the history list in your browser.

Hits – The number of times a web site has been visited.

Host – A host is the computer where a particular file or domain is present.

HotBot – This is a popular internet search engine used to find pages relating to any keywords you decide to enter. 'Bot' is short for robot. In internet terms it means a piece of software that performs a task on the internet, such as searching.

Hot spots – Areas of a web page, usually in a graphic, that can be clicked on to lead to another page.

HTML – This is the computer language used to create pages on the world wide web – hyper text markup language.

Infoseek – One of the leading internet search engines.

Internet – This is the broad term for the fast-expanding network of global computers that can access each other in a standard way. If you have a modem on your computer, you too are part of the internet. The term encompasses email, web pages, internet chat, newsgroups, gopher and telnet, rather as the term 'the printed word' for example refers to books, magazines, newspapers, catalogues, leaflets and posters. The 'internet' does not exist in one place or under one authority any more than 'the printed word' does.

Internet Explorer – The world's most popular browser software, a product of MicroSoft and keen rival to Netscape (recently taken over by America Online).

Internet service provider – ISPs are commercial, educational or official organisations which offer internet access to users. Commercial ISPs usually have a monthly fixed charge. Services typically include access to the world wide web, electronic mail, access to newsgroups, as well as a number of other services such as news, chat, and entertainment.

ISDN– Integrated Services Digital Network. A high speed telephone network that can send computer data from the internet to your PC faster than a normal telephone line.

Links – Many web sites have 'links'. These are buttons you can click on with your mouse to get to another site on the world wide web.

Log on – You may be asked to 'log on' to certain sites and particular pages. You will normally need to enter your name and a password.

Log on/log off – To access/leave a network. In the early days of computing this literally involved making a record in a log book.

Lurk – The slang term used to describe reading a newsgroup's messages without actually taking part in that newsgroup. Despite the connotations of the word, it is a perfectly respectable activity on the internet.

Mail server – A remote computer that enables you to send and receive emails. Your internet access provider will usually act as your mail server.

Mailing list – An electronic facility of the internet. You can subscribe to any number of mailing lists on the internet: there are tens of thousands of them catering for every conceivable interest. Any new information that might be of interest to you is then downloaded to your PC automatically, for example every day or every week. A good place to find them is Liszt (http://www.liszt.com). You can normally quit a mailing list by sending an email message to request removal. You can of course have your own conventional mailing list of customers.

Mall (or I-mall) – An online shopping centre: a collection of online traders.

Marquee – A moving ('scrolling') line of text on a web site, often used for eye-catching advertising purposes.

Microcash – Small payments made on the internet (see also Barclaycoin).

Millennium compliant – Anything that is 'millennium compliant' will work in the year 2000 (and up to the year 2038). Some computers will not operate after the year 2000 due to programming problems.

Modem – The word is short for MOdulator/DEModulator. It is an internal or external piece of hardware plugged into your PC. It links into a standard phone socket, giving you access to the internet.

Navigate – To click on the hyperlinks on a web site in order to move to other web pages or internet sites.

Net – A slang term for the internet. In the same way, the world wide web is often just called the web.

Netiquette – Popular term for the unofficial rules and language used to keep electronic communication in an acceptably polite form.

Netscape – After Internet Explorer, Netscape is the most popular browser software available for surfing the internet. An excellent browser, Netscape has suffered in the wake of the rise of Microsoft's Internet Explorer, mainly because of the success of Microsoft in getting it installed on most new PCs. Netscape has recently been taken over by America Online for $4 billion.

Newsgroup – A newsgroup is a collection of messages, usually unedited and not checked by anyone. Messages can be placed within the newsgroup by anyone including you. Newsgroups are an endless source of information, gossip and ideas. The 30,000-plus newsgroups are collectively referred to as usenet.

News reader – A type of software that enables you to search, read, post and manage messages in a newsgroup.

News server – A remote computer (e.g. your internet service provider) that enables you to access newsgroups.

Online – Whenever you connect to the internet you are technically 'online'. However, many people now refer to 'online' banking as direct connection to the bank's computer, rather than via the internet.

Password – Your secret code word that will let you enter certain sites. You will need a password to conduct online banking transactions, for example.

PoP – Point of Presence. This refers to the number of local-dial telephone numbers available from your ISP. If your ISP does not have a local access number or POP, then don't sign up – your telephone bill will rocket. All the big ISPs have local numbers all over the UK.

Portal site – Portal means gateway. A portal site is one loaded into your web browser as soon as you connect to the internet. It could for example be the front page of your internet service provider such as AOL, Demon or Virgin Net. Or you can set your browser to make it some other front page, for example a search engine such as Yahoo!, or even your own front page.

Post, to – The common term used for sending ('posting') messages to a newsgroup. Posting messages is very like sending emails.

Protocol – Technical term for the method by which computers communicate, for example http (hyper text transfer protocol) or ftp (file transfer protocol). It's not something to worry about in ordinary life.

Refresh, reload – You can refresh or reload a page if it doesn't appear properly first time, or if you want to get the most up-to-date version. Essentially your computer gets the most recent version of the page you are viewing.

Register – You may have to give your name, personal details and financial information to some sites before you can continue to use the pages. This is done so that site owners can produce a mailing list to offer you products and services. It is also done to reduce use of the site by people who are not really interested. An additional benefit of registering is that it can help increase security, since the owners of the site know details of everyone using it.

Registered user – Someone who has filled out an online form and then been granted special access to restricted areas of a web site. Access is then usually obtained by entering a password and user name.

Search engine – A piece of software that allows you to access information by typing in any key words of your choice. There are lots of free search engines on the internet – Yahoo!, AltaVista, Infoseek, Excite, Ask Jeeves, Lycos and Webcrawler to name but a few. Many bigger web sites have their own search engines to help you find what you are looking for on their sites.

Secure servers – The hardware and software provided so that people can use their credit cards and leave other details without the risk of others seeing them online.

Secure sockets layer (SSL) – You will see 'SSL' whenever shopping or conducting financial transactions. It means your data is coded and is almost impossible for hackers to get at.

Secure transactions – Transactions that are coded to avoid hacking (see **Secure sockets layer**).

Server – A server is a computer that stores material for access by people using the internet.

Service provider – See access provider.

Shareware – Software that, although free, comes with a moral obligation to send a small donation to the author should you continue use of the software after a trial period – usually between 30 and 90 days. A vast amount of shareware is now available on the internet.

Shockwave – A popular piece of software produced by Macromedia, which enables you to view animations and other special effects on web sites. You can download it free and in a few minutes from Macromedia's web site.

Signature file – This is a computer file in which you can place your address details, and which you can add to email and newsgroup messages. You only need to create a signature file once and you can then append it to your emails as often as you like.

Spam – The popular term for electronic junk mail, i.e. unsolicited and unwelcome email messages sent across the internet. There are various forms of spam-busting software which you can now obtain to filter out unwanted messages.

Subscribe – Term for accessing a newsgroup in order to read and post messages in the newsgroup. There is no charge, and you can subscribe, unsubscribe and resubscribe at any time at the click of your mouse.

Surfing – The act of browsing the internet, especially following trails of links on pages on the world wide web.

TCP/IP – Transmission Control Protocol/Internet Protocol, the essential technology of the internet. It's not normally something you need worry about.

Thread – An ongoing topic in a usenet newsgroup or mailing list discussion. The term refers to the original message on a particular topic, and all the replies and other messages which spin off from it. With news reading software, you can easily 'view thread' and read these messages in a convenient batch.

UNIX – This is an operating system that has been in use for many years, and still is used in many larger systems. Most ISPs use this operating system.

URL – Uniform Resource Locator – the address of each internet page. For instance the URL of Internet Handbooks is:

http://www.internet-handbooks.co.uk

Usenet – The collection of more than 30,000 active newsgroups that make up a substantial part of the internet.

User name, user ID – Any name you use to enter certain parts of the internet, including your service provider.

Virus – A piece of computer code that can cause damage to any other piece of computer code.

Wallet – An electronic purse that you can fill up with e-cash.

Webcrawler – A popular internet search engine used to find pages relating to specific keywords entered.

Webmaster – The person who runs a particular web site.

Windows – The ubiquitous operating system for personal computers, developed by Bill Gates and the Microsoft Corporation. The Windows 3.1 version was followed by Windows 95 and, most recently, Windows 98.

WWW – The world wide web has become the most popular part of the internet, made up of often highly designed pages with numerous hyperlinks to other pages. The world wide web is the part of the internet on which all financial institutions and other business organisations make their pages available.

Yahoo! – Probably the world's most popular internet directory and search engine.

Zip/unzip – Many files that you download from the internet will be in compressed format, especially if they are large files. This is to make them quicker to download. These files are said to be zipped or compressed. Unzipping these compressed files generally refers to the process of returning them to their original size on receipt. Zip files have the extension '.zip' and are created (and unzipped) using WinZip or a similar popular software package.

Site index

This section includes a handy guide to the following types of web site:

- *general financial information*
- *credit and loans*
- *home buying and mortgages*
- *homes and property*
- *internet banking*
- *pensions and insurance*
- *savings and investments*
- *share dealing*
- *supermarkets*
- *taxation*

This is a quick index of web sites mentioned in this book. They are presented as a handy guide in A to Z order, to save you going back through the book if all you need is an address in a hurry.

General financial information

AAA Investment Guide	http://www.wisebuy.co.uk/sg-tx0.htm
Euro	http://www.euro.gov.uk/http://www.euro-emu.co.uk/
	http://europa.eu.int/euro/html/entry.html
	http://www.eubusiness.com/emu/euroamue.htm
Financial Info Net Directory	http://www.find.co.uk/
Financial Times	http://www.ft.com
IMRO	http://www.imro.co.uk/
Money Central	http://www.moneycentral.com/home.asp
MoneyExtra	http://moneyextra.com/
MoneyWeb	http://www.moneyweb.co.uk/
Moneywise magazine	http://www.readersdigest.co.uk/finance.htm
MoneyWorld UK	http://www.moneyworld.co.uk/
MoneyXtra	http://moneyxtra.com/default.asp
MoneyZone	http://www.lineone.net/moneyzone/content.fhtml
Motley Fool	http://www.fool.co.uk/
PIA	http://www.pia-limited.co.uk/
Quicken	http://www.quicken.co.uk
SFA	http://www.sfa.org.uk/home.htm
SIB	http://www.sib.co.uk
This Is Money	http://www.thisismoney.com/
Times-Money	http://www.times-money.co.uk
UK Portfolio	http://www.ukportfolio.freeserve.co.uk/research2.htm

Note:
you will find all these available on the Internet Handbooks web site site at

http://www.internet-handbooks.co.uk

Site index

Credit and loans

Affinity cards	http://www.footballcard.co.uk/
	http://www.unioncard.co.uk/
	http://www.graduatecard.co.uk/
Bank of Scotland	http://www.bankofscotland.co.uk/
Barclaycard	http://www.barclaycard.co.uk
Barclaycoin	http://www.barclaycoin.co.uk/
Bradford & Bingley	http://www.bradford-bingley.co.uk
Business Credit Management	http://www.creditman.co.uk/
Capital Investors	http://www.capital-investors.co.uk/main.htm
Checkfree	http://www.checkfree.com/index-ecomcon.html
Credit Status	http://www.creditstatus.com/
CyberCash	http://www.cybercash.com/
Digicash	http://www.digicash.com/index_e.html
E-bank	http://www.e-banking.org/
Egg	http://www3.egg.com/loans/default.asp
Freeway	http://www.freeway.ltd.uk
Halifax	http://www.halifax.co.uk/card/card.html
Hamilton Direct Bank	http://www.hdb.co.uk/
Instant Credit Search	http://www.instant-search.com/
Instant Search	http://www.instant-search.com/
Jonathan Comerie	http://www.knowledge.co.uk/xxx/credit/
Judgment Removal Co	http://www.judgmentremoval.demon.co.uk/
Lloyds	http://www.lloydsbank.co.uk/
Loan Corporation	http://www.loancorp.co.uk/index.htm
Lombard	http://www.lombard.co.uk/index.htm
M Molloy	http://www.knowledge.co.uk/xxx/molloy/
Marks & Spencer	https://www.marks-and-spencer.co.uk/financial-services/
MasterCard	http://www.mastercard.com/press/
MBNA	http://www.mbnainternational.com/cards/index.htm
Midland	http://www.midlandbank.com/cards/
Mondex	http://www.mondex.com
Nationwide	http://www.nationwide.co.uk/fserv/banking/credit/creditcard.htm
NatWest	http://www.natwest.co.uk
Netchex	http://www.netchex.com/
Paragon	http://www.paragon-cars.co.uk
Priority Loans	http://www.btinternet.com/~priorityloans/index.htm
Purple Loans	http://www.purpleloans.com
Royal Bank of Scotland	http://www.royalbankscot.co.uk/personal/credit/
Status International	http://www.status-int.co.uk/
Sterling Direct	http://www.sterlingdirect.co.uk/Home.htm
Templeton Ross	http://www.templeton-ross.co.uk/index2.html
TSB	http://www.tsb.co.uk
UK Credit Files	http://www.ukcreditfiles.co.uk/
UK Data On Line	http://www.ukdata.com/
UK Loans	http://www.ukloans.co.uk
Universal Finance	http://ourworld.compuserve.com/homepages/universal_finance/uftop.htm
VISA	http://www.visa.com/cgi-bin/vee/ct/main.html?2+0
Wise Money	https://www.wisemoney.com/homepage.asp
Woolwich	http://www.woolwich.co.uk/creditcard/

Site index

Home buying and mortgages

A1 Removals	http://www.informationdesign.co.uk/a1moves/
Abbey National	http://www.abbeynational.co.uk
Alliance and Leicester	http://www.alliance-leicester.co.uk/
Ashton Thomas	http://www.internetlink.co.uk/ashton_thomas.htm
Avoncourt	http://www.avoncourt.co.uk/
Bank of Scotland	http://www.bankofscotland.co.uk/newmortgages.html
Barclays	http://www.personal.barclays.co.uk/
Bath Building Society	http://www.bibs.co.uk/
Birmingham Midshires BS	http://www.worldserver.pipex.com/bmbs/mortgage/msummary.htm?
Bradford and Bingley	http://www.bradford-bingley.co.uk/home.htm
Bristol and West	http://www.bristol-west.co.uk/mortgage_hub.htm
Cambridge BS	http://www.cambridge-building-society.co.uk/
Cheltenham and Gloucester	http://www.cheltglos.co.uk/
Conveyancing Marketing	http://www.conveyancing-cms.co.uk/
Coutts	http://www.coutts.com/enhanced/index.htm
Coventry BS	http://www.covbsoc.co.uk/mortgages/mtgframe.htm
Darlington BS	http://www.darlington.co.uk/mort.htm
Dunfermline BS	http://www.dunfermline-bs.co.uk/mortgage/index.html
First Direct	http://www.firstdirect.co.uk
First Peoples Mortgage	http://www.first.co.uk/
Freedman and Co	http://www.moneysense.co.uk/
Furness BS	http://www.furnessbs.co.uk/mortgages_menu.htm
Halifax	http://www.halifax.co.uk/mort/mort.html
Hinckley and Rugby BS	http://www.hrbs.co.uk/mortgage.html
Homeloans Direct	http://www.homeloans.co.uk/
John Charcol	http://www.johncharcol.co.uk/mortgages/
Lambeth BS	http://www.lambeth.co.uk/
Leeds and Holbeck	http://www.leeds-holbeck.co.uk/frmmorts.htm
Leek United BS	http://www.leek-united.co.uk
Legal and General	http://www.landg.com/mortgage/mortgage1.html
Mansfield BS	http://www.emnet.co.uk/mansfield-bs/
Market Harborough BS	http://www.mhbs.co.uk/mortgage.htm
Marsden BS	http://www.marsdenbs.co.uk/#
Midland	http://www.midlandbank.com/borrow/home/choose/choose.htm
MoneyNet	http://www.moneynet.co.uk/
Mortgage Alliance	http://www.magreen.demon.co.uk/
Mortgage Clinic	http://uk.zarcrom.com/mortgages/
Mortgage Help Desk UK	http://www.mortgageman.u-net.com/
MortgageKey	http://www.ftech.net/~mortgage/
Moves	http://www.moves.co.uk/
Terry Smith Mortgages	http://www.net.dircon.co.uk/
Trustguard Homeloans	http://members.aol.com/trustguard/
National Counties BS	http://www.ncbs.co.uk/mortgage/mortgage.htm
Nationwide	http://www.nationwide.co.uk/
NatWest	http://www.natwest.co.uk
Newbury BS	http://www.newbury.co.uk/frame.htm
Newcastle BS	http://www.newcastle.co.uk/resident/index.htm
Northern Rock	http://www.northernrock.co.uk/html/mortgages/mortgages.htm
Norwich & Peterborough BS	http://www.norwichandpeterborough.co.uk/

Nottingham BS	http://www.nottingham-bs.co.uk/mortgage/index.htm
Skipton BS	http://www.skipton.co.uk/pp.htm
Staffordshire BS	http://www.staffordshirebuildingsociety.co.uk/Hp-rm.htm
Standard Life	http://www.standardlifebank.com/mortgages.html
Stroud & Swindon BS	http://www.stroudandswindon.co.uk/mortgage.html
Teachers BS	http://www.teachersbs.co.uk/index.html
The Principality BS	http://www.principality.co.uk/front.html
Universal BS	http://www.ubs.uk.com/nav-mor.htm
Virgin	http://www.virgin-direct.co.uk/one/html/body_home.html
West Bromwich BS	http://www.westbrom.co.uk/mort.htm
Woolwich	http://www.woolwich.co.uk/lending/index.htm
Yorkshire BS	http://www.ybs.co.uk/wel_mort.htm

Homes and property

Beechwood Homes	http://www.beechwood.co.uk/
Berkeley Homes	http://www.berkeleygroup.com/index2.html
Bewley Homes	http://www.bewley.co.uk/
CALA Homes	http://www.pwave.co.uk/pwave/cala/
Fairclough Homes	http://www.fairclough.co.uk/
Home Hunter	http://www.homehunter.co.uk/
Home Pages	http://www.homepages.co.uk/index.html
Homes UK	http://www.homes-uk.co.uk/hfs_home_uke.html
Homes On Line	http://www.homes-on-line.co.uk/
House Directory	http://www.house-directory.co.uk/
HouseWeb	http://www.houseweb.co.uk/
Independent Financial Advisors	http://www.ifap.org.uk/home/homeword.htm
Internet Property Finder	http://www.propertyfinder.co.uk/
Internet Property Register	http://www.propreg.com/
National Property Register	http://www.national-property-register.co.uk/
Persimmon Homes	http://www.persimmon.plc.uk/
Premier Properties	http://www.premier-property.net/home.asp
Premier Property Network	http://www.premier-property.net/home.asp
Prestige Properties	http://www.prestigeproperty.co.uk/
Property Bunny	http://www.propertybunny.co.uk/
Property Gold	http://www.ukpg.co.uk/
Property Platform	http://www.property-platform.com/
Property Sight	http://www.property-sight.co.uk/
Property Warehouse	http://www.uk-property.com/
Property Zone	http://www.property-zone.com/uk/
UK Property Sales	http://www.ukpropertysales.com/
UK Property	http://www.uk-property.co.uk/
Up My Street	http://www.upmystreet.com/

Internet banking

Barclays	http://www.personal.barclays.co.uk/online/
British Bankers Association	http://www.bankfacts.org.uk/
Citibank	http://www.citibank.com/uk/intbank/index.htm
Co-operative Bank	http://www.co-operativebank.co.uk/ib_registration.html
Lloyds	http://www.lloydsbank.co.uk/ibank/index.htm

Nationwide	http://www.nationwide.co.uk
Norwich and Peterborough	http://www.norwichandpeterborough.co.uk/intro.htm

Pensions and insurance

Allied Dunbar	http://www.allieddunbar.co.uk
Assured Travel Insurance	http://www.britsurf.org/dial-direct/assured.html
AssureNet	http://www.assurenet.sonnet.co.uk/
AXA Equity & Law	http://www.axaassurance.co.uk
Bequest Wills	http://dspace.dial.pipex.com/bequest/index.htm
BUPA	http://www.bupa.com
Butcher Robinson & Staples	http://www.brasil.co.uk/ http://www.screentrade.com/
C J Erwood	http://www.atlantica.co.uk/personal/cjlegacy.html
Carquote	http://www.carquote.co.uk/
Car Source	http://www.carsource.co.uk/
Consultant Insurance Brokers	http://www.consultant-insurance.co.uk/
Co-operative Insurance	http://www.cis.co.uk/products/life.html
County Wills	http://members.aol.com/countywill/index.htm
Direct Line	http://www.directline.com/Life/index.htm
DSS	http://www.dss.gov.uk/ca/
E&L Insurance	http://fido.k9.co.uk/e&l/index.htm
Edinburgh Fund Managers	http://www.edfd.com/
Equitable Life	http://www.equitable.co.uk/
Exotic Direct	http://www.exoticdirect.co.uk/
First Medical Healthplans	http://www.1stmedical.co.uk/
Fogg Travel	http://www.itsnet.co.uk/insure/fogg/
Garrison & Co	http://www.garrison.co.uk/
Guardian	http://www.guardianfs.co.uk/public/html/lifetitle.html
Healthy Pets Insurance	http://www.healthy-pets.co.uk/
	http://www.biiba.org.uk/brokingonline.html
IFA Direct	http://www.ifadirect.co.uk/
Independent Advice	http://www.independent-advice.co.uk/
Insurance Connections	http://www.demon.co.uk/dayco/phatrav.html
Lawnet	http://qvartnadecet.mkn.co.uk/HELP/LAW/WILLINFO
Legal & General	http://www.landg.com/lifeass/family/protfamily.html
	http://www.landg.com/pensions/pensions1.html
Marks and Spencer	https://www.marks-and-spencer.co.uk/financial-services/
Medibroker	http://www.medibroker.co.uk/main.html
Medical Sickness	http://www.medical-sickness.co.uk
Mediquote	http://www.mediquote.co.uk/main.htm
Merchant Investors	http://test.merchant-investors.co.uk/
National Insurance	http://ssa.nics.gov.uk/
Nomad Travel Insurance	http://www.nomad-insurance.co.uk/
Norwich Union	http://www.norwichunion.co.uk
	http://www.norwich-union.co.uk/homepage.htm
	http://www.norwich-union.co.uk/life_menu.htm
Pace	http://www.paceltd.co.uk/
Permanent	http://www.permanent.co.uk/
Pet Healthcare	http://www.pethealthcare.co.uk/
Pet Plan	http://www.petplan.co.uk/
Pet Shield	http://www.petproducts.co.uk/

Site index

Pet Wise	http://www.swireblanch.co.uk/petwise/
PPP Healthcare	http://www.ppphealthcare.co.uk/
PPP	http://www.longtermcare.co.uk
Prime Health	http://www.primehealth.co.uk
Private Health Associates	http://www.demon.co.uk/dayco/pha.html
Private Health Partnership	http://www.php.co.uk/php/
Professional Will Writing Co	http://www.pwc.ndirect.co.uk/
Prudential	http://www.pru.co.uk/
Quicken Family Lawyer	http://www.parsonstech.com/software/famlaw.html
Royal & Sun Alliance	http://www.royalsunalliance.co.uk/direct/life/index.htm
Royal Liver	http://www.royal-liver.com/
	http://www.royal-liver.com/royaliver/lifeassu.htm
SAGA	http://www.saga.co.uk/insurance/index.html
Scottish Amicable	http://www.scottishamicable.com/products/index.html
	http://www.scottishamicable.com/products/index.html
Scottish Life	http://www.scottishlife.co.uk/Scottish%20Life/products/pensions.htm
Scottish Widows	http://www.scottishwidows.co.uk/
Snowcard	http://www.ski.co.uk/snowcard/
Society of Will Writers	http://freespace.virgin.net/society.willwriters/
St Christopher Driver Plan	http://www.st-christopher.com/
Standard Life	http://www.standardlife.co.uk/products/lifeassurance.html
Standard Life (pensions)	http://www.standardlife.co.uk/products/pensions.html
Travel Insurance Agency	http://www.travelinsurers.com/
Travel Insurance Club	http://www.travelinsuranceclub.co.uk/
Western Provident	http://www.wpahealth.co.uk
Willmaker	http://www.nolo.com/item/wd7.html
Willwriters	http://www.willwriters.co.uk/
Winterthur Life	http://www.winterthur-life.co.uk/
Woolwich Pet Guard	http://www.woolwich.co.uk/petguard/petad.htm
World Cover Direct	http://www.worldcover.co.uk/
World Wide Travel Insurance	http://www.wwtis.co.uk/

Savings and investments

Aberdeen Prolific	http://www.iii.co.uk/aberdeen-prolific/
Absolute Assigned Policies	http://www.aap.co.uk/main.htm
Ass. of Unit Trust & Inv. Funds	http://www.autif.co.uk/
Auctions	http://www.ebid.co.uk/
	http://www.onlineauctions.co.uk/index.htm
Baillie Gifford	http://www.bailliegifford.co.uk/home.html
Bank of Wales	http://www.bankofwales.co.uk/jersey/index.htm
Barclays Offshore	http://www.offshorebanking.barclays.com/
BBC Watchdog	http://www.bbc.co.uk/watchdog/
Beale & Dobie	http://www.bealedobie.co.uk/home.htm
Cazenove	http://www.cazenove.co.uk/cc/1home.htm
Chartered	http://www.chartered-tci.com/
Consumers Association	http://www.which.net/upfront/contents.html
Direct Debit	http://www.directdebit.co.uk/discounts.htm
Discounts	http://www.ukpower.com/
	http://www.buy.co.uk/
Fidelity Investments	http://www.fidelity.co.uk

Fidelity	http://www.fidelity.co.uk/direct/index.html
Flemings	http://www.flemings.co.uk/fitm/homepage/
Flemings	http://www.flemings.com/
Friends Provident	http://www.friendsprovident.co.uk
Garrison Discount Investments	http://www.garrison.co.uk/
Herald Investment Trust	http://www.heralduk.com/herald98/himl/default/Default.htm
Heritage Capital	http://www.heritage-capital.co.uk/
Hill Samuel	http://www.hillsamuel.co.uk
Holloway Friendly	http://www.holloway.co.uk/main.htm
Homeowners Friendly Society	http://www.homeowners.co.uk/home.htm
Internet Shopping	http://www.shopguide.co.uk
Investec	http://www.investecguinnessflight.com/uk/ukframe.htm
Investments Online	http://www.investments-online.co.uk/
Jersey	http://www.jersey-mail.co.uk/finance/index.htm
Legal & General	http://www.legalandgeneral.co.uk
M&G	http://www.mandg.iii.co.uk/html/top_home.htm
	http://www.mandg.co.uk/
Martin Currie	http://www.martincurrie.com/i-trusts-infof.html
Martin Currie	http://www.martincurrie.com/u-trustinfof.html
Mercury Asset Management	http://www.mam.com/frameset.htm
National Savings	http://www.nationalsavings.co.uk/
Northern Rock	http://www.northernrock-guernsey.co.gg/index.htm
Norwich Union	http://www.norwich-union.co.uk/index.htm
Perpetual Offshore	http://www.perpetual-offshore.com/home.nsf/offshore
Policy Plus	http://www.policyplus.com/main.html
Royal Liver Assurance	http://www.royal-liver.com/royaliver/fram.htm
SAGA	http://www.saga.co.uk/investment/index.html
Save & Prosper	http://www.prosper.co.uk/entry/content.html
Scottish Friendly	http://www.scottishfriendly.co.uk/find/inxleaf.htm
	http://www.scottishfriendly.co.uk/find/mcone.htm
Scottish Investment Trust	http://www.sit.co.uk/
SEP Marketing	http://www.zynet.co.uk/childs/sepm.htm
Standard Life	http://www.standardlife.co.uk/products/savings.html
Surrenda Link	http://www.surrendalink.u-net.com/
Templeton	http://www.templeton.co.uk/
Traded Endowments	http://www.endowments.com/

Share dealing

AMEX	http://www.amex.com/cgi-bin/WebObjects/AmexWeb
Australian Stock Exchange	http://www.asx.com.au/
Barclays Stockbrokers	http://www.barclays-stockbrokers.co.uk/
Bloomberg	http://www.bloomberg.com/welcome.html
CAROL	http://www.carol.co.uk
Charles Schwab	http://www.schwab-worldwide.com/europe
Charles Stanley	http://www.charles-stanley.co.uk/
Durlacher and Co	http://www.durlacher.co.uk/
EASDAQ	http://www.easdaq.be/pb/enb_00.asp
Electronic Share Information	http://www.esi.co.uk
Ellis & Partners	http://www.ellisandpartners.co.uk/
Frankfurt Stock Exchange	http://www.exchange.de/fwb/fwb.html

Site index

FTSE	http://www.ftse.com/
Internet Investor	http://www.iionline.com/
Johannesburg Stock Exchange	http://www.jse.co.za/
Kyte Securities	http://www.kytesecurities.com/
London Stock Exchange	http://www.londonstockex.co.uk/
Money	http://www.pathfinder.com/money/plus?page=index.oft
Montreal Stock Exchange	http://www.me.org/
NASDAQ	http://www.nasdaq.com/
NYSE	http://www.nyse.com
Pilling and Co	http://www.pilling.co.uk/
Quote.com	http://www.quote.com
Share Centre	http://www.share.co.uk/
SmartMoney	http://www.smartmoney.com/
Stocktrade	http://www.stocktrade.co.uk/
Tokyo Stock Exchange	http://www.tse.or.jp/eindex.html
Tradepoint	http://www.tradepoint.co.uk/
UK Equities Direct	http://www.hemscott.com/EQUITIES/
Xest	http://www.xest.com

Supermarkets

ASDA	http://www.asda.co.uk/
Groceries	http://www.groceries.org.uk/
Sainsburys	http://www.sainsburys.co.uk/
Somerfield	http://www.somerfield.co.uk/
Tesco	http://www.tesco.co.uk/

Taxation

Chartered Institute of Taxation	http://www.tax.org.uk/
Consumers Association	http://www.which.net
Contributions Agency	http://www.dss.gov.uk/ca/index.htm
Financial Software	http://www.financialsoftware.co.uk/
HM Customs and Excise	http://www.hmce.gov.uk/
Inland Revenue	http://www.inlandrevenue.gov.uk
LineOne Tax Club	http://www.lineone.net/clubs/money/tax/
QuickTax	http://www.intuit.co.uk/marketing/quicken/features.htm#quicktax
TaxSoft	http://www.taxsoft.co.uk/
Treasury	http://www.hm-treasury.gov.uk/
UK Tax Links	http://www.uktax.demon.co.uk